Praise for *CSS Secrets*

❝ This is a new generation of CSS books, for a new generation of CSS. No longer a simple language tied to complicated browser hacks and workarounds, CSS is now a richly powerful and deeply complex ecosystem of over 80 W3C specifications. Nobody is better at making sense of this new CSS, and of providing design principles that help you solve problems with it, than Lea Verou—among the handful of truly amazing coders I've known. ❞

— **Jeffrey Zeldman**
author, Designing with Web Standards

❝ Lea Verou's encyclopaedic mind is one of a kind, but thanks to this generous book, you too can get an insight into what it's like to wield CSS to do just about anything you can think of. Even if you think you know CSS inside-out, I guarantee that there are still secrets in this book waiting to be revealed. ❞

— **Jeremy Keith**
Shepherd of Unknown Futures, Clearleft

❝ If you want the inside scoop on fascinating CSS techniques, smart best practices, and some flat-out brilliance, don't hesitate—read this book. I loved it! ❞

— **Eric A. Meyer**

" Lea is an exceedingly clever coder. This book is absolutely packed with clever and useful ideas, even for people who know CSS well. Even better, you'll feel more clever in your work as this book encourages pushing beyond the obvious."

— Chris Coyier
CodePen

" CSS Secrets is an instant classic—so many wonderful tips and tricks you can use right away to enhance your UX designs!"

— Christopher Schmitt
author of CSS Cookbook

" There aren't many books that provide as many practical techniques as Lea Verou's CSS Secrets. Filled with dozens of solutions to common design problems, the book is a truly valuable collection of smart tips and tricks for getting things done well, and fast. Worth reading, even if you think that you know the ins and outs of CSS!"

— Vitaly Friedman
cofounder and editor-in-chief of Smashing Magazine

" Without fail, whenever I read something written by Lea Verou, I manage to learn something new. CSS Secrets is no different. The book is broken down into easy-to-digest chunks filled with lots of juicy bits of knowledge. While some of the book is very forward looking, there is plenty that I've been able to take away and apply to my own projects right away."

— Jonathan Snook
web designer and developer

" Lea's book is fantastic. She bends and contorts CSS to do things I'm pretty sure even the spec authors never imagined! You will learn multiple ways of accomplishing each graphic effect by trying out the techniques she walks through in each chapter. Later, in your work, you'll find yourself saying, "hmm, that thing Lea did will work perfectly here!" Before you know it, your site is almost image free because your graphics are all in easy to maintain CSS components. What's more, her techniques are fun, walking the line between practical and improbable!"

— Nicole Sullivan
Principal Software Engineer, creator of OOCSS

" Lea Verou's *CSS Secrets* is useful not so much as a collection of CSS tips, but as a textbook on how to solve problems with CSS. Her in-depth explanation of the thought process behind each secret will teach you how to create your own solutions to CSS problems. And don't miss the Introduction, which contains some must-read CSS best practices."

— Elika J. Etemad (aka fantasai)
W3C CSS Working Group Invited Expert

" Lea's presentations have long been must-see events at web development conferences around the world. A distillation of her years of experience, *CSS Secrets* provides elegant solutions for thorny web design issues, while also—and more importantly—showing how to solve problems in CSS. It's an absolute must-read for every frontend designer and developer."

— Dudley Storey
designer, developer, writer, web education specialist

" I thought I had a pretty advanced understanding of CSS, then I read Lea Verou's book. If you want to take your CSS knowledge to the next level, this is a must-own."

— Ryan Seddon
Team Lead, Zendesk

" *CSS Secrets* is by far the most technical book that I have ever read on the topic. Lea has managed to push the boundaries of a language as simple as CSS so far that you will not be able to distinguish this from magic. Definitely not a beginner's read; it's heavily recommended to anyone thinking they know CSS all too well."

— Hugo Giraudel
frontend developer, Edenspiekermann

" I often think that CSS can seem a bit like magic: a few rules can transform your web pages from blah to beautiful. In *CSS Secrets*, Lea takes the magic to a whole new level. She is a master magician of CSS, and we get to explore that magical world along with her. I can't count how many times I said out loud while reading this book, "That's so cool!" The only trouble with *CSS Secrets* is that after reading it, I want to stop everything else I'm doing and play with CSS all day."

— Elisabeth Robson
cofounder of WickedlySmart.com and coauthor of Head First JavaScript Programming

CSS SECRETS

BETTER SOLUTIONS TO EVERYDAY WEB DESIGN PROBLEMS

LEA VEROU

Beijing · Boston · Farnham · Sebastopol · Tokyo

CSS Secrets

by Lea Verou

Published by O'Reilly Media, Inc., 1005 Gravenstein Highway North, Sebastopol, CA 95472.

O'Reilly books may be purchased for educational, business, or sales promotional use. Online editions are also available for most titles (*http://safaribooksonline.com*). For more information, contact our corporate/institutional sales department: 800-998-9938 or *corporate@oreilly.com*.

Editors: Mary Treseler and Meg Foley	**Proofreader:** Charles Roumeliotis
Production Editor: Kara Ebrahim	**Interior Designer:** Lea Verou
Copyeditor: Jasmine Kwityn	**Cover Designer:** Monica Kamsvaag
Indexer: WordCo Indexing Services	**Illustrator:** Lea Verou

See *http://www.oreilly.com/catalog/errata.csp?isbn=0636920031123* for release details.

The O'Reilly logo is a registered trademark of O'Reilly Media, Inc. The cover image and related trade dress are trademarks of O'Reilly Media, Inc.

Print History: First Edition, June 2015

Revision History for the First Edition:

2015-06-03	First Release
2015-07-17	Second Release

ISBN: 978-1-4493-7263-7

[TI]

In loving memory of
my mother & best friend, Maria Verou (1952–2013),
who left this world way too early.

Table of Contents

Secrets by Specification

Foreword

Ah, the good old days. Back in the previous millennium, we had just two CSS-capable browsers, and what they did was a fairly limited subset of a fairly limited specification, so you could fairly easily keep a complete map of what worked and what didn't in your head. That map included the bugs in each implementation, as they had many errors and oversights, some of them verging on the comical. Heck, some bugs were so fundamental that they made the browsers' layout behavior completely incompatible, forcing us to come up with a whole army of parser-bug-exploiting hacks just to work around the differences!

Wait a minute. The old days were *horrible*. Glad we're done with all that!

Things really have gotten so much better in the last several years, CSS-wise. Browsers have, for the most part, converged on compatibility, and where they are incompatible, it's nearly always because one browser doesn't support a feature that another does, as opposed to both of them trying to support the same thing differently, and usually badly. The specifications have pushed capabilities forward even as they've added features that re-create the convoluted tricks of old in much simpler, more compact ways. CSS has far more features and far more power than ever before—but, as we all know, with great power comes great complexity. It's not even a case of intentional complexity: when you combine enough working parts, no matter how simple each may be, interesting things can and do emerge. (For more on this topic, see *The LEGO Movie*.)

But it's exactly that unintended complexity that gives CSS the ability to surprise us with emergent features we never expected, or even planned. There are secrets to be found in the intersections of properties and the bending of values. You can carve corners with gradients, animate elements, increase clickable areas, even create pie charts...and so much more. CSS has capabilities that we only dreamed of back when I was but a lad, possibilities beyond anything we imagined. It's added abilities that I once thought could never be expressed in a compact, human-readable manner—animations, to pick one example. It's advanced far enough that I'm confident there are many, many secrets yet to be discovered. Perhaps you'll discover some of them.

Until that day arrives, there are plenty of fascinating techniques that have already been unearthed, and few have done more than Lea Verou to find and share them with the world. From her blog posts to her open source contributions to her dynamic, interactive talks all over the world, Lea has amassed a formidable reserve of CSS knowledge. This book is a beautiful distillation of that knowledge. You now possess a guide to some of the most interesting, surprising, and useful techniques that CSS has yielded, a guide compiled by one of the brightest minds in the field. What Lea has prepared for you in these pages will enrich, delight, and—yes—even astonish.

Go forth, learn well, and let these discoveries be secrets no more.

— Eric A. Meyer

Preface

In the past few years, **CSS has undergone a transformation**, similar to the JavaScript revolution circa 2004. It went from being a dead-simple styling language with limited power, to a complex technology defined by **over 80 W3C specifications** (including drafts), with its own developer ecosystem, its own conferences, and its own frameworks and tooling. **CSS has grown so much that it's practically impossible for any single person to hold all of it in their brain.** Even in the W3C CSS Working Group that defines the language, nobody is an expert on every single aspect of CSS— and few even come close. Instead, most WG members focus on certain CSS specifications and might know very little about others.

Up until roughly 2009, CSS expertise was not defined by how well the language was known. This was more or less a given for any serious CSS work. Instead, CSS prowess was defined by the number of browser bugs and workarounds that had been committed to memory. Fast-forward to 2015, and browsers are now designed to support standards, and flimsy browser-specific hacks are frowned upon. There are still some unavoidable incompatibilities, but—especially because most browsers now auto-update —the pace of change is so fast, that attempting to document them in a book would be a waste of time and space.

The challenge in modern CSS has little to do with working around transient browser bugs. The challenge now is using the CSS features we have in a creative way, in order to come up with **DRY, maintainable,**

DRY is an acronym that stands for "Don't Repeat Yourself." It's a popular programming mantra to promote an aspect of maintainable code: being able to change its parameters with as few edits as possible, ideally one. Emphasis on DRY CSS code is a recurring theme in this book. The opposite of DRY is **WET**, which stands for "We Enjoy Typing" or "Write Everything Twice."

flexible, lightweight, and as much as possible, **standards-compliant solutions**. This is exactly what this book is all about.

There are many books out there that document certain CSS features from A to Z. *CSS Secrets*, for better or for worse, is not one of them. Its purpose is to fill the knowledge gaps that are left after you've already familiarized yourself with the reference material—to open your mind to new ways to take advantage of the features you already know about, or to let you know about useful CSS features that aren't as shiny and popular, and that deserve more love. However, above all, the main purpose of this book is to teach you **how to solve problems with CSS**.

CSS Secrets is not a cookbook either. Each "secret" is not a canned recipe, with rigid steps you must follow to achieve a specific effect. Instead, I've tried to describe the thinking behind every technique in detail, as I believe that **understanding the process of finding a solution is far more valuable than the solution itself**. Even if you don't think that a certain technique is relevant to your work, learning how to reach a solution might still prove valuable for tackling even completely different problems. Long story short, **you will hopefully get many proverbial fish from this book, but its main goal is to "feed you for a lifetime," by teaching you how to catch them.**

Words of thanks

This book would not have been possible without the help and support of a number of fantastic people, to whom I'm deeply grateful. A big, heartfelt thank you goes to:

- All those who supported my work over the years, otherwise I wouldn't have found myself in the position of writing a book in the first place. To readers of **my blog** *(Lea.verou.me)*, **Twitter** *(twitter.com/leaverou)*, and elsewhere, and even more to **you**, dear reader of my first book! To everyone who has used **my open source work** *(github.com/leaverou)* and even more to those who contributed.

- All the conference organizers who have invited me for talks and workshops over the years, especially to **Damian Wielgosik** and **Paweł Czerski** who first believed in me and invited me to the inaugural Front-Trends conference in 2010. And to **Vasilis Vassalos** who trusted me to design a web development course for Athens University of Economics and Business back in 2010, as all these experiences taught me a great deal about teaching (and a technical book is basically teaching).

- Everyone in the **CSS Working Group** who voted to bring me on as an Invited Expert, which has transformed my perspective on web technologies in general and on CSS in particular.

- My editors, **Mary Treseler** and **Meg Foley**, who gave me control over the entire process and have been incredibly patient with me when I missed deadlines (which happened more often than I'd care to admit).

- My production editor, **Kara Ebrahim**, who spent copious amounts of time fixing layout issues and manually compensating for CSS rendering bugs and limitations in the PDF renderer used for this book.

- My technical editors: **Elika Etemad**, **Tab Atkins**, **Ryan Seddon**, **Elisabeth Robson**, **Ben Henick**, **Robin Nixon**, and **Hugo Giraudel**. They not only helped me correct factual mistakes, but also provided invaluable feedback regarding the understandability of the prose.

- **Eric Meyer**, who I still cannot believe agreed to write a Foreword for my book.

- My research advisor, **David Karger**, who was extremely understanding when I arrived at MIT without having finished this book, which was supposed to be done long before then. Without his continued patience, the fate of this book would have been bleak.

- My dad, **Miltiades Komvoutis**, who taught me art and aesthetics very early on. Without him, I would probably have zero interest in design and CSS, and this book would have been about something else, like C++ or kernel programming.

- My uncle/second dad, **Stratis Veros**, and his lovely wife, **Maria Brere**, who put up with me when I was at my most cranky while writing this book. Also to their kids, **Leonie** and **Phoebe**, who are the cutest little girls in the world and without whom, this book would have finished around a month earlier.

- My incredible late mother, **Maria Verou**, to whom this book is dedicated. For the 27 years our lives overlapped, she was my best friend and biggest supporter. Her own life was a huge inspiration: she moved to the other side of the world to do postgraduate research at MIT in the 1970s, a time when most women in Greece barely made it to college, and got her degree with distinction. She taught me ambition, kindness, integrity, independence, open-mindedness. But most importantly, she taught me to not take life too seriously. I miss her sorely.

Photo credits

A big thanks to the lovely people who publish their photos with permissive Creative Commons licenses; otherwise, every example in this book would feature pictures of my cat (and many examples do, regardless). Here is a list of the CC photos I used and where you can find them:

"House Made Sausage from Prairie Grass Cafe, Northbrook," Kurman Communications, Inc.

flickr.com/kurmanphotos/7847424816

"Cats that Webchick Is Herding," Kathleen Murtagh

flickr.com/ceardach/4549876293

"Stone Art," by Josef Stuefer

flickr.com/josefstuefer/5982121

"A Field of Tulips," Roman Boed

flickr.com/romanboed/867231576

"Resting in the Sunshine," Steve Wilson

flickr.com/pokerbrit/10780890983

"Naxos Island, Greece," Chris Hutchison

flickr.com/employtheskinnyboy/3904743709

Making of

This is a book that eats its own dog food, proverbially speaking. It was **written in clean HTML5**, with a few `data-` attributes, defined by O'Reilly's **HTMLBook standard** *(oreillymedia.github.io/HTMLBook)*. This means that everything you see in this book—the layout, the figures, the colors—**is HTML styled with CSS**. A lot of the figures are also generated with **SVG** or use SVG data URIs, generated via SCSS functions. The few math formulas were written in **LaTeX** and then converted to **MathML** behind the scenes. You may find it amusing that the page numbers, chapter numbers, and secret numbers are merely CSS counters.

Many of the books O'Reilly publishes these days are made that way. They have built a system especially for this purpose, called **Atlas** *(atlas.oreilly.com)*. The best thing about Atlas is that it's also available for the public, not just for official O'Reilly use.

However, this book was not a typical Atlas use case. It pushed the limits of what is possible today with CSS for printing, in a way that—to my knowledge—no other book has. It helped us find many bugs in Atlas and Antenna House (the PDF renderer used by Atlas) and even many issues with the print-related CSS specifications themselves, which I took to the CSS WG.

"How much code does it take to make a book like this with web technologies?" you might ask. Let's look at a few statistics (before production):

- This book is styled with **4,700** lines of SCSS, compiling to **3,800** lines of CSS.
- A little over **10,000** lines of HTML.

- There are **322** figures in the entire book, but only **140** image files (including SVG images and screenshots), as most figures are just a series of divs styled with CSS. (Figure styling accounts for 65% of the book's CSS and SCSS code!)

Here is a list of tools used in making this book, besides Atlas:

- **Git** for version control
- **SCSS** for CSS preprocessing
- The entire book was written in the **Espresso** *(macrabbit.com/espresso)* text editor
- **CodeKit** was used for compiling SCSS to CSS
- **Dabblet** *(dabblet.com)* was used for the live demos and for the few figures that are screenshots of the demos
- The SVG-based figures that were not hand coded were created in **Adobe Illustrator**
- **Adobe Photoshop** was used to edit screenshots, when needed

The fonts used were **Rockwell** for the headings, Frutiger for the body text, `Consolas` for the code, and Baskerville for the dedication and many figures.

The book was written on a 13″ MacBook Air, in a variety of countries, including Greece, Kenya, Australia, New Zealand, the Philippines, Singapore, Chile, Brazil, the United States, France, Spain, the UK, Wales, Poland, Canada, and Austria.

About this book

Who this book is for

The primary target audience for this book is **intermediate to advanced CSS developers**. By getting the introductory stuff out of the way, we can explore more advanced use cases of modern CSS features and combinations thereof. This, however, means that quite a few **assumptions** have been made about you, dear reader:

- I assume **you know CSS 2.1 inside out**, and have a few years of experience with it. You don't struggle to understand how positioning works. You've used generated content to enhance your designs without extraneous markup or images. You don't resort to plastering `!important` all over your code because you actually understand specificity, inheritance, and the cascade. You know what the different parts of the box model are, and you are not fazed by margin collapsing. You are familiar with the different length units and know when it's best to use each one.

- You've read quite a bit about **the most popular CSS3 features**, online and/or in books, and have tried them out, even if only in personal projects. Even if you haven't studied them in depth, you know how to create rounded corners, add a `box-shadow`, or create a linear gradient. You've played with some basic 2D transforms, and have enhanced interactions with basic transitions and animations.

- You have seen **SVG** and know what it's used for, even if you don't quite know how to write it yourself.

- You can read and understand **basic, vanilla JavaScript**, such as creating elements, manipulating their attributes, and adding them to the document.

- You've heard of **CSS preprocessors** and know what they can do, even if you choose not to use one.

- You're familiar with **middle school level math**, such as square roots, the Pythagorean theorem, sines, cosines, and logarithms.

However, to enable readers that don't meet all these assumptions to enjoy this book, there is a **"Prerequisites"** box in the beginning of some secrets, briefly listing any CSS knowledge or previous secrets that need to be known for the secret to make sense (excluding CSS 2.1 features, otherwise the box would get really long). It looks like this:

> ## Prerequisites
>
> `box-shadow`, basic CSS gradients, the "Flexible ellipses" secret on page 76

This way, even if certain things are not already known, one can read up about them and come back to the secret afterward. **As long as their prerequisites are met, the secrets can actually be read in any order**, though there is value in reading them in the book order, as a lot of thought has been put into what the optimal order is.

Note that I mentioned "CSS developers" and that "design skills" are not in the list of assumptions above. It's important to note that **this is not a design book**. While it unavoidably touches on certain design principles and describes a few UX improvements, *CSS Secrets* is first and foremost a book **about solving problems with code**. CSS might have a visual output, but it is still code, just like SVG, WebGL/OpenGL, or the JavaScript Canvas API is code, not design. Writing good, flexible CSS requires the same kind of analytical thinking that programming does. Nowadays, most people use preprocessors for their CSS, with variables, math, conditionals, and loops, so it's almost starting to look like programming!

This is not to imply that designers are discouraged from reading this book. Anybody who has sufficient coding experience with CSS can benefit from it, and there are many talented designers who can also write excellent CSS code. However, it's important to note that teaching you how to improve the visual design or usability of a website is **not** among the goals of this book, even if it happens as a side effect.

Format & conventions used

The book consists of **47 "secrets,"** grouped by topic in **seven chapters**. These secrets are more or less independent and—as long as their prerequisites are met—can be read in any order. The demos in every secret are not complete websites, or even parts thereof. They are purposefully as small and simple as possible, in order to facilitate understanding. The assumption is that you already know what you want to implement. The purpose of this book is not to give design ideas, but implementation solutions.

FIGURE P.1

This is an example sidebar figure, introducing the great Sir Adam Catlace

Notes, such as this one, provide additional information or explain a term mentioned in the text.

This is a warning. Its purpose is to warn you (surprising, I know!) about possible false assumptions and certain things that could go wrong.

Every secret is split into two or more sections. The first section, titled "**The problem,**" introduces a common CSS challenge that we are going to solve. Sometimes this introduction might describe widely popular solutions that are suboptimal (e.g., solutions that require a lot of markup, hardcoded values, etc.), and usually concludes with variations of the question *"Is there a better way to achieve this?"*

After introducing the problem, one or more solutions follow. This book was inspired by the CSS talks I have presented at various conferences so I tried to maintain the interactive presentation format as much as a book allows. Therefore, every solution is illustrated by a number of figures, demonstrating the visual output for every step of the solution that results in a visual change. Because figures are not always directly next to the text that describes what they demonstrate, they are numbered and referenced in the text. You can see an example of a figure in **Figure P.1** and the current sentence was an example of a reference to it.

Inline code is denoted by `monospace text` and colors often have a small preview next to them as well (e.g., ■ `#f06`). Block-level code looks like this:

```css
background: url("adamcatlace.jpg");
```

or this:

```html
<figure>
    <img src="adamcatlace.jpg" />
    <figcaption>Sir Adam Catlace</figcaption>
</figure>
```

As you might have noticed, when the language of a code block is not CSS, it's noted in the top-right corner. Also, when the example discussed only involves a single element, and no pseudo-classes or pseudo-elements are involved, there is usually no selector or braces (**{}**) included in the code blocks, for brevity.

All JavaScript examples in the book are vanilla JavaScript, with no frameworks or libraries required. There is only one helper function used, **$$()**, in order to make it easier to loop over a set of elements that match a certain CSS selector. The function's definition is:

```js
function $$(selector, context) {
    context = context || document;
    var elements = context.querySelectorAll(selector);
    return Array.prototype.slice.call(elements);
}
```

TRIVIA Side trivia

Dark "Trivia" sections at the bottom of pages introduce tangentially related trivia, such as the historical or technical background behind a CSS feature. They are not necessary for using or understanding the main material, but readers might find them interesting nevertheless.

Every secret includes one or more live examples that can be accessed with short, memorable URLs in **play.csssecrets.io**. The references to them look like this:

▶ **PLAY!** `play.csssecrets.io/polka`

It is strongly recommended that you check out the "Play!" examples, especially if you are confused by the techniques described or if you get stuck while following along.

HAT TIP

Credit where it's due: *When a technique described was first documented by someone else in the community, credit will be given in a "Hat Tip" paragraph like this one, referencing the URL of the source as well. We all know that having to find the "References" section at the end of a book is a hassle, so these essentially provide **references in context**.*

FUTURE Future solutions

"Future" sections (positioned at the bottom of pages and set on a dark background) introduce techniques that are already in draft specifications, but at the time of writing have no implementations. Readers should always check if these techniques are supported, as they might have been implemented after the publication of this book. In cases where the feature is obscure enough that browser support websites might not include it, the section will include a test that the reader can load, in short memorable URLs, such as the one shown here in the "Test!" example. These tests are usually designed so that shades of green appear when the feature is supported and shades of red otherwise. The exact instructions are mentioned in the code, as a comment.

TEST! `play.csssecrets.io/test-conic-gradient`

At the end of almost every secret you'll find a list of related specifications that looks like this:

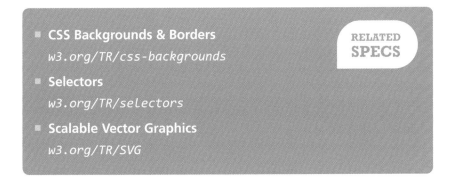

- **CSS Backgrounds & Borders**
  w3.org/TR/css-backgrounds
- **Selectors**
  w3.org/TR/selectors
- **Scalable Vector Graphics**
  w3.org/TR/SVG

RELATED
SPECS

This includes references to all the specifications from which features were mentioned. However, just like the "Prerequisites" box, this does not apply to **CSS 2.1** *(w3.org/TR/CSS21)*, otherwise it would be listed in the "Related Specs" section of every single secret. This means that the few secrets that only discuss CSS 2.1 features have no "Related Specs" section at all.

Browser support & fallbacks

**LIMITED
SUPPORT**

Possibly the biggest peculiarity of this book is the **complete lack of browser compatibility tables**. This was a conscious decision, as with today's browser release cycles, such information is bound to get out of date before this book even hits the shelves. I believe that **inaccurate browser support information is misleading, and is actually worse than no information.**

However, most secrets described either currently have decent browser support and/or degrade gracefully. In cases where a technique described presently has particularly poor browser support, there is a "Limited Support" warning icon next to the relevant solution, like the one next to this paragraph. This should be enough to hint that you should not use the solution without looking up browser support for it and taking extra care for providing good fallbacks.

There are plenty of excellent websites containing up-to-date browser support information. Here are some suggestions:

- **Can I Use...?** *(caniuse.com)*
- **WebPlatform.org**
- **Mozilla Developer Network** *(developer.mozilla.org)*
- **Wikipedia's "Comparison of Layout Engines (Cascading Style Sheets)"** *(en.wikipedia.org/wiki/ Comparison_of_layout_engines_(Cascading_Style_Sheets))*

Sometimes you might find that a certain feature is supported, but slightly differently across browsers. For example, it might need a **vendor prefix**, or **slightly different syntax**. Only the standards-compliant, unprefixed syntax will be included in the examples. However, you can almost always use different syntaxes alongside and let the cascade take care of which one wins. For this reason, **always place the standard version last**. For example, to get a vertical linear gradient from **yellow** to **red**, the book would only list the standard version:

```
background: linear-gradient(90deg, yellow, red);
```

However, if you want to support very old browsers, you might end up having to write something like the following:

You can read more on vendor prefixes, why they exist, and how to abstract them away from your code in the **"A story of ice, fire, and vendor prefixes" section on page 6**.

```
background: -moz-linear-gradient(0deg, yellow, red);
background: -o-linear-gradient(0deg, yellow, red);
background: -webkit-linear-gradient(0deg, yellow, red);
background: linear-gradient(90deg, yellow, red);
```

Because the landscape of these differences is just as fluid as browser support, it is expected that things like this are part of your standard research before using a CSS feature and are not discussed further in the solutions presented.

Similarly, most of the time it's good practice to provide fallbacks, so that your website doesn't break in older browsers, even if it doesn't look as fancy in them. These are not discussed extensively when they are obvious, as the assumption is that you know how the cascade works. For example, when specifying a gradient, such as the one just shown, you should also add a solid color version before all of them. A good idea for the solid color might be the average of the two gradient colors (in this case, ■ `rgb(255, 128, 0)`):

```
background: rgb(255, 128, 0);
background: -moz-linear-gradient(0deg, yellow, red);
background: -o-linear-gradient(0deg, yellow, red);
background: -webkit-linear-gradient(0deg, yellow, red);
background: linear-gradient(90deg, yellow, red);
```

However, sometimes it's not possible to provide decent fallbacks through the cascade. As a last resort, you could use tools like **Modernizr** (*modernizr.com*), which adds classes like **textshadow** or **no-textshadow** to the root element (`<html>`), so you can use them to **target elements only when certain features are (not) supported**, like so:

```
h1 { color: gray; }

.textshadow h1 {
    color: transparent;
    text-shadow: 0 0 .3em gray;
}
```

If the feature you are trying to create a fallback for is sufficiently new, you could use the **@supports** rule, which is the "native" Modernizr. For example, the preceding code would become:

```
h1 { color: gray; }

@supports (text-shadow: 0 0 .3em gray) {
    h1 {
        color: transparent;
```

```
        text-shadow: 0 0 .3em gray;
    }
}
```

However, for now, **be wary of using @supports**. By using it here we just limited our effect not only to browsers that support text shadows, but also to browsers that support the **@supports** rule—a much more limited set.

Last, but not least, there is always the option of using a few lines of home-baked JavaScript to perform feature detection and add classes to the root element in the same fashion as Modernizr. The main way to determine whether a property is supported is to check its existence on the **element.style** object of any element:

```js
var root = document.documentElement; // <html>

if ('textShadow' in root.style) {
    root.classList.add('textshadow');
}
else {
    root.classList.add('no-textshadow');
}
```

If we need to test for multiple properties, we can easily turn this into a function:

```js
function testProperty(property) {
    var root = document.documentElement;

    if (property in root.style) {
        root.classList.add(property.toLowerCase());
        return true;
    }
```

```
        root.classList.add('no-' + property.toLowerCase());
        return false;
}
```

If we want to test a value, we need to assign it to the property and check if the browser retains it. Because we are modifying styles here and not just testing for their existence, it makes sense to use a dummy element:

```
var dummy = document.createElement('p');
dummy.style.backgroundImage = 'linear-gradient(red,tan)';

if (dummy.style.backgroundImage) {
    root.classList.add('lineargradients');
}
else {
    root.classList.add('no-lineargradients');
}
```

This can easily be converted to a function as well:

```
function testValue(id, value, property) {
    var dummy = document.createElement('p');
    dummy.style[property] = value;

    if (dummy.style[property]) {
        root.classList.add(id);
        return true;
    }

    root.classList.add('no-' + id);
    return false;
}
```

Testing selectors and @rules is a bit more complex, but follows the same principle: when it comes to CSS, browsers drop anything they don't understand, so we can check if a feature is recognized by dynamically applying it and checking if it was retained. Of course, keep in mind that a browser being able to **parse** a CSS feature offers **no guarantee that the feature is correctly implemented, or even that it's implemented at all**.

Introduction 1

Web standards: friend or foe?

The standards process

Contrary to popular belief, the **W3C (World Wide Web Consortium) does not "make" standards**. Instead, it acts as a forum for interested parties to get together and do so, in its W3C Working Groups. Of course, the W3C is not a mere observer: it sets the ground rules and it oversees the process. But **it's not (primarily) W3C staff that actually write the specifications**.

CSS specifications, in particular, are written by the members of the CSS Working Group, often abbreviated as CSS WG. At the time of writing, the CSS WG includes 98 members, and its composition is as follows:

- **86** members from W3C member companies (88%)
- **7** Invited Experts, including yours truly (7%)
- **5** W3C staff members (5%)

As you might notice, the vast majority of WG members (88%) come from *W3C member companies*. These are companies—such as browser vendors, popular websites, research institutes, general technology companies, etc.— that have a vested interest in seeing web standards flourish. Their yearly membership dues represent the majority of the W3C's funding, enabling

FIGURE 1.1

"Standards are like sausages: it's better not to see them being made" —Anonymous W3C WG member the Consortium to distribute its specifications **freely** and **openly**, unlike other standards bodies that have to charge for them.

Invited Experts are web developers who have been asked to participate in the standards process, after demonstrating a continuous commitment to helping out, and a sufficient technical background to participate in the discussions.

Last, but not least, *W3C staff members* are people who actually work at the Consortium and facilitate communication between the WG and the W3C.

A widespread misconception among web developers is that the W3C creates standards from up high that the poor browsers then have to follow, whether they like them or not. However, this couldn't be further from the truth: browser vendors have **much more of a say than the W3C** in what goes into standards, as evidenced by the numbers listed before.

Also contrary to popular belief, **standards are not created in a vacuum**, behind closed doors. The CSS WG is committed to transparency and all its communications are open to the public, inviting review and participation:

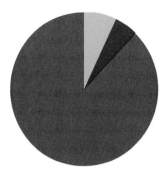

FIGURE 1.2

The composition of the CSS WG:
- Member companies
- Invited Experts
- W3C staff members

- Most discussions happen in its **mailing list**, **www-style** *(lists.w3.org/Archives/Public/www-style)*. www-style is publicly archived, and is open to participation from anyone.

- There is a **weekly telcon**, with a duration of one hour. This is not open to participation by non-WG members, but is minuted in real time in the **#css** channel on **the W3C's IRC server** *(irc.w3.org/)*. These minutes are then cleaned up and posted to the mailing list a few days later.

- There are also **quarterly face-to-face meetings**, which are also minuted in the same fashion as telcons. They are also often open to **observation** (auditing), after requesting permission from the WG *chairs*.

All this is part of the W3C process and has to do with decision making. However, the ones that are actually responsible for putting these decisions to writing (i.e., authoring the specifications) are the *Spec Editors*. Spec Editors might be W3C staff members, browser developers, interested Invited Experts, or member company employees who are doing it as a full-time job, paid by their companies to advance standards for the common good.

Each specification goes through multiple stages as it evolves from initial inception to maturity:

Interested in learning more? Elika Etemad (fantasai) has written **a series of amazing articles on how the CSS WG operates** *(fantasai.inkedblade.net/ weblog/2011/inside-csswg)*. Very highly recommended.

1. **Editor's Draft (ED):** The first stage of a spec could be as messy as being just a collection of ideas by the spec editor. There are no requirements for this stage and no guarantee that it's approved by the WG. However, this is also the first stage of every revision: all changes are first made in an ED, then published.

2. **First Public Working Draft (FPWD):** The first published version of a spec, after it's deemed ready for public feedback by the WG.

3. **Working Draft (WD):** There are many WDs after the first one, each slightly better, incorporating feedback from the WG and the broader community. First implementations often start at this stage, but it's not unheard of to have experimental implementations of earlier stage specs.

4. **Candidate Recommendation (CR):** This is considered a relatively stable version. Now it's time for implementations and tests. A spec cannot advance past this stage without a full test suite and at least two independent implementations.

5. **Proposed Recommendation (PR):** Last chance for W3C member companies to express disagreement with the specification. This rarely happens, so it's usually just a matter of time for every PR spec to move to the next, final stage.

6. **Recommendation (REC):** The final stage of a W3C specification.

One or two WG members have the role of being *chairs*. Chairs are responsible for organizing meetings, coordinating calls, timekeeping, and generally moderating the whole thing. Being chair is a very time-consuming and energy-draining role, and is frequently compared to **herding cats**. Of course, everyone involved in standards knows that such a comparison is moot: herding cats is actually considerably easier.

FIGURE 1.3
Chairing a W3C Working Group is frequently compared to herding cats

CSS3, CSS4, and other mythical creatures

CSS 1 was a very short and relatively simple specification, published in 1996 by Håkon Wium Lie and Bert Bos. It was so small that it was all included in a single HTML page, which required around 68 sheets of A4 paper to print.

CSS 2, published in 1998, was more strictly defined, and included much more power and two more spec editors: Chris Lilley and Ian Jacobs. At this point, the length of the specification had grown to 480 (!) printed pages and was already getting too big to be held in human memory in its entirety.

After CSS Level 2, the CSS WG realized that the language was getting too big to be contained in a single specification. Not only was it extremely unwieldy to read and edit, but it was also holding CSS back. Remember that **for a specification to advance to the final stages, every single feature in it needs at least two independent implementations and exhaustive tests**. This was no longer practical. Therefore, it was decided that going forward, CSS was going to be broken into multiple specifications (modules), each with its own versioning. Those that expand on features that were already present in CSS 2.1 would have a level number of 3. For example, some of these modules are:

- **CSS Syntax** *(w3.org/TR/css-syntax-3)*
- **CSS Cascading and Inheritance** *(w3.org/TR/css-cascade-3)*
- **CSS Color** *(w3.org/TR/css3-color)*
- **Selectors** *(w3.org/TR/selectors)*
- **CSS Backgrounds & Borders** *(w3.org/TR/css3-background)*
- **CSS Values and Units** *(w3.org/TR/css-values-3)*
- **CSS Text** *(w3.org/TR/css-text-3)*
- **CSS Text Decoration** *(w3.org/TR/css-text-decor-3)*
- **CSS Fonts** *(w3.org/TR/css3-fonts)*
- **CSS Basic User Interface** *(w3.org/TR/css3-ui)*

However, modules that introduce entirely new concepts start from Level 1. Here are a few examples:

- **CSS Transforms** (*w3.org/TR/css-transforms-1*)
- **Compositing and Blending** (*w3.org/TR/compositing-1*)
- **Filter Effects** (*w3.org/TR/filter-effects-1*)
- **CSS Masking** (*w3.org/TR/css-masking-1*)
- **CSS Flexible Box Layout** (*w3.org/TR/css-flexbox-1*)
- **CSS Grid Layout** (*w3.org/TR/css-grid-1*)

Despite the popularity of the "CSS3" buzzword, there is actually no specification defining such a thing, like there was for CSS 2.1 or its predecessors. Instead, what most authors are referring to is an arbitrary set of Level 3 specs, plus some Level 1 specs. Although there is some good degree of consensus among authors on which specs are included in "CSS3," as CSS modules evolve at different rates over the years, it will become more and more difficult to refer to things like CSS3, CSS4, and so on and be universally understood.

A story of ice, fire, and vendor prefixes

In standards development, there is always a big catch-22: standards groups need input from developers to create specifications that address real development needs. However, developers are generally not interested in trying out things they can't use in production. When experimental technologies get widely used in production, the WG is forced to stick with the early, experimental version of the technology, to avoid breaking several existing websites if they change it. Obviously, this completely negates the benefits of getting developers to try out early standards.

Over the years, many solutions have been proposed to address this conundrum, none of them perfect. The universally despised vendor prefixes were one of them. The idea was that every browser would be able to implement experimental (or even proprietary) features with their own prefix prepended to its name. The most common prefixes are `-moz-` for Firefox, `-ms-` for IE, `-o-` for Opera, and `-webkit-` for Safari and Chrome. Developers would be able to freely experiment with these prefixed features and provide feedback to the WG, which would then incorporate this feedback into the specs and slowly perfect the design of the feature. Because the final, standardized version would have a different name (no prefix), it wouldn't collide with the existing uses of its prefixed counterparts.

Sounds great, right? Of course, as you probably know, the reality was quite different from the vision. When developers realized that these experimental, vendor-prefixed properties could make it so much easier to create effects that previously required messy workarounds, they started using them everywhere. Vendor-prefixed properties quickly became the CSS trend of the time. Tutorials were written, StackOverflow replies were given, and soon almost every self-respecting CSS developer was using them all over the place.

Eventually, authors realized that using only existing vendor prefixes meant they would have to go back to previous work and add new declarations every time another browser implemented their favorite cool new CSS feature. Not to mention how hard it became to keep up with which prefixes were needed for what feature. The solution? Add all possible vendor prefixes preemptively, including the unprefixed version at the end, to future-proof it. We ended up with code like the following:

```
-moz-border-radius: 10px;
-ms-border-radius: 10px;
-o-border-radius: 10px;
-webkit-border-radius: 10px;
border-radius: 10px;
```

Two of the declarations here are completely redundant: **-ms-border-radius** and **-o-border-radius** never existed in any browser, as IE and Opera implemented **border-radius** unprefixed from the get-go.

Obviously, repeating every declaration up to five times was tedious and unmaintainable. It was only a matter of time until tools were built to automate this:

■ Websites like **CSS3, Please!** *(css3please.com)* or **pleeease** *(pleeease.io/playground.html)* allow you to paste your unprefixed CSS code and get back CSS with all necessary prefixes added. Such apps were among the first ideas devised to automate vendor prefix addition, but are not very popular anymore, as using them incurs quite a lot of overhead compared to other solutions.

- **Autoprefixer** *(github.com/ai/autoprefixer)* uses the database from **Can I Use...** *(caniuse.com)* to determine which prefixes to add to unprefixed code and compiles it locally, like a preprocessor.

- My own **-prefix-free** *(leaverou.github.io/prefixfree)* performs feature testing in the browser to determine which prefixes are needed. The benefit is that it rarely needs updating, as it gets everything from the browser environment, including the list of properties.

- Preprocessors like **LESS** *(lesscss.org)* or **Sass** *(sass-lang.com)* don't offer any means of prefixing out of the box, but many authors create mixins for the features they prefix most often, and there are several libraries of such mixins in circulation.

Because authors were using the unprefixed version of features as a means to future-proof their code, it became impossible to change them. We were basically stuck with half-baked early specs that we could change in very limited ways. It didn't take long for everyone involved to realize that **vendor prefixes were an epic failure**.

These days, vendor prefixes are rarely used for new experimental implementations. Instead, experimental features require **config flags** to be turned on, effectively preventing developers from using them in production, as you can't really tell users to change their settings in order to view your website properly. Of course, this has the consequence that fewer authors get to play with experimental features, but we still get enough feedback, and arguably, better quality feedback, without the drawbacks of vendor prefixes. However, it will be a long time before the ripple effects of vendor prefixes stop haunting us all.

CSS coding tips

Minimize code duplication

Keeping code DRY and maintainable is one of the biggest challenges in software development, and that applies to CSS as well. In practice, one big component of maintainable code is **minimizing the amount of edits necessary to make a change**. For example, if to enlarge a button you need to make 10 edits in many different rules, chances are you will miss a few of them, especially if you are not the one who wrote the original code. Even if the edits are obvious, or you eventually find them, you have just wasted time that could be put to better use.

Furthermore, this is not just about future changes. Flexible CSS makes it easier to write CSS once, and then create variations with very little code, as there are only a few values you need to override. Let's look at an example.

Take a look at the following CSS, which styles the button shown in **Figure 1.4**:

FIGURE 1.4

The button we are going to use in our example

```
padding: 6px 16px;
border: 1px solid #446d88;
background: #58a linear-gradient(#77a0bb, #58a);
border-radius: 4px;
box-shadow: 0 1px 5px gray;
color: white;
```

```
text-shadow: 0 -1px 1px #335166;
font-size: 20px;
line-height: 30px;
```

There are several issues with the maintainability of this code that we can fix. The low-hanging fruit is the font metrics. If we decide to change the font size (perhaps to create a variation that will be used for important, bigger buttons), we also need to adjust the line spacing, as they are both absolute values. Furthermore, the line spacing doesn't reflect what its relationship is to the font size, so we would even need to perform calculations to figure out what it should be for a different font size. **When values depend on each other, try to reflect their relationship in the code.** In this case, the line spacing is 150% the line height. Therefore, it would be much more maintainable to show this in the code:

```
font-size: 20px;
line-height: 1.5;
```

While we're at it, why did we specify the font size as an absolute length? Sure, absolute lengths are easy to work with, but they come back to bite you every single time you make changes. Now, if we decide to make the parent font size bigger, we would have to change every single rule in the stylesheet that uses absolute font measurements. It's much better to use percentages or **em**s:

FIGURE 1.5

Enlarging the font size breaks other effects in our button (corner rounding being the most noticeable), as they are specified using absolute lengths

```
font-size: 125%; /* Assuming a 16px parent font size */
line-height: 1.5;
```

Now if I change the parent font size, the button will instantly become bigger. However, it will look quite different (**Figure 1.5**), because all other effects were designed for a smaller button and did not scale. We can make all the other effects scalable as well, by specifying any lengths in **em**s, so that they all depend on the font size. This way, we can control the size of the button in one place:

```css
padding: .3em .8em;
border: 1px solid #446d88;
background: #58a linear-gradient(#77a0bb, #58a);
border-radius: .2em;
box-shadow: 0 .05em .25em gray;
color: white;
text-shadow: 0 -.05em .05em #335166;
font-size: 125%;
line-height: 1.5;
```

Here we wanted our font size and measurements to be relative to the parent font size, so we used **ems**. In some cases, you want them to be relative to the **root font size** (i.e., the font size of <html>), and ems result in complex calculations. In that case, you can use the **rem** unit. Relativity is an important feature in CSS, but you do have to **think** about what things should be relative **to**.

Now our larger button looks much more like a scaled version of the original (**Figure 1.6**). Notice that we still left some lengths as absolute values. **It's a judgment call which effects should scale with the button and which ones should stay the same.** In this case, we wanted our border thickness to stay **1px** regardless of the button dimensions.

However, making the button smaller or larger is not the only thing we might want to change. Colors are another big one. For example, what if we want to create a red Cancel button, or a green OK button? Currently, we would need to override four declarations (**border-color**, **background**, **box-shadow**, **text-shadow**), not to mention the hassle of recalculating all the different darker/lighter variants of our main color, ■ **#58a**, and figuring out how much lighter or darker each color is. Also, what if we want to place our button on a non-white background? Using ■ **gray** for its shadow will only look as intended on a white background.

We could easily eliminate this hassle by using semi-transparent white and black for lighter/darker variants, respectively, overlaid on our main color:

FIGURE 1.6

Now we can make our button larger, and all its effects scale too

```css
padding: .3em .8em;
border: 1px solid rgba(0,0,0,.1);
background: #58a linear-gradient(hsla(0,0%,100%,.2),
                                 transparent);
```

TIP! Use HSLA instead of RGBA for semi-transparent white, as it has slightly fewer characters and is quicker to type, due to the lack of repetition.

```
border-radius: .2em;
box-shadow: 0 .05em .25em rgba(0,0,0,.5);
color: white;
text-shadow: 0 -.05em .05em rgba(0,0,0,.5);
font-size: 125%;
line-height: 1.5;
```

Now all it takes to create variations with different colors is to override **background-color** (**Figure 1.7**):

FIGURE 1.7

All it took to create these color variations was changing the background color

```
button.cancel {
    background-color: #c00;
}

button.ok {
    background-color: #6b0;
}
```

Our button is already much more flexible. However, this example doesn't demonstrate every opportunity to make your code more DRY. You will find a few more tips in the following sections.

Maintainability versus brevity

Sometimes, **maintainability and brevity can be mutually exclusive**. Even in the previous example, our final code is a bit longer than our original. Consider the following snippet to create a **10px** thick border on every side of an element, **except the left one**:

```
border-width: 10px 10px 10px 0;
```

It's only one declaration, but to change the border thickness we would need to make three edits. It would be much easier to edit as two declarations, and it's arguably easier to read that way too:

```
border-width: 10px;
border-left-width: 0;
```

currentColor

In **CSS Color Level 3** *(w3.org/TR/css3-color)*, we got many new color keywords like `lightgoldenrodyellow`, which aren't that useful. However, we also got a special new color keyword, borrowed from SVG: `currentColor`. This does not correspond to a static color value. Instead, it always resolves to the value of the `color` property, effectively making it **the first ever variable in CSS**. A very limited variable, but a variable nevertheless.

For example, let's assume we want all of the horizontal separators (all `<hr>` elements) to automatically have the same color as the text. With `currentColor`, we could do this:

```
hr {
    height: .5em;
    background: currentColor;
}
```

You might have noticed similar behavior with many existing properties. For example, if you specify a border with no color, it automatically gets the text color. This is because `currentColor` is also the initial value of many CSS color properties: `border-color`, the `text-shadow` and `box-shadow` colors, `outline-color`, and others.

In the future, when we get functions to manipulate colors in native CSS, `currentColor` will become even more useful, as we will be able to use variations of it.

Some would argue that the **em** unit was actually the first variable in CSS, as it referred to the value of **font-size**. Most percentages play a similar role, though in less exciting ways.

Inheritance

While most authors are aware of the **inherit** keyword, it is often forgotten. The **inherit** keyword can be used in any **CSS** property and it always corresponds to the computed value of the parent element (in pseudo-elements that is the element they are generated on). For example, to give form elements the same font as the rest of the page, you don't need to re-specify it, just use **inherit**:

```css
input, select, button { font: inherit; }
```

Similarly, to give hyperlinks the same color as the rest of the text, use **inherit**:

```css
a { color: inherit; }
```

The **inherit** keyword can often be useful for backgrounds as well. For example, to create speech bubbles where the pointer automatically inherits the background and border (**Figure 1.8**):

Your username:

leaverou

Only letters, numbers, underscores (_) and hyphens (-) allowed!

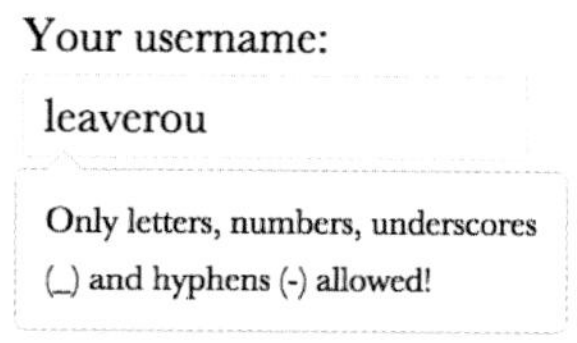

FIGURE 1.8

A speech bubble where the pointer gets the background color and border from the parent

```css
.callout { position: relative; }

.callout::before {
    content: "";
    position: absolute;
    top: -.4em; left: 1em;
    padding: .35em;
    background: inherit;
    border: inherit;
    border-right: 0;
    border-bottom: 0;
    transform: rotate(45deg);
}
```

Trust your eyes, not numbers

The human eye is far from being a perfect input device. Sometimes accurate measurements result in looking inaccurate and designs need to account for that. For example, it's well known in visual design literature that our eyes don't perceive something as being vertically centered when it is. Instead, it needs to be slightly above the geometrical middle to be perceived as such. See that phenomenon for yourself, in **Figure 1.9**.

Similarly, in type design, it is well known that round glyphs such as "O" need to be slightly larger than more rectangular glyphs, as we tend to perceive round shapes as smaller than they actually are. Check that out for yourself in **Figure 1.10**.

Such **optical illusions are very common in any form of visual design**, and need to be accounted for. An extremely common example is padding in containers with text. The issue is present regardless of the amount of text—it could be a word or several paragraphs. If we specify the same amount of padding on all four sides of a box, it actually ends up looking uneven, as **Figure 1.11** demonstrates. The reason is that **letterforms are much more straight on the sides than their top and bottom**, so our eyes perceive that extra space as extra padding. Therefore, we need to specify **less padding for the top and bottom sides** if we want it to be perceived as being the same. You can see the difference this makes in **Figure 1.12**.

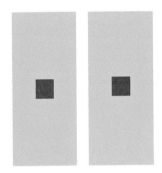

FIGURE 1.9

In the first rectangle, the brown square is mathematically vertically centered, but doesn't look so; in the second one, it is actually placed slightly above the geometrical center, but it looks more centered to the human eye

FIGURE 1.10

The circle looks smaller, but its bounding box is exactly the same as the square

On Responsive Web Design

RWD (Responsive Web Design) has been all the rage over the past few years. However, the emphasis is often placed on how important it is for websites to be "responsive," leaving a lot unsaid about what good RWD entails.

The common practice is testing a website in multiple resolutions and adding more and more media queries to fix the issues that arise. However, **every media query adds overhead** to future CSS changes, and they should not be added lightly. Every future edit to the CSS code requires

FIGURE 1.11

Specifying the same padding (`.5em` here) on all four sides of a container with text makes it look larger on the top and bottom sides

FIGURE 1.12

Specifying larger padding (here: `.3em .7em`) on the left and right side makes it look much more uniform

TIP! Consider using **ems** in your media queries instead of pixels. This allows text zoom to trigger layout changes as necessary.

checking whether any media queries apply, and potentially editing those too. This is often forgotten, resulting in breakage. The more media queries you add, the more fragile your CSS code becomes.

That is not to say that media queries are a bad practice. **Used right, they can be indispensable.** However, they should be a last resort, after every other attempt to make a website design flexible has failed, or when we want to completely change an aspect of the design in smaller/larger viewports (e.g., making the sidebar horizontal). The reason is that media queries do not fix issues in a continuous manner. They are all about specific thresholds (a.k.a. "breakpoints"), and unless the rest of the code is written to be flexible, media queries will only fix specific resolutions, essentially sweeping issues under the rug.

Of course, it goes without saying that **media query thresholds should not be dictated by specific devices**, but by the design itself. Not only because there are so many different devices (especially if we take future devices into account) that a website should look good at any possible resolution, but also because a website on the desktop might be viewed in a window of any size. If you are confident that your design works well in every possible viewport size, who cares about what resolution specific devices have?

Following the principles described in the **"Minimize code duplication" section on page 9** will also help with this, as you won't have to override as many declarations in your media queries, essentially minimizing the overhead they cause.

Here are a few more tips to avoid needless media queries:

- Use percentages instead of fixed widths. When that's not possible, use viewport-relative units (**vw**, **vh**, **vmin**, **vmax**), which resolve to a fraction of the viewport width or height.
- When you want a fixed width for larger resolutions, use **max-width**, not **width**, so it can still adapt to smaller ones without media queries.
- Don't forget to set a **max-width** of **100%** for replaced elements such as **img**, **object**, **video**, and **iframe**.
- In cases when a background image needs to cover an entire container, **background-size: cover** can help maintain that regardless of said container's size. However, bear in mind that bandwidth is not unlimited, and

it's not always wise to include large images that are going to be scaled down via CSS in mobile designs.

- When laying out images (or other elements) in a grid of rows and columns, let the number of columns be dictated by the viewport width. Flexible Box Layout (a.k.a. Flexbox) or `display: inline-block` and regular text wrapping can help with that.

- When using multi-column text, specify `column-width` instead of `column-count`, so that you get one column only in small resolutions.

In general, the idea is to strive for **liquid layouts and relative sizing between media query breakpoints**. When a design is sufficiently flexible, making it responsive shouldn't take more than a few short media queries. The designers of Basecamp wrote about this very matter in late 2010:

> "As it turned out, making the layout work on a variety of devices was just a matter of adding a few CSS media queries to the finished product. The key to making it easy was that the layout was already liquid, so optimizing it for small screens meant collapsing a few margins to maximize space and tweaking the sidebar layout in the cases where the screen is too narrow to show two columns."
>
> — **Experimenting with responsive design in Iterations** *(signalvnoise.com/posts/2661-experimenting-with-responsive-design-in-iterations)*

If you find yourself needing a boatload of media queries to make your design adapt to smaller (or larger) screens, take a step back and reexamine your code structure, because in all likelihood, responsiveness is not the only issue there.

Use shorthands wisely

As you probably know, the following two lines of CSS are not equivalent:

```
background: rebeccapurple;
```

```
background-color: rebeccapurple;
```

The former is a shorthand and will always give you a ■ rebeccapurple background, whereas the element with the longhand (**background-color**) could end up with a pink gradient, a picture of a cat, or anything really, as there might also be a **background-image** declaration in effect. This is the problem when you mainly use longhands: you are not resetting all the other properties that could be affecting what you're trying to accomplish.

You could of course try to set **all the longhands** and call it a day, but then you might forget some. Or the CSS WG might introduce more longhands in the future, and your code will have failed to reset those. Don't be afraid of shorthands. It is **good defensive coding and future-proofing** to use them, **unless we intentionally want to use cascaded properties** for everything else, like we did for the colored button variants in the **"Minimize code duplication" section on page 9**.

Longhands are also very useful in combination with shorthands, to make code DRY-er in properties whose values are a comma-separated list, such as the **background** properties. This is best explained with an example:

```
background: url(tr.png) no-repeat top right / 2em 2em,
            url(br.png) no-repeat bottom right / 2em 2em,
            url(bl.png) no-repeat bottom left / 2em 2em;
```

Notice how the **background-size** and **background-repeat** values are repeated three times, despite being the same for every image. We can take advantage of CSS list expansion rules which say that **if only one value is provided, it is expanded to apply to every item in the list**, and move these repeated values to longhands:

```
background: url(tr.png) top right,
            url(br.png) bottom right,
            url(bl.png) bottom left;
background-size: 2em 2em;
background-repeat: no-repeat;
```

Now we can change the `background-size` and `background-repeat` with only one edit instead of three. You will see this technique used throughout the book.

Should I use a preprocessor?

You've probably heard of CSS preprocessors such as **LESS** *(lesscss.org)*, **Sass** *(sass-lang.com)*, or **Stylus** *(learnboost.github.io/stylus)*. They offer several conveniences for authoring CSS, such as variables, mixins, functions, rule nesting, color manipulation, and more.

Used properly, they can help keep code more flexible in a large project, when CSS itself proves too limited to let us do so. As much as we strive to code robust, flexible, DRY CSS, sometimes we just stumble on the limitations of the language. However, preprocessors also come with a few issues of their own:

- You lose track of your CSS' **filesize and complexity**. Concise, small code might compile to a CSS behemoth that is sent down the wires.

TRIVIA Weird shorthand syntax

You might have noticed in the shorthand and longhand example that specifying **background-size** in the **background** shorthand requires also providing a **background-position** (even if it's the same as the initial one) and using a slash (**/**) to separate them. Why do some shorthands have such weird rules?

This is almost always done for disambiguation purposes. Sure, in the example here, it's obvious that **top right** is a **background-position** and **2em 2em** a **background-size** regardless of their ordering. However, think of values like **50% 50%**. Is it a **background-size** or a **background-position**? When you are using the longhands, the CSS parser knows what you mean. However, in the shorthand, the parser needs to figure out what that **50% 50%** refers to without any help from the property name. This is why the slash is needed.

For most shorthands, there is no such disambiguation issue and their values can be specified in any order. However, it's always good practice to look up the exact syntax, to avoid nasty surprises. If you are familiar with regexes and grammars, you could also check the grammar for the property in the relevant specification, which is probably the quickest way to see if there is a specific ordering.

- **Debugging becomes harder**, as the CSS you see in the developer tools is not the CSS you wrote. This is becoming less of an issue, as *SourceMaps* get more debugger support. SourceMaps are a cool new technology that aims to mitigate this issue by telling the browser what preprocessor CSS corresponds to what generated CSS, down to the line number.

- They introduce some degree of **latency** in our development process. Even though they are generally fast, it still takes a second or so to compile your code to CSS, which you have to wait for before previewing its result.

- With every abstraction, comes more effort required by someone to start working on our codebase. We either have to only collaborate with people fluent in the preprocessor dialect of our choice, or teach it to them. So we are either **restricted in our choice of collaborators or need to spend extra time for training,** both of which are suboptimal.

- Let's not forget the *Law of Leaky Abstractions*: "All non-trivial abstractions, to some degree, are leaky." Preprocessors are written by humans, and like every non-trivial program humans have ever written, **they have their own bugs**, which can be very insidious as we rarely suspect that a preprocessor bug might be the culprit behind our CSS issues.

In addition to the issues listed here, preprocessors also pose the risk of making authors dependent on them, perpetuating their use even when unnecessary, such as in smaller projects or in the future, after their most popular features have been added to native CSS. Surprised? Yes, **many preprocessor-inspired features have been making their way into pure CSS**:

- There is already a draft about variable-like custom properties, under the title of **CSS Custom Properties for Cascading Variables** *(w3.org/TR/css-variables-1)*.

- The function `calc()` from CSS Values & Units Level 3 not only is very powerful for performing calculations, but also very well supported, even today.

- The `color()` function in **CSS Color Level 4** *(dev.w3.org/csswg/css-color)* will provide means to manipulate colors.

- There are several serious discussions in the CSS WG about nesting, and even a draft spec (ED) existed about it in the past.

Note that native features like these are generally **much more powerful than the ones provided by preprocessors**, as they are dynamic. For example, a preprocessor has no clue how to perform a calculation like **100% - 50px**, because the value percentages resolve to is not known until the page is actually rendered. However, native CSS **calc()** has no trouble evaluating such expressions. Similarly, variable use like the following is not possible with preprocessor variables:

Don't forget that native CSS features like these can be manipulated through scripting too. For example, you could use JS to change the value of a variable.

```
ul { --accent-color: purple; }
ol { --accent-color: rebeccapurple; }
li { background: var(--accent-color); }
```

Can you see what we did there? The background of list items in ordered lists will be ⬛ rebeccapurple, whereas the background of list items in unordered lists will be ⬛ purple. Try doing that with a preprocessor! Of course, in this case, we could have just used descendant selectors, but the point of the example was to show how dynamic these variables will be.

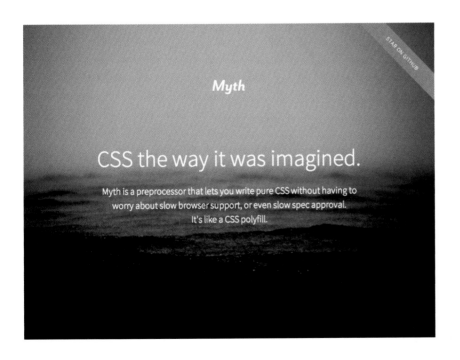

FIGURE 1.13

Myth *(myth.io)* is an experimental preprocessor that emulates these native CSS features, instead of introducing proprietary syntax, essentially acting like a CSS polyfill

Because most of the aforementioned native CSS features are not well supported today, in many cases using preprocessors is unavoidable if maintainability matters (and it should). My advice would be to start off every project with pure CSS, and when it starts being impossible to keep it DRY, switch to using a preprocessor then. To avoid becoming completely dependent on preprocessors or using them when they are not actually needed, **their use needs to be a conscious decision**, not a mindless first step performed by default in every new project.

In case you were wondering (and haven't read the first chapter, tsk-tsk), **the style of this book was authored in SCSS**, although it started as pure CSS and only switched when the code grew too complex to be maintainable. Who said CSS and its preprocessors are only for the Web?

Backgrounds & Borders

1 Translucent borders

The problem

By now, you've probably dabbled quite a bit with semi-transparent colors in CSS, such as `rgba()` and `hsla()`. They were a huge revolution back in 2009, when we were finally able to use them in our designs, despite the required fallbacks, shims, and even ugly IE filter hacks for the daring. However, their uses in the wild were mostly centered around backgrounds. There were a few reasons for this:

- Some early adopters hadn't quite realized that these new color formats were actually colors just like ■ `#ff0066` or ● **orange**, and treated them like images, using them only in backgrounds.
- It was much easier to provide fallbacks for backgrounds than for other properties. For example, the fallback for a semi-transparent background

could be a single pixel semi-transparent image. For other properties, the only possible fallback was a solid color.

- Using them in other properties, such as borders, wasn't always as straightforward. We'll see why next.

FIGURE 2.1

24ways.org was one of the first websites to really utilize semi-transparent colors in its design, as early as 2008, although they were also mostly backgrounds (design by Tim Van Damme)

Suppose we want to style a container with a white background and a semi-transparent white border, through which our body background shows. Our first attempt would probably look like this:

```
border: 10px solid hsla(0,0%,100%,.5);
background: white;
```

FIGURE 2.2

Our initial attempt to achieve semi-transparent borders

Unless you have a good understanding of how backgrounds and borders work, the result (shown in **Figure 2.2**) can be quite baffling. Where did our border go? And if we cannot achieve semi-transparent borders by using a semi-transparent color for the border, then how can we do it?!

The solution

Although it might not look like it, our border is still there. By default, backgrounds extend underneath the border area, which you can easily check by applying a good ol' dashed border to an element with a background (**Figure 2.3**). This doesn't make much of a difference when you're using solid opaque borders, but in this case, it completely changes our design. Instead of having a semi-transparent white border through which our nice body background shows, we ended up having semi-transparent white borders on opaque white, which are indistinguishable from plain white borders.

In CSS 2.1, this was just how backgrounds worked. We just had to accept it and move on. Thankfully, since **Backgrounds & Borders Level 3** *(w3.org/TR/css3-background)*, we are able to adjust this behavior when it's not convenient, through the **background-clip** property. Its initial value is **border-box**, which means that backgrounds are clipped at the outer edge of the element's *border box*. If we want our background to not extend underneath the border, all we have to do is to give it the value **padding-box**, which tells the browser to clip the background at the padding edge:

```
border: 10px solid hsla(0,0%,100%,.5);
background: white;
background-clip: padding-box;
```

The much nicer result can be seen in **Figure 2.4**.

▶ **PLAY!** play.csssecrets.io/**translucent-borders**

- **CSS Backgrounds & Borders**
  w3.org/TR/css-backgrounds

RELATED
SPECS

2 Multiple borders

Prerequisites
Basic **box-shadow** use

The problem

Back in the day, when **Backgrounds & Borders Level 3** *(w3.org/TR/ css3-background)* was still a draft, there was a lot of discussion in the CSS WG about whether multiple borders should be allowed, just like multiple background images. Unfortunately, the consensus at the time was that there weren't enough use cases, and authors could always use **border-image** to achieve the same effect. However, what the Working Group missed is that we usually want the flexibility of being able to adjust borders in CSS code, so developers ended up resorting to ugly hacks such as using multiple elements to emulate multiple borders. However, there are better ways to solve this without polluting our markup with useless extra elements.

box-shadow solution

By now, most of us have probably (over)used **box-shadow** to create shadows. However, it is little known that it accepts a fourth parameter (called **"spread radius"**), which **makes the shadow larger** (positive lengths) or **smaller** (negative lengths) by the amount you specify. A positive spread radius combined with zero offsets and zero blur creates a "shadow" that looks more like a solid border (**Figure 2.5**):

```
background: yellowgreen;
box-shadow: 0 0 0 10px #655;
```

This is not particularly impressive, as you can create the same kind of border by using the **border** property. However, the good thing about **box-shadow** is that **we can have as many of them as we want, comma separated**. So, we can pretty easily add a second ■ **deeppink** "border" to the previous example:

```
background: yellowgreen;
box-shadow: 0 0 0 10px #655, 0 0 0 15px deeppink;
```

The only thing to keep in mind is that **box-shadow**s are overlaid one on top of the other, with the first one being the topmost. Therefore, you need to adjust the spread radius accordingly. For example, in the preceding code, we wanted a **5px** outer border, so we specified a spread radius of **15px** (**10px + 5px**). You can even specify a regular shadow after all the "outlines," if you want:

```
background: yellowgreen;
box-shadow: 0 0 0 10px #655,
            0 0 0 15px deeppink,
            0 2px 5px 15px rgba(0,0,0,.6);
```

The shadow solution works quite well in most cases, but has a few caveats:

- Shadows don't work *exactly* like borders, as they don't affect layout and are oblivious to the `box-sizing` property. However, you can emulate the extra space a border would occupy via padding or margins (depending on whether the shadow is `inset` or not).

- The method we demonstrated creates fake "borders" on the **outside** of elements. These do not capture mouse events such as hovering or clicking. If this is important, you can add the `inset` keyword to make the shadows be drawn on the **inside** of your element. Note that you will need to add extra padding to produce sufficient spacing.

▶ **PLAY!** play.csssecrets.io/**multiple-borders**

outline solution

In some cases, **if we only need two borders**, we can use a regular border and the `outline` property for the outer one. This also gives us flexibility regarding the border style (what if we want a `dashed` second border?), whereas with the `box-shadow` method, we can only emulate solid borders. Here is how the code for **Figure 2.6** would look with this method:

```
background: yellowgreen;
border: 10px solid #655;
outline: 15px solid deeppink;
```

Another good thing about outlines is that you can control their distance from the boundaries of the element, via `outline-offset`, which even accepts negative values. This can be useful for a number of effects. For example, check out **Figure 2.8** for a basic stitching effect.

However, this method has a few limitations:

- As mentioned, it only works for two "borders," as `outline` does not accept a comma-separated list of outlines. If we need more, the previous technique is our only option.

- Outlines do not have to follow rounding (through **border-radius**), so even if your corners are round, the outline may have straight corners (**Figure 2.9**). Note this behavior is considered a bug by the CSS WG, and is likely to be changed to match the **border-radius** in the future.

- Per the **CSS User Interface Level 3 specification** *(w3.org/TR/css3-ui)*, "Outlines may be non-rectangular." Although in most cases they tend to be rectangular, if you use this method, make a mental note to test the result thoroughly in different browsers.

FIGURE 2.9

Outlines created through the **outline** property do not follow the element's rounding, although that could change in the future

- **CSS Backgrounds & Borders**
  w3.org/TR/css-backgrounds
- **CSS Basic User Interface**
  w3.org/TR/css3-ui

RELATED SPECS

Flexible background positioning

The problem

FIGURE 2.10

`background-position:`
`bottom right;` doesn't usually
yield very aesthetically pleasing
results, as the image has no spacing
from the sides

Fairly often, we want to position a background image with offsets from a different corner than the top-left one, such as the bottom right. In CSS 2.1, we could only specify offsets from the top-left corner or keywords for the other three corners. However, we often want to leave some space (akin to padding) between the background image and the corner it's on, to avoid things that look like **Figure 2.10**.

For containers with fixed dimensions, this is possible with CSS 2.1, but it's messy: we can calculate what offset your background image would have from the top-left corner based on its dimensions and the offset we want from the bottom-right corner, and apply that. However, on elements with variable dimensions (due to variable contents), this is not possible. Developers often end up approximating it by setting the background position to some percentage that is slightly smaller than 100%, such as 95%. Surely, with modern CSS, there must be a better way!

Extended background-position solution

The `background-position` property was extended to allow specifying **offsets from any corner** in **CSS Backgrounds & Borders Level 3** *(w3.org/TR/css3-background)*, by providing **keywords before the offsets**. For example, if we want our background image to have a **20px** offset from the right side and a **10px** offset from the bottom side, we can do this:

```
background: url(code-pirate.svg) no-repeat #58a;
background-position: right 20px bottom 10px;
```

You can see the result in **Figure 2.11**. The last step is to provide a decent fallback. As it currently stands, on browsers that don't support the extended `background-position` syntax, the background image will be stuck on the top-left corner (the default position) and will look awful, not to mention it will render the text unreadable (**Figure 2.12**). Providing a fallback is as easy as including a good ol' `bottom right` position in the `background` shorthand:

FIGURE 2.12

We need to specify a fallback, if we don't want users of older browsers to see this

```
background: url(code-pirate.svg)
            no-repeat bottom right #58a;
background-position: right 20px bottom 10px;
```

▶ PLAY! play.csssecrets.io/**extended-bg-position**

background-origin solution

One of the most common cases for wanting to apply offsets from a corner is to make the background image follow padding. With the extended background position we just described, the code would look like this:

Applying offsets to the background image that are equal to the padding value

The box model

```
padding: 10px;
background: url(code-pirate.svg) no-repeat #58a;
background-position: right 10px bottom 10px;
```

You can see the result in **Figure 2.13**. As you can see, it works, but it's not very DRY: every time we change the padding value, we need to update it in three different places! Thankfully, there is a simpler way to do this, which automatically follows the padding we specify, without the need to redeclare the offsets.

You've probably written things like **background-position: top left;** quite a few times over the course of your web development career. Have you ever wondered: *which top-left corner?* As you may know, there are four boxes in every element (**Figure 2.14**): the margin box, the border box, the padding box, and the content box. Which box's **top left** corner does **background-position** refer to?

By default, **background-position** refers to the **padding box**, so that borders don't end up obscuring background images. Therefore, **top left** is by default the **top-left outer corner of the padding box**. In **Backgrounds & Borders Level 3** *(w3.org/TR/css3-background)*, however, we got a new property that we can use to change this behavior: **background-origin**. By default, its value is (quite predictably) **padding-box**. If we change it to **content-box**, as in the following code, the side and corner keywords we use in **background-position** will refer to the edge of the content box (effectively, this means that any background images will be offset from the sides/corners as much as our padding is):

```
padding: 10px;
background: url("code-pirate.svg") no-repeat #58a
            bottom right; /* or 100% 100% */
background-origin: content-box;
```

The visual result is exactly the same as in **Figure 2.13**, just with more DRY code. Keep in mind that you can also combine the two techniques we showed if needed! If you want offsets that generally vary with the padding, but are inset/outset a little more than that, you can use **background-origin: content-box** together with additional offsets via the extended **background-position**.

▶ **PLAY!** play.csssecrets.io/**background-origin**

calc() solution

Let's revisit our original challenge: we want to position our background image **10px** from the bottom and **20px** from the right side. However, if we think of it **in terms of offsets from the top-left corner**, we basically want an offset of **100% - 20px** horizontally and **100% - 10px** vertically. Thankfully, the **calc()** function allows us to do exactly that sort of calculation and it works perfectly with **background-position**:

> Don't forget to include white-space around any – and + operators in **calc()**, otherwise it's a parsing error! The reason for this weird rule is forward compatibility: in the future, keywords might be allowed inside **calc()**, and they can contain hyphens.

```
background: url("code-pirate.svg") no-repeat;
background-position: calc(100% - 20px) calc(100% - 10px);
```

▶ **PLAY!** play.csssecrets.io/**background-position-calc**

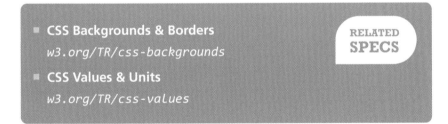

■ **CSS Backgrounds & Borders**
w3.org/TR/css-backgrounds

■ **CSS Values & Units**
w3.org/TR/css-values

RELATED
SPECS

4 Inner rounding

Prerequisites

box-shadow, **outline**, the "Multiple borders" secret on page 28

The problem

Sometimes we want a container that is only rounded on the inside, but the outer corners of its border/outline are sharp, such as the one in **Figure 2.15**. It's an interesting effect that's not overdone yet. It's trivial to achieve this effect with two elements:

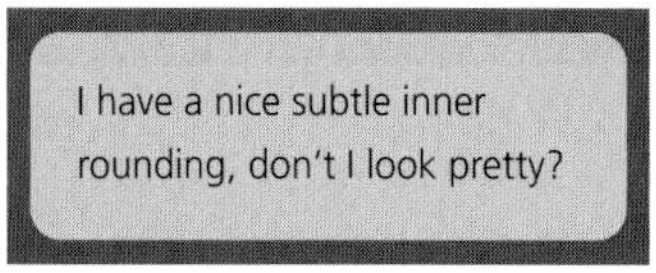

I have a nice subtle inner rounding, don't I look pretty?

FIGURE 2.15

A container with an outline and rounding only on the inside

```html
HTML
<div class="something-meaningful"><div>
    I have a nice subtle inner rounding,
    don't I look pretty?
</div></div>
```

```
.something-meaningful {
    background: #655;
    padding: .8em;
}


.something-meaningful > div {
    background: tan;
    border-radius: .8em;
    padding: 1em;
}
```

This works fine, but it forces us to use two elements when we only need one. Is there a way to achieve the same effect with only one element?

The solution

The previous solution is more flexible, as it allows us to use the full power of backgrounds. For example, if we want our "border" to not just be a solid color, but have a noise texture as well, it's pretty easy to do. However, when we're dealing with good ol' solid colors, there is a way to do this, with just one element (granted it is a bit hacky). Take a look at the following CSS:

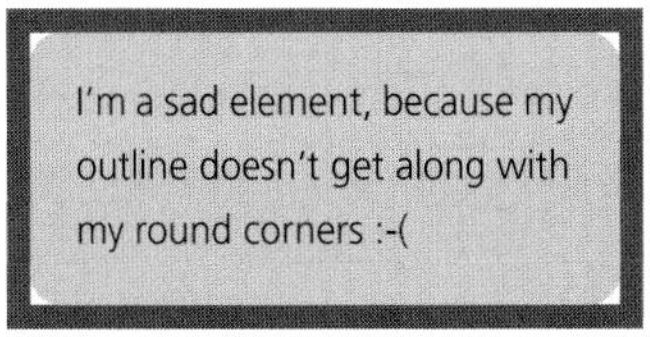

```
background: tan;
border-radius: .8em;
padding: 1em;
box-shadow: 0 0 0 .6em #655;
outline: .6em solid #655;
```

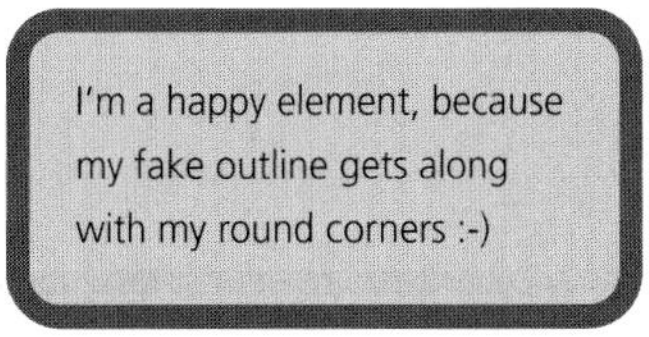

Can you guess what the visual result is? It produces the effect in **Figure 2.15**. We basically took advantage of the fact that outlines do not follow the element's rounding (and thus, have sharp corners) but **box-shadow**s do. Therefore, if we overlay one on top of the other, the **box-shadow** covers the gaps that the outline leaves on the corners (**Figure 2.17**), so their

FIGURE 2.16

Using the **outline** property on a rounded element

FIGURE 2.17

Using the **box-shadow** property with no offsets and no blur on an element with rounded corners

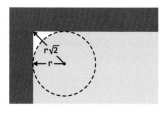

I have a nice subtle inner rounding, don't I look pretty?

FIGURE 2.18

Here the outline is shown in black and the shadow in magenta, to make it clearer what is going on; notice that the outline is the one drawn on top

Why is this **hacky**? Because it **depends on the fact that outlines do not follow corner rounding**, but there is no guarantee this will stay that way. The spec currently gives browsers a lot of leeway in outline drawing, but in the future **it will explicitly recommend following rounding, per a recent CSS WG decision**. Whether browsers will honor that decision remains to be seen.

FIGURE 2.19

When our border radius is *r*, the length from the center of the **border-radius** circle to the corner of the outline rectangle is $r\sqrt{2}$, which means the minimum possible spread is $r\sqrt{2} - r = (\sqrt{2} - 1)r$

combination gives us the desired effect. **Figure 2.18** displays the shadow and outline with different colors, to provide a clearer visual explanation.

Note that we didn't really need to specify a **box-shadow** spread that is equal to the outline, we only need to specify a large enough spread to cover those "gaps." In fact, specifying a spread equal to our outline width can cause rendering artifacts in some browsers, so I would recommend something a bit smaller. This begs the question: **what is the smallest spread we could specify that covers these gaps?**

To answer this question, we need to remember the *Pythagorean theorem* we learned at school about calculating the lengths of the sides of right triangles. The theorem states that the hypotenuse (the longest, diagonal side of the triangle) is equal to $\sqrt{a^2 + b^2}$ where *a* and *b* are the lengths of its legs. When both legs are of equal length, the formula becomes $\sqrt{2a^2} = a\sqrt{2}$.

You might be wondering how on Earth middle school geometry is relevant to our inner rounding effect. Check out **Figure 2.19** for a visual explanation of how it can be used to calculate the minimum spread we need. In our case, **border-radius** is **.8em**, so the minimum spread is $.8(\sqrt{2} - 1) \approx .33137085$em. All we need is to round it up a little and specify a spread radius of **.34em**. To avoid having to make the calculation every time, you can just use half of your corner radius, which is guaranteed to be large enough, because $\sqrt{2} - 1 < 0.5$.

Note that these calculations uncover **another constraint of this method**: for this effect to work, our spread radius needs to be smaller than our outline width, but it also needs to be larger than $(\sqrt{2} - 1)r$, where r is our **border-radius**. This means that if our outline width is smaller than $(\sqrt{2} - 1)r$, this is not possible and we cannot apply this effect.

▶ PLAY! play.csssecrets.io/**inner-rounding**

- **CSS Backgrounds & Borders**
  w3.org/TR/css-backgrounds
- **CSS Basic User Interface**
  w3.org/TR/css3-ui

RELATED
SPECS

5 Striped backgrounds

The problem

Stripes of all sizes, colors, and angles are at least as ubiquitous on the Web as in any other medium of visual design, from magazines to wallpaper. However, the workflow of implementing them is far from ideal. Usually, we would create a separate bitmap image and need an image editor every time we needed to make changes. Some might use SVG instead, but it's still a separate file and the syntax is far from friendly. Wouldn't it be awesome if we could create stripes directly in our CSS? You might be surprised to find that we actually can.

The solution

Assume we have a basic vertical linear gradient, from  ◻ #fb3 to ◼ #58a (**Figure 2.20**):

```
background: linear-gradient(#fb3, #58a);
```

Now let's try to bring the color stops a little closer together (**Figure 2.21**):

```
background: linear-gradient(#fb3 20%, #58a 80%);
```

Now the top 20% of our container is filled with solid ◻ #fb3 and the bottom 20% with solid ◼ #58a. The actual gradient only occupies 60% of our container height. If we bring the color stops even closer together (**40%** and **60%** respectively, seen in **Figure 2.22**), the actual gradient becomes even smaller. One starts to wonder, what happens if the color stops meet at the exact same position?

```
background: linear-gradient(#fb3 50%, #58a 50%);
```

> *"If multiple color stops have the same position, they produce an infinitesimal transition from the one specified first in the rule to the one specified last. In effect, the color suddenly changes at that position rather than smoothly transitioning."*
>
> — **CSS Image Values Level 3** *(w3.org/TR/css3-images)*

As you can see in **Figure 2.23**, there is no longer any gradient, just two solid colors, each occupying half of our **background-image**. Essentially, we have already created two big horizontal stripes.

Because gradients are just generated background images, we can treat them the same as any other background image and adjust their size with **background-size**:

FIGURE 2.20

Our starting point

FIGURE 2.21

Gradient now occupies 60% of total height, the rest being solid colors; color stop positions are shown with dashed lines

FIGURE 2.22

Gradient now occupies 20% of total height, the rest being solid colors; color stop positions are shown with dashed lines

Both stops are now at 50%

Our generated background without the repetition

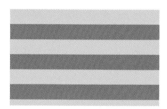

The final horizontal stripes

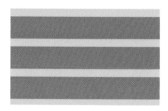

Stripes with unequal widths

```
background: linear-gradient(#fb3 50%, #58a 50%);
background-size: 100% 30px;
```

As you can see in **Figure 2.24**, we shrunk the size of our two stripes to **15px** height each. Because our background is repeated, we now have our whole container filled with horizontal stripes (**Figure 2.25**).

We can similarly create stripes with unequal widths, by adjusting the color stop positions (**Figure 2.26**):

```
background: linear-gradient(#fb3 30%, #58a 30%);
background-size: 100% 30px;
```

To avoid having to adjust two numbers every time we want to change the stripe width, we can take advantage of the specification:

> *"If a color stop has a position that is less than the specified position of any color stop before it in the list, set its position to be equal to the largest specified position of any color stop before it."*
>
> —**CSS Images Level 3** *(w3.org/TR/css3-images)*

This means that if we set the second color's position at **0**, its position will be adjusted by the browser to be equal to the position of the previous color stop, which is what we wanted anyway. Therefore, the following code also creates the exact same gradient we saw in **Figure 2.26**, but is a little more DRY:

```
background: linear-gradient(#fb3 30%, #58a 0);
background-size: 100% 30px;
```

It's just as easy to create stripes with more than two colors. For example, the following snippet will produce horizontal stripes of three colors (**Figure 2.27**):

```
background: linear-gradient(#fb3 33.3%,
            #58a 0, #58a 66.6%, yellowgreen 0);
background-size: 100% 45px;
```

▶ PLAY! play.csssecrets.io/**horizontal-stripes**

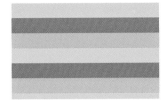

FIGURE 2.27
Stripes with three colors

Vertical stripes

Horizontal stripes are the easiest to code, but not all striped backgrounds we see on the Web are horizontal. Just as many are vertical stripes (**Figure 2.28**), and probably the most popular and visually interesting are some form of diagonal stripes. Thankfully, CSS gradients can help us recreate those too, with varying degrees of difficulty.

The code for vertical stripes is almost the same, with one main difference: an extra first argument that specifies the gradient direction. We could have specified it for horizontal stripes too, but the default (**to bottom**) was exactly what we needed for them. We also need to set a different **background-size**, for obvious reasons:

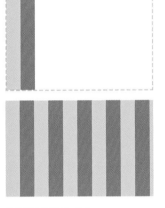

FIGURE 2.28
Our vertical stripes
Top: Our background tile without the repetition
Bottom: The repeated stripes

```
background: linear-gradient(to right, /* or 90deg */
            #fb3 50%, #58a 0);
background-size: 30px 100%;
```

▶ PLAY! play.csssecrets.io/**vertical-stripes**

Diagonal stripes

After creating horizontal and vertical stripes, we might attempt to create diagonal stripes (45°) by just changing the **background-size** and direction of the gradient again, like so:

FIGURE 2.29
Our first failed attempt for diagonal stripes

```
background: linear-gradient(45deg,
            #fb3 50%, #58a 0);
background-size: 30px 30px;
```

FIGURE 2.30

The kind of image that tiles seamlessly to create diagonal stripes; does it look familiar?

FIGURE 2.31

Our 45° stripes; the dashed lines indicate the repeating tile

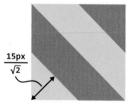

FIGURE 2.32

A background size of **20px** results in a stripe width of
$\frac{15}{\sqrt{2}} \approx 10.606601718$ pixels

However, as you can see in **Figure 2.29**, this doesn't work. The reason is that we just rotated the gradient *inside* each tile by 45 degrees, not the repeated background as a whole. Try to remember the bitmap images we usually use to create diagonal stripes, such as the one in **Figure 2.30**. They include four stripes instead of two, so that they tile seamlessly. This is the kind of tile we need to recreate in CSS, so we will need quite a few more color stops:

```
background: linear-gradient(45deg,
            #fb3 25%, #58a 0, #58a 50%,
            #fb3 0, #fb3 75%, #58a 0);
background-size: 30px 30px;
```

You can see the result in **Figure 2.31**. As you can see, we were successful at creating diagonal stripes, but they look thinner than our horizontal and vertical ones. To understand why this happened, we need to remember the *Pythagorean theorem* we learned at school about calculating the lengths of the sides of right triangles. The theorem states that the hypotenuse (the longest, diagonal side of the triangle) is equal to $\sqrt{a^2 + b^2}$ where a and b are the lengths of its legs. On a 45° right triangle, both its legs are of the same length, so the formula becomes $\sqrt{2a^2} = a\sqrt{2}$. In our diagonal stripes, the background size specifies the length of the hypotenuse, but the stripe width is actually the length of the leg. Check out **Figure 2.32** for a visual explanation.

This means that to get our original stripe width of **15px**, we need to specify a background size of $2 \times 15\sqrt{2} \approx 42.426406871$ pixels:

```
background: linear-gradient(45deg,
            #fb3 25%, #58a 0, #58a 50%,
```

```
        #fb3 0, #fb3 75%, #58a 0);
background-size: 42.426406871px 42.426406871px;
```

You can see the final result in **Figure 2.33**. However, unless somebody is pointing a gun at your head threatening to kill you unless you are able to produce diagonal stripes that are exactly 15 pixels wide (in which case, you would die anyway, because $\sqrt{2}$ is not a rational number, so even this is an approximation—though a very high-precision one), I would strongly recommend rounding this unwieldy number, to something like **42.4px** or even **42px**.

FIGURE 2.33

Our final 45° stripes; note that now the stripe width is the same as our other examples

▸ PLAY! play.csssecrets.io/**diagonal-stripes**

Better diagonal stripes

The method shown in the previous section is not very flexible. What if we want stripes that are 60° instead of 45°? Or 30°? Or 3.1415926535°? If we just try to change the angle of the gradient, the result looks awful (check out **Figure 2.34** for a failed attempt at 60° stripes).

Thankfully, there is a better way to create diagonal stripes. A little-known fact is that `linear-gradient()` and `radial-gradient()` also have repeating versions: `repeating-linear-gradient()` and `repeating-radial-gradient()`. These work exactly the same way, with one difference: the color stops are repeated indefinitely, until they fill up the whole image. So, for example, this repeating gradient (shown in **Figure 2.35**):

FIGURE 2.34

Our failed naïve attempt at 60° stripes

```
background: repeating-linear-gradient(45deg,
          #fb3, #58a 30px);
```

would be equivalent to this simple linear gradient:

FIGURE 2.35

A repeating linear gradient

```
background: linear-gradient(45deg,
                 #fb3, #58a 30px,
                 #fb3 30px, #58a 60px,
                 #fb3 60px, #58a 90px,
                 #fb3 90px, #58a 120px,
                 #fb3 120px, #58a 150px, ...);
```

Repeating linear gradients are perfect for—you guessed it—stripes! Due to their repeating nature, it means our whole background can be in the generated gradient image. Therefore, we don't need to worry about creating seamless tiles that can be repeated.

For comparison, the background we created in **Figure 2.33** could have been produced by this repeating gradient:

```
background: repeating-linear-gradient(45deg,
                 #fb3, #fb3 15px, #58a 0, #58a 30px);
```

The first obvious benefit is reduced repetition: we can change any of the colors with two edits instead of three. Also note that our measurements are now in the gradient color stops instead of **background-size**. The background size is the initial one, which for gradients is the size of the element. This means that the lengths are also more straightforward, as they are measured on the *gradient line*, which is perpendicular to our stripes. No more clunky $\sqrt{2}$ calculations!

However, the biggest benefit is that now we can just change the angle to whatever we want, and it just works without having to think hard and long about how to make a seamless tile. For example, here are our 60° stripes (**Figure 2.36**):

```
background: repeating-linear-gradient(60deg,
                 #fb3, #fb3 15px, #58a 0, #58a 30px);
```

FIGURE 2.36

Our actual 60° stripes

It was as easy as just changing the angle! Note that with this method we need four color stops for two stripe colors, regardless of the stripe angle. This means it's usually better to use the first method for horizontal and vertical stripes and this one for diagonal stripes. If we're dealing with 45° stripes, we could even combine the two methods, by essentially using repeating linear gradients to simplify the code that creates our repeating tile:

```
background: repeating-linear-gradient(45deg,
            #fb3 0, #fb3 25%, #58a 0, #58a 50%);
background-size: 42.426406871px 42.426406871px;
```

▶ PLAY!   play.csssecrets.io/**diagonal-stripes-60deg**

FUTURE **Color stops with two positions**

Soon, we will be able to specify two positions on the same color stop, as one of the simpler planned additions in **CSS Image Values Level 4** *(w3.org/TR/css4-images)*. This will work as **a shortcut to two consecutive color stops with the same color and different positions**, something very commonly needed to create gradient-based patterns. For example, the code for the diagonal stripes in **Figure 2.36** would become:

```
background: repeating-linear-gradient(60deg, #fb3 0 15px, #58a 0 30px);
```

Not only is this significantly more concise, but also considerably more DRY: the colors are no longer duplicated, so we can change them with only one edit. Unfortunately, at the time of writing, this is not yet supported in any browser.

TEST!   play.csssecrets.io/**test-color-stop-2positions**

Flexible subtle stripes

More often than not, our stripes are not completely different colors but subtle brightness variations of the same color. For example, take a look at these stripes:

```
background: repeating-linear-gradient(30deg,
                #79b, #79b 15px, #58a 0, #58a 30px);
```

FIGURE 2.37

Stripes with subtle lightness variation

You can see in **Figure 2.37** that they are stripes of one color (■ #58a) and a lighter variant of that. However, that relationship between the colors is not easy to tell by reading the code. Moreover, if we wanted to change the base color, we would have to make four (!) edits.

Thankfully, there is a better way: instead of specifying separate colors for every stripe, we can specify our darkest color as the background color, which will show through stripes with semi-transparent white:

```
background: #58a;
background-image: repeating-linear-gradient(30deg,
                hsla(0,0%,100%,.1),
                hsla(0,0%,100%,.1) 15px,
                transparent 0, transparent 30px);
```

The result looks exactly the same as **Figure 2.37**, but we can now change the color in only one place. We also get the added benefit of our base color functioning as a fallback color for browsers that don't support CSS gradients. Furthermore, as we will see in the next secret, gradient patterns with transparent regions allow us to create very complex patterns by superimposing multiple different ones.

▸ **PLAY!** play.csssecrets.io/**subtle-stripes**

- **CSS Image Values**
  w3.org/TR/css-images

- **CSS Backgrounds & Borders**
  w3.org/TR/css-backgrounds

- **CSS Image Values Level 4**
  w3.org/TR/css4-images

RELATED
SPECS

6 Complex background patterns

Prerequisites

CSS gradients, the "Striped backgrounds" secret on page 40

The problem

In the previous section, we learned how to use CSS gradients to create all sorts of stripes. However, stripes are not the be-all and end-all of background patterns or even just geometric patterns. We quite often need many other different types, such as grids, polka dots, checkerboards, and many others.

Thankfully, CSS gradients can help with many of these too. It's possible to create almost **any kind of geometric pattern with CSS gradients**, although it's **not always practical**. If we're not careful, we might end up with an insane amount of unmaintainable code. CSS patterns are also one case where it really pays off to use a CSS preprocessor, such as

Sass *(sass-Lang.com)* to reduce repetition, as the more complex they get, the less DRY they become.

FIGURE 2.38

My CSS3 Patterns Gallery (found at **lea.verou.me/css3patterns**) showed what is possible with CSS gradients as early as 2011. It was included in almost every article, book, and conference talk that mentioned CSS gradients between 2011 and 2012 and was used by several browser vendors to fine-tune their CSS gradients implementations. However, not every pattern showcased in it would be a good use case for a production website. Some of them are included only to show what is possible, but their code is extremely long and repetitive. For those cases, SVG is a better choice. For some examples of SVG patterns, visit **philbit.com/svgpatterns**, which was created as the SVG answer to the CSS Patterns Gallery.

In this secret, we will focus on creating some of the easiest and commonly needed patterns.

Grids

When using only one gradient, there aren't that many patterns we can create. The magic starts to unfold when we **combine multiple gradients**, having them show through each other's transparent regions. Perhaps the easiest such pattern is overlaying horizontal and vertical stripes to create various types of grids. For example, the following code creates the tablecloth-reminiscent (gingham) pattern shown in **Figure 2.39**:

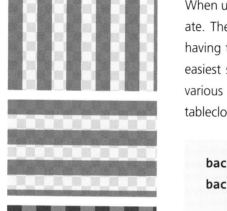

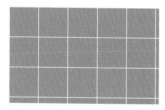

FIGURE 2.39

Our tablecloth (gingham) pattern, as well as the two gradients that comprise it (transparency shown here as the conventional gray checkerboard)

```
background: white;
background-image: linear-gradient(90deg,
                    rgba(200,0,0,.5) 50%, transparent 0),
                  linear-gradient(
                    rgba(200,0,0,.5) 50%, transparent 0);
background-size: 30px 30px;
```

In some cases, we want to be able to **adjust the cell size of the grid, and have the width of its lines remain constant**—for example, to create grid lines that serve as guides. This is a great use case for using **lengths instead of percentages** as gradient color stops:

```
background: #58a;
background-image:
    linear-gradient(white 1px, transparent 0),
    linear-gradient(90deg, white 1px, transparent 0);
background-size: 30px 30px;
```

FIGURE 2.40

A basic blueprint grid CSS pattern whose lines remain **1px** regardless of the size of the grid

The result (seen on **Figure 2.40**) is a grid of **1px** white lines with a grid cell size of **30px**. Just like in the **"Flexible subtle stripes" section on page 48**, the base color is also functioning as a fallback color.

This grid is a good example of a pattern that can be made with reasonably maintainable (though not completely DRY) CSS code:

- It's quite easy to figure out what to edit if we need to change the grid size, line thickness, or any of the colors.

- We don't have to make tons of edits to change any of this; we only need to edit one or two values.

- It's also quite short, at only four lines of code and 170 bytes. An SVG would not have been shorter.

We can even overlay two grids with different line widths and colors to create a more realistic blueprint grid (**Figure 2.41**):

To calculate the file size of your CSS pattern, paste the code in **bytesizematters.com**.

```
background: #58a;
background-image:
    linear-gradient(white 2px, transparent 0),
    linear-gradient(90deg, white 2px, transparent 0),
    linear-gradient(hsla(0,0%,100%,.3) 1px,
        transparent 0),
    linear-gradient(90deg, hsla(0,0%,100%,.3) 1px,
        transparent 0);
background-size: 75px 75px, 75px 75px,
                15px 15px, 15px 15px;
```

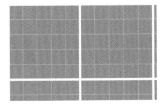

FIGURE 2.41

A more complex blueprint grid, comprised of two grids with different parameters

▶ PLAY! play.csssecrets.io/**blueprint**

Polka dot

So far, we have only used linear gradients to make patterns. However, radial gradients can be very useful as well, as they allow us to create circles, ellipses, or parts thereof. The simplest pattern we can create with a radial gradient is an array of dots (**Figure 2.42**):

```
background: #655;
background-image: radial-gradient(tan 30%, transparent 0);
background-size: 30px 30px;
```

FIGURE 2.42

An array of dots; the repeating tile is shown with dashed lines

Admittedly, this is not very useful on its own. However, we can combine two of those gradients and give them different background positions, to create a polka dot pattern (**Figure 2.43**):

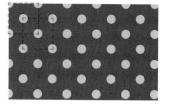

```
background: #655;
background-image: radial-gradient(tan 30%, transparent 0),
                  radial-gradient(tan 30%, transparent 0);
background-size: 30px 30px;
background-position: 0 0, 15px 15px;
```

FIGURE 2.43

Polka dot pattern; both repeating tiles are shown with dashed lines

▸ PLAY! play.csssecrets.io/**polka**

Note that for the effect to work, the second background position must be half of the tile size. Unfortunately, this means that to change the tile size, we need to make four edits. This is on the brink of being unmaintainable, although whether it has crossed the line is debatable. If you are using a preprocessor, you may want to convert it into a mixin:

SCSS

```
@mixin polka($size, $dot, $base, $accent) {
    background: $base;
    background-image:
        radial-gradient($accent $dot, transparent 0),
        radial-gradient($accent $dot, transparent 0);
    background-size: $size $size;
    background-position: 0 0, $size/2 $size/2;
}
```

Then, to create the polka dot pattern, we would call it like this:

```scss
@include polka(30px, 30%, #655, tan);
```

Checkerboards

Checkerboard patterns are used in a number of cases. For instance, subtle checkerboards can be an interesting alternative to a bland solid color background. Also, a gray checkerboard pattern is the de facto standard way to depict transparency, which is required in a number of different UIs. Making a checkerboard pattern in CSS is possible, but considerably trickier than one might expect.

The typical tile that generates a checkerboard when repeated consists of two squares from each color, like the one indicated in **Figure 2.44**. It looks like it should be easy to recreate with CSS: we would just create two squares with different background positions, right? Not exactly. Yes, we can technically create squares with CSS gradients, but with no spacing around them, the result will look like a solid color. However, there is no way to create squares with space around them with one CSS gradient. If you're having doubts, try to find a gradient that, when repeated, produces the image in **Figure 2.45**.

The trick is to **compose the square from two right triangles**. We already know how to create right triangles (remember our failed attempt at diagonal stripes in **Figure 2.29**?). To refresh your memory, the code looked like this (here with different colors and transparency):

```
background: #eee;
background-image:
    linear-gradient(45deg, #bbb 50%, transparent 0);
background-size: 30px 30px;
```

You might be wondering how this helps with anything. Sure, if we tried to compose squares from two triangles like the ones in **Figure 2.29**, we would

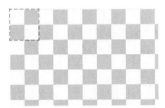

FIGURE 2.44

A gray checkerboard pattern to indicate transparency; if this was created by repeating an image, the tile would be the one denoted by the dashed line

FIGURE 2.45

Repeating a square with space around it; the tile is shown with dashed lines

end up with a solid color. However, what if we reduce the legs of these triangles to half their original size, so that they occupy $\frac{1}{8}$ of the tile, instead of the current $\frac{1}{2}$? We can easily do that by **changing the color stop position to 25% instead of 50%**. Then we would end up with something like **Figure 2.46**.

Similarly, we can create triangles of the opposite direction if we flip the color stops (**Figure 2.47**):

FUTURE Conical gradients

In the future, we won't have to resort to meticulously overlaying triangles to create checkerboards. **CSS Image Values Level 4** *(w3.org/TR/css4-images)* defines a new set of gradient functions to generate *conical gradients* (a.k.a. "angle gradients"). These gradients often look like a cone observed from above, hence the name "conical." They are generated by a line that gradually changes color as it rotates around a fixed point. For example, the hue wheel shown here would be created with the following gradient:

```
background: conic-gradient(red, yellow, lime, aqua, blue, fuchsia, red);
```

Conical gradients are useful for far more things than hue wheels: starbursts, brushed metal effects, and many other kinds of backgrounds, including (you guessed it!) checkerboards. They would enable us to create the repeating tile of **Figure 2.44** in just one gradient:

```
background: repeating-conic-gradient(#bbb 0, #bbb 25%, #eee 0, #eee 50%);
background-size: 30px 30px;
```

Unfortunately, there is no browser support for conical gradients at the time of writing.

TEST! play.csssecrets.io/**test-conic-gradient**

```
background: #eee;
background-image:
    linear-gradient(45deg, transparent 75%, #bbb  0);
background-size: 30px 30px;
```

Can you guess what happens if we combine the two? The code would look
like this:

```
background: #eee;
background-image:
    linear-gradient(45deg, #bbb 25%, transparent 0),
    linear-gradient(45deg, transparent 75%, #bbb 0);
background-size: 30px 30px;
```

At first, the result in **Figure 2.48** doesn't look like we're getting any-
where. However, we just need to **move the second gradient by half the
tile size**, in order to combine them into a square:

```
background: #eee;
background-image:
    linear-gradient(45deg, #bbb 25%, transparent 0),
    linear-gradient(45deg, transparent 75%, #bbb 0);
background-position: 0 0, 15px 15px;
background-size: 30px 30px;
```

Can you guess what the result looks like? It's exactly what we were
trying to achieve earlier, and looks like **Figure 2.49**. Notice that this is essentially **half a checkerboard**. All we need to turn this into a full checkerboard is to repeat the two gradients to create another set of squares and
offset their positions again, a bit like applying the polka dot technique twice:

```
background: #eee;
```

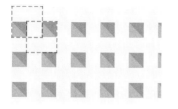

FIGURE 2.49

Our combined triangles now form squares with space around them; the two tiles are shown with dashed lines and the second gradient is shown slightly darker

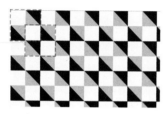

FIGURE 2.50

This is a complex pattern and it's often difficult to wrap one's head around how it works, especially after reducing it to two gradients. It usually aids understanding of how a pattern works to give a random color to one of the gradients or color stops. For example, here the first gradient is shown with

■ rebeccapurple instead of the semi-transparent black and the two tiles are outlined with dashed lines.

WET stands for "We Enjoy Typing" and is the opposite of DRY code (i.e., it refers to repetitive, unmaintainable code).

```
background-image:
    linear-gradient(45deg, #bbb 25%, transparent 0),
    linear-gradient(45deg, transparent 75%, #bbb 0),
    linear-gradient(45deg, #bbb 25%, transparent 0),
    linear-gradient(45deg, transparent 75%, #bbb 0);
background-position: 0 0, 15px 15px,
                        15px 15px, 30px 30px;
background-size: 30px 30px;
```

The result is a checkerboard, identical to the one in **Figure 2.44**. We can improve the code a bit by combining the opposite facing triangles (i.e., the first with the second and the third with the fourth) and making the darker gray semi-transparent black, so that we can change the base color without always having to adjust the top color accordingly:

```
background: #eee;
background-image:
    linear-gradient(45deg,
        rgba(0,0,0,.25) 25%, transparent 0,
        transparent 75%, rgba(0,0,0,.25) 0),
    linear-gradient(45deg,
        rgba(0,0,0,.25) 25%, transparent 0,
        transparent 75%, rgba(0,0,0,.25) 0);
background-position: 0 0, 15px 15px;
background-size: 30px 30px;
```

Now we have two gradients instead of four, but the code is almost as WET as before. To change the accent color or the cell size, we need to make four edits. At this point, it might be a good idea to use a preprocessor mixin to reduce duplication. For example, in Sass it would look like this:

```
@mixin checkerboard($size, $base,
                    $accent: rgba(0,0,0,.25) {
```

```scss
    background: $base;
    background-image:
        linear-gradient(45deg,
            $accent 25%, transparent 0,
            transparent 75%, $accent 0),
        linear-gradient(45deg,
            $accent 25%, transparent 0,
            transparent 75%, $accent 0);
    background-position: 0 0, $size $size,
    background-size: 2*$size 2*$size;
}


/* Used like… */
@include checkerboard(15px, #58a, tan);
```

In any case, this is so much code that it might actually be better to go the SVG route. An SVG tile for **Figure 2.44** would be as small and simple as:

```
                                          SVG
<svg xmlns="http://www.w3.org/2000/svg"
     width="100" height="100" fill-opacity=".25" >
    <rect x="50" width="50" height="50" />
    <rect y="50" width="50" height="50" />
</svg>
```

One could reply, "But CSS gradients save us HTTP requests!" However, with modern browsers, we can embed the SVG file in our stylesheet as a data URI, and we don't even need to base64 or URLencode most of it:

```
background: #eee url('data:image/svg+xml,\
            <svg xmlns="http://www.w3.org/2000/svg" \
                width="100" height="100"
                fill-opacity=".25">\
            <rect x="50" width="50" height="50" /> \
```

```
            <rect y="50" width="50" height="50" /> \
          </svg>');
background-size: 30px 30px;
```

TIP! Note how you can break a CSS string into multiple lines for readability, by just escaping the line breaks with a backslash (\)!

The SVG version is not only 40 characters shorter, but also considerably less repetitive. For example, we can change the colors in only one place and the size with two edits.

▸ **PLAY!** play.csssecrets.io/**checkerboard-svg**

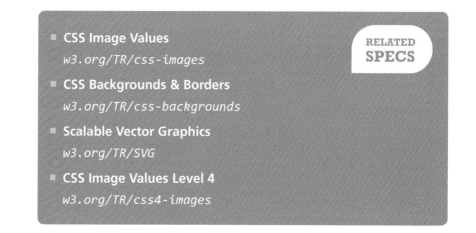

- **CSS Image Values**
  w3.org/TR/css-images
- **CSS Backgrounds & Borders**
  w3.org/TR/css-backgrounds
- **Scalable Vector Graphics**
  w3.org/TR/SVG
- **CSS Image Values Level 4**
  w3.org/TR/css4-images

RELATED
SPECS

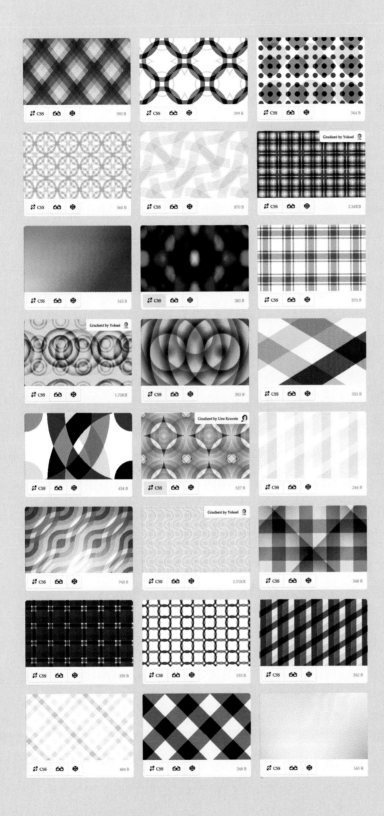

FIGURE 2.51

Combining these techniques with **blending modes** *(w3.org/TR/compositing-1)*, by using `background-blend-mode` with values other than `normal` for some (or even all) of the layers a background pattern is made of can yield very interesting results, as this **pattern gallery by Bennett Feely** *(bennettfeely.com/gradients)* demonstrates. Most of these patterns only use the `multiply` blending mode, but other values such as `overlay`, `screen`, or `difference` can be very useful too.

7 (Pseudo)random backgrounds

Prerequisites

CSS gradients, the "Striped backgrounds" secret on page 40, the "Complex background patterns" secret on page 50

The problem

FIGURE 2.52

Nature doesn't repeat itself in "seamless" tiles

Repeating geometric patterns are nice, but can be a bit boring. **Hardly anything in nature ever repeats in identical tiles.** Even in repetition, there is always variation and randomness. Look at a field with flowers: while it's uniform enough to be beautiful, it is also random enough to be interesting. No two flowers are ever exactly the same. This is why when we are trying to make background patterns appear as natural as possible, we are also trying to have as few and as hard to notice "seams" between the repeating tiles as possible, which directly conflicts with our desire to keep the filesize low.

> "[W]hen you notice a distinctive feature—for instance, a knot in some woodgrain—repeating at regular intervals, it really breaks the illusion of organic randomness."
>
> — Alex Walker, **The Cicada Principle and Why It Matters to Web Designers**
> (sitepoint.com/the-cicada-principle-and-why-it-matters-to-web-designers)

Replicating randomness can be challenging, because CSS does not offer any inherent randomness capabilities. Let's take the example of stripes. Assume we want vertical stripes of various colors and widths (let's keep it simple and say four colors), with no visible "seams" of repeating tiles. Our first thought might be to create one gradient with all four stripes, like so:

```
background: linear-gradient(90deg,
            #fb3 15%, #655 0, #655 40%,
            #ab4 0, #ab4 65%, hsl(20, 40%, 90%) 0);
background-size: 80px 100%;
```

FIGURE 2.53

Our original attempt at pseudorandom stripes, with all the colors generated by the same linear gradient

As you can see in **Figure 2.53**, the repetition is obvious, as the pattern repeats itself every **80px** (our **background-size**). Can we do better?

The solution

One first idea might be to enhance the illusion of randomness by splitting the flat stripe tile into layers: one base color and three layers of stripes, repeating in different intervals. We can easily achieve this by hardcoding the stripe width in the color stops and using **background-size** to control their spacing. The code might look like this:

```
background: hsl(20, 40%, 90%);
background-image:
    linear-gradient(90deg, #fb3 10px, transparent 0),
    linear-gradient(90deg, #ab4 20px, transparent 0),
    linear-gradient(90deg, #655 20px, transparent 0);
background-size: 80px 100%, 60px 100%, 40px 100%;
```

FIGURE 2.54

Our second attempt, involving overlaying different gradients with different background sizes; the (perceived) repeating tile is shown with dashed lines

Note that here *"tile"* is used a bit liberally: it's not referring to the repeated image of any individual gradient, but the **perceived repeating tile of their composition** (i.e., if we weren't using multiple backgrounds, what size would our repeated background image have to be to achieve the same result?).

Because the repetition in the topmost tile will be most noticeable (as it's not covered by anything), **we want to put the tile with the largest repeat interval on top** (in this case, the orange stripes).

As you can see in **Figure 2.54**, these look significantly more random, but if we look closely, we can still see the repeating tile every **240px**. The end of the first repeating tile of such a composition is the offset at which **all our individual background images have repeated an integer amount of times**. As you might remember from school, if we have a few numbers, the minimum number that can contain any of them an integer amount of times is their *least common multiple* (often abbreviated as LCM). Therefore, here **the size of the tile is the LCM of the background sizes** and the LCM of 40, 60, and 80 is 240.

It logically follows that to increase perceived randomness, we need to **maximize the size of the repeating tile**. Thanks to math, we don't have to think long and hard about how to achieve this, because we already know the answer. **To achieve maximum LCM, the numbers need to be**

FIGURE 2.55

Our final stripes, using prime numbers to increase perceived randomness

*relatively prime.** In that case, their LCM is their product. For example, 3, 4, and 5 are relatively prime, so their LCM is 3 × 4 × 5 = 60. An easy way to achieve this is to choose **prime numbers, because they're always relatively prime with any other number**. Lists of primes up to very large numbers are widely available on the Web.

To maximize randomness even further, we can even use prime numbers for the stripe widths. This is what our code would look like:

```
background: hsl(20, 40%, 90%);
background-image:
    linear-gradient(90deg, #fb3 11px, transparent 0),
    linear-gradient(90deg, #ab4 23px, transparent 0),
    linear-gradient(90deg, #655 41px, transparent 0);
background-size: 41px 100%, 61px 100%, 83px 100%;
```

Yes, the code is not pretty, but good luck trying to find any seams in **Figure 2.55**. The size of our repeating tile is now 41 × 61 × 83 = 207,583 pixels, larger than any screen resolution one could possibly imagine!

This technique was dubbed **"The Cicada Principle"** by **Alex Walker**, who first had the idea of using primes to increase perceived randomness of backgrounds. Note that this is not only useful for backgrounds, but also for anything that involves repetition. Other applications include:

---

* *Prime numbers* are integers that **can't be divided by any other number besides 1 and themselves**. For example, the first 10 prime numbers are 2, 3, 5, 7, 11, 13, 17, 19, 23, 29. On the other hand, *relatively prime* is a **relation between numbers**, not an attribute of a single number. Relatively prime numbers have **no common divisors**, but may have many divisors in general (e.g., 10 and 27 are relatively prime, but neither is prime). **Of course, a prime number is relatively prime with any other number.**

- Applying small pseudorandom rotations on the images in a photo gallery, with multiple `:nth-child(an)` selectors where *a* is a prime.

- Making an animation that doesn't seem to ever repeat exactly in the same way, by applying multiple animations with prime durations. (Check out **play.csssecrets.io/cicanimation** for an example.)

> ▶ **PLAY!** play.csssecrets.io/**cicada-stripes**

HAT TIP

*Hat tip to **Alex Walker** for coming up with an idea that inspired this technique in **"The Cicada Principle and Why It Matters to Web Designers"** (sitepoint.com/the-cicada-principle-and-why-it-matters-to-web-designers). **Eric Meyer** (meyerweb.com) later had the idea of creating something called **"Cicadients"** (meyerweb.com/eric/thoughts/2012/06/22/cicadients), which involves applying the technique on background images generated via CSS gradients. **Dudley Storey** has also written a **very informative piece on this concept** (demosthenes.info/blog/840/Brood-X-Visualizing-The-Cicada-Principle-In-CSS).*

> **RELATED SPECS**
>
> - **CSS Image Values**
>   w3.org/TR/css-images
> - **CSS Backgrounds & Borders**
>   w3.org/TR/css-backgrounds

8 Continuous image borders

The problem

Sometimes we want to apply a pattern or image **not as a background, but as a border**. For example, check out **Figure 2.57** for an element with a decorative border that is basically an image clipped to the border area. In addition, we want the image to resize to cover the entire border area regardless of the dimensions of our element. How would we attempt to do something like this with CSS?

At this point, there might be a very loud voice in your head screaming, *"border-image, border-image, we can use border-image, that's not a problem anymore!!!11."* **Not so fast, young padawan.** Recall how **border-image** actually works: it's basically **9-slice scaling**. You slice the

FIGURE 2.56

Our stone art image, used throughout this secret

image into nine boxes and apply them to the corners and sides accordingly. **Figure 2.58** offers a visual reminder of how this works.

How could we possibly slice our image via **border-image** to create the example in **Figure 2.57**? Even if we meticulously get it right for specific dimensions and border width, it wouldn't adjust properly for different ones. The issue is that there is no specific part of the image that we want to be at the corners; the part of the image shown in the corner squares changes with the dimensions of the element and border width. If you try it for a bit, you will likely also conclude that this is not possible with **border-image**. But then what can we do?

The easiest way is to use two HTML elements: one using a background with our stone art image, and one with a white background covering it for our content area:

```html
<div class="something-meaningful"><div>
    I have a nice stone art border,
    don't I look pretty?
</div></div>
```

FIGURE 2.57

Our image used as a border with varying heights

```css
.something-meaningful {
    background: url(stone-art.jpg);
    background-size: cover;
    padding: 1em;
}


.something-meaningful > div {
    background: white;
    padding: 1em;
}
```

This works fine to create the "border" shown in **Figure 2.57**, but it requires an extra HTML element. This is suboptimal: not only does it mix presentation and styling, but modifying the HTML is simply not an option in certain cases. Can we do this with only one element?

The solution

Thanks to CSS gradients and the background extensions introduced in **Backgrounds & Borders Level 3** *(w3.org/TR/css3-background)*, we can achieve the exact same effect with only one element. The main idea is to use **a second background of pure white, covering the stone art image**. However, to make the second image show through the border area, we should apply different values of `background-clip` to them. One last thing is that we can only have a background color on the last layer, so we need to fake the white via a CSS gradient from white to white.

This is how our first attempt to apply this idea might look:

```
padding: 1em;
border: 1em solid transparent;
background: linear-gradient(white, white),
            url(stone-art.jpg);
background-size: cover;
background-clip: padding-box, border-box;
```

As we can see in **Figure 2.59**, the result is very close to what we wanted, but there is some weird repetition. The reason is that the default **background-origin** is **padding-box**, and thus, the image is sized based on the padding box and placed on the 0,0 point on the padding box. The rest is just repetitions of that first background tile. To correct this, we just need to set **background-origin** to **border-box** as well:

```
padding: 1em;
border: 1em solid transparent;
background: linear-gradient(white, white),
            url(stone-art.jpg);
background-size: cover;
background-clip: padding-box, border-box;
```

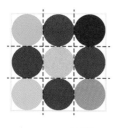

FIGURE 2.58

A quick primer on **border-image**

Top: Our sliced image; the dashed lines indicate its slicing

Middle: `border-image: 33.34% url(…) stretch;`

Bottom: `border-image: 33.34% url(…) round;`

Play with the code at

play.csssecrets.io/border-image

```
background-origin: border-box;
```

These new properties are also available on the **background** shorthand, which can help us reduce our code significantly here:

```
padding: 1em;
border: 1em solid transparent;
background:
    linear-gradient(white, white) padding-box,
    url(stone-art.jpg) border-box 0 / cover;
```

FIGURE 2.59

Our first attempt is very close to what we wanted

▶ **PLAY!** play.csssecrets.io/**continuous-image-borders**

Of course, we can use the same technique with **gradient-based patterns**. For example, take a look at the following code, which generates a **vintage envelope themed border**:

```
padding: 1em;
border: 1em solid transparent;
background: linear-gradient(white, white) padding-box,
        repeating-linear-gradient(-45deg,
            red 0, red 12.5%,
            transparent 0, transparent 25%,
            #58a 0, #58a 37.5%,
            transparent 0, transparent 50%)
        0 / 5em 5em;
```

FIGURE 2.60

An actual vintage envelope

You can see the result in **Figure 2.61**. You can easily change the width of the stripes via the **background-size** and the thickness of the border via the **border** declaration. Unlike our stone art border example, this effect **is doable with** **border-image** too:

 TIP! To see these issues in action, visit **play.csssecrets.io/vintage-envelope-border-image** and experiment with changing values.

```
padding: 1em;
border: 16px solid transparent;
border-image: 16 repeating-linear-gradient(-45deg,
                        red 0, red 1em,
                        transparent 0, transparent 2em,
                        #58a 0, #58a 3em,
                        transparent 0, transparent 4em);
```

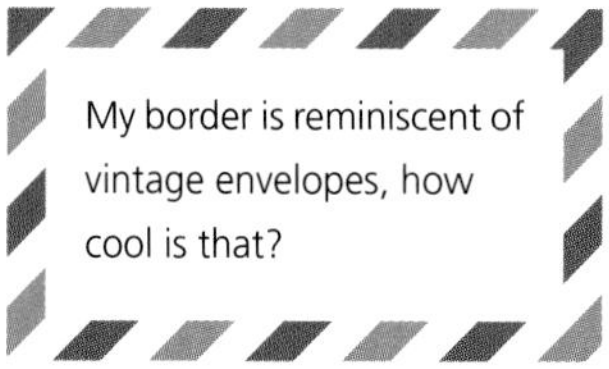

FIGURE 2.61

Our "vintage envelope" border

My border is reminiscent of vintage envelopes, how cool is that?

However, the **border-image** approach has several issues:

- We need to update **border-image-slice** every time we change the **border-width** and make them match.

- Because we cannot use **em**s in **border-image-slice**, we are **restricted to only pixels** for the border thickness.

- The stripe thickness needs to be encoded in the color stop positions, so we need to make four edits to change it.

▸ PLAY! play.csssecrets.io/**vintage-envelope**

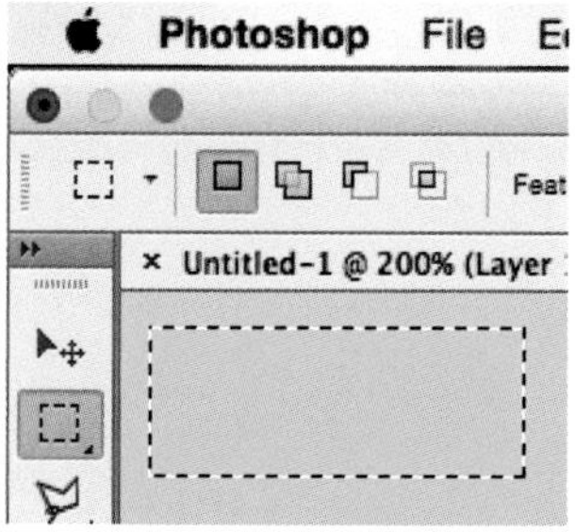

FIGURE 2.62

Marching ants are also used in Adobe Photoshop to indicate area selection

Another fun application of this technique is using it to make **marching ants borders**! Marching ants borders are dashed borders that seem to scroll like marching ants (if you imagine that the dashes are ants). These are incredibly common in GUIs; image editors use them almost always to indicate area selection (**Figure 2.62**).

To create marching ants, we are going to use a variation of the "vintage envelope" effect. We will convert the stripes to just black and white, reduce the width of the border to **1px** (notice how the stripes now turn to a dashed border?), and change the **background-size** to something appropriate. Then, we animate the **background-position** to **100%** to make it scroll:

```
@keyframes ants { to { background-position: 100% } }

.marching-ants {
    padding: 1em;
```

```
    border: 1px solid transparent;
    background:
        linear-gradient(white, white) padding-box,
        repeating-linear-gradient(-45deg,
          black 0, black 25%, white 0, white 50%
        ) 0 / .6em .6em;
    animation: ants 12s linear infinite;
}
```

You can see a still of the result in **Figure 2.63**. Obviously, this is not only useful for marching ants, but also for **creating all sorts of custom dashed borders, with different color dashes and custom dash-gap width**.

Currently, the only way to achieve a similar effect via `border-image` is to use an animated GIF for `border-image-source`, as shown in **chrisdanford.com/blog/2014/04/28/marching-ants-animated-selection-rectangle-in-css**. When browsers start supporting gradient interpolation, we will also be able to do it with gradients, though in a messy, WET way.

▶ **PLAY!** play.csssecrets.io/**marching-ants**

FIGURE 2.63

It's not really possible to show marching ants in a book (a still just looks like dashed borders); visit the live example—it's fun!

FIGURE 2.64

Top border clipping, to mimic traditional footnotes

¹ This is a footnote.

However, `border-image` can also be quite powerful, and even more when used with gradients. For example, assume we want a clipped top border, like the one commonly used in footnotes. All it takes is `border-image` and a vertical gradient, with the clipping length hardcoded. The border width is controlled by ...`border-width`. The code would look like this:

```
border-top: .2em solid transparent;
border-image: 100% 0 0 linear-gradient(90deg,
                          currentColor 4em,
                          transparent 0);
padding-top: 1em;
```

The result is identical to **Figure 2.64**. In addition, because we specified everything in **ems**, the effect will adjust with **font-size** changes, and because we used **currentColor**, it will also adapt to **color** changes (assuming we want the border to be the same color as the text).

► PLAY! play.csssecrets.io/**footnote**

■ **CSS Backgrounds & Borders**
   w3.org/TR/css-backgrounds

■ **CSS Image Values**
   w3.org/TR/css-images

RELATED
SPECS

Shapes 3

9 Flexible ellipses

The problem

You have probably noticed at some point that any square element with a sufficiently large **border-radius** can turn into a circle, with CSS code akin to the following:

FIGURE 3.1

A circle, generated by fixed dimensions and a **border-radius** of half that

```
background: #fb3;
width: 200px;
height: 200px;
border-radius: 100px; /* >= half the side */
```

You might have also noticed that you could specify **any** radius larger than **100px** and it will still result in a circle. The reason is outlined in the specification:

However, we often cannot provide a specific width and height on an element, as we want it to **adjust to its content**, which may not be known ahead of time. Even if we are designing a static website and its exact content is predetermined, we might want to modify it at some point, or it could be displayed in a fallback font with different metrics. In that case, we usually want it to be **an ellipse when the width and height are not exactly equal and a circle when they are**. However, with our previous code, that is not the case. The resulting shape when the width is larger than the height is shown in **Figure 3.2**. Can we even use `border-radius` to make an ellipse, let alone a flexible one?

FIGURE 3.2

Our previous circle example, when the height is smaller than the width; the **border-radius** circle is shown here with dashed lines

The solution

One lesser known fact is that `border-radius` accepts **different horizontal and vertical radii**, if you use a slash (/) to separate the two. This allows us to create **elliptical rounding** at the corners (**Figure 3.3**). So, if we had an element with dimensions of 200px × 150px, for example, we could turn it into an ellipse with radii equal to half its width and height, respectively:

FIGURE 3.3

A box with unequal horizontal and vertical **border-radius**; our corner curving now follows an ellipse with horizontal and vertical radii equal to the **border-radius** we specified, shown here with dashed lines

```
border-radius: 100px / 75px;
```

You can see the result in **Figure 3.4**.

However, this has a **major flaw**: if the dimensions change, the `border-radius` values need to change as well. You can see in **Figure 3.5** how the `border-radius` looks when you have a 200px × 300px element instead. When our dimensions vary depending on content, we have a problem.

Or, do we? Another lesser known feature of **border-radius** is that **it accepts percentages, not just lengths**. The percentage **resolves to the corresponding dimension**, width for the horizontal radius and height for the vertical one. This means **the same percentage can compute to different horizontal and vertical radii**. Therefore, to create a flexible ellipse, we can replace both radii with **50%**:

```
border-radius: 50% / 50%;
```

And because the parts before and after the slash are now the same (even though they don't compute to the same value), we can further simplify it to:

```
border-radius: 50%;
```

The result is a flexible ellipse with just one line of CSS, regardless of width and height.

▶ **PLAY!**   play.csssecrets.io/**ellipse**

Half ellipses

Now that we know how to make a flexible ellipse with CSS, it naturally follows to wonder if we can make other common shapes, like **fractions of**

<hr/>

TRIVIA **Why "border-radius"?**

Many wonder why **border-radius** was named that way, as it doesn't require borders to work. It seems that **corner-radius** would have been much more appropriate. The reason for this (admittedly confusing) name is that **border-radius** rounds the edge of the element's *border box*. When the element has no borders, this makes no difference, but when it does, it's the outer corner of the border that is rounded. The rounding of the inner corner is smaller (**max(0, border-radius - border-width)** to be precise).

an ellipse. Let's take a moment to think about a half ellipse (e.g., the one in **Figure 3.6**).

It's symmetrical across the vertical axis, but not across the horizontal one. Even if we can't know the exact **border-radius** values (or if it's at all possible) yet, it starts to become obvious that we will need different radii **per corner**. However, the values we've examined so far only allow for one value for all four corners.

Fortunately, the **border-radius** syntax is more flexible than that. You might be surprised to find that **border-radius** is actually a shorthand. We can provide different values for each corner, and there are two different ways to do that. One way would be to use the longhand properties it's comprised of:

A half ellipse can become a semicircle when the width is double the height (or when the height is double the width, for ellipses cut down the vertical axis).

FIGURE 3.6
A half ellipse

- border-top-left-radius
- border-top-right-radius
- border-bottom-right-radius
- border-bottom-left-radius

However, the more concise way is to use the **border-radius** shorthand and to provide **multiple whitespace-separated values**. If we provide four values, they each apply to one corner, **in clockwise order, starting from the top left**. If we provide fewer than four values, they are multiplied in the usual CSS way, akin to properties like **border-width**. Three values mean the fourth is the same as the second. Two values mean the third is the same as the first. **Figure 3.7** provides a visual explanation of how this works. We can even provide **different horizontal and vertical radii for all four corners**, by specifying 1–4 values before the slash and 1–4 different values after it. Note that these are expanded into four values individually. For example, a **border-radius** value of **10px / 5px 20px** is equivalent to **10px 10px 10px 10px / 5px 20px 5px 20px**.

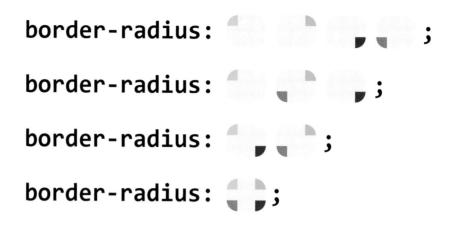

Let's now examine the half ellipse problem again with this newfound knowledge. Is it possible to specify such `border-radius` values that would generate a shape like this? We cannot know until we've tried. Let's start by making a few observations:

- The shape is **symmetrical horizontally**, which means both the **top left and top right radii should be the same**; likewise, the **bottom left and bottom right radii** should also match.

- There are no straight horizontal edges at the top (i.e., the entire top side is curved), which means **the top left and top right radii together should total 100% of the shape's width**.

- From the previous two observations, we can deduce that the horizontal left and right radii should be **50%**.

- Vertically, it seems that **the rounding for the two top corners occupies the entire element's height** and there is **no rounding at the bottom corners**. Therefore, it seems that a reasonable value for the vertical part of the `border-radius` would be `100% 100% 0 0`.

- Because the vertical rounding of the bottom corners is zero, it doesn't matter what horizontal rounding they have, as that will always compute to zero anyway. (Can you imagine a corner with zero vertical rounding and positive horizontal rounding? Yup, neither could the spec writers.)

Putting all this together, we can come up with the CSS code for the flexible half ellipse in **Figure 3.6** pretty easily:

```
border-radius: 50% / 100% 100% 0 0;
```

It's equally simple to come up with values that create half ellipses cut down the vertical axis instead, like the one shown in **Figure 3.8**:

```
border-radius: 100% 0 0 100% / 50%;
```

As an exercise, try to write CSS code for the other half of the ellipse.

▶ PLAY! play.csssecrets.io/**half-ellipse**

FIGURE 3.8

A half ellipse cut down the vertical axis

Quarter ellipses

After creating a whole ellipse and a half ellipse, the natural next question is whether we can make a quarter ellipse, like the one shown in **Figure 3.9**. Following a similar thought process as before, we can notice that to create a quarter ellipse, **one of the corners needs to have a 100% radius both horizontally and vertically, and the other four will have no rounding**. Because the percentage will be the same for both horizontal and vertical radii of all four corners, no slash notation is needed. The code would look like this:

Similarly to the half ellipse example, when the width and height are equal, this will be a quarter **circle**.

```
border-radius: 100% 0 0 0;
```

FIGURE 3.9

A quarter ellipse

Unfortunately, in case you are now wondering what other fractions of ellipses are possible with **border-radius** (e.g., is $\frac{1}{8}$th of an ellipse possible? One third?), I'm afraid you will be disappointed, because there are no possible **border-radius** values to generate that.

FIGURE 3.10

Simurai masterfully used **border-radius** to its full extent to create all sorts of shapes for his **BonBon buttons** (*simurai.com/archive/ buttons*)

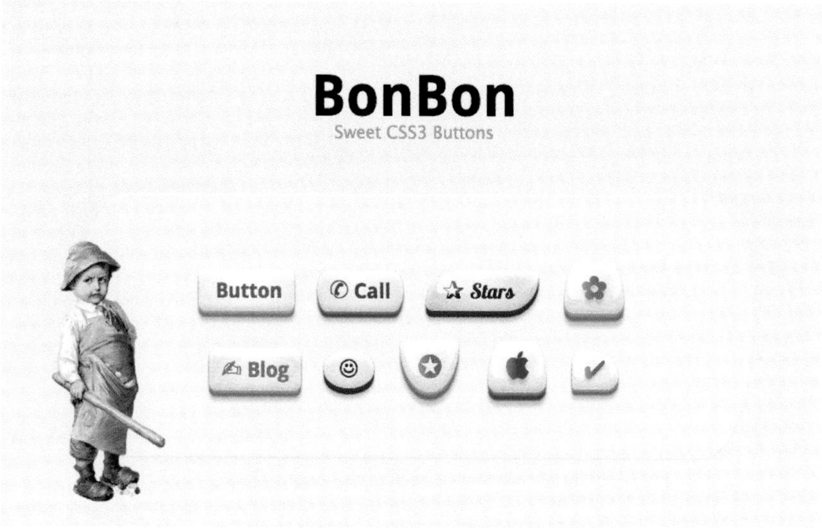

▸ **PLAY!** `play.csssecrets.io/`**`quarter-ellipse`**

■ **CSS Backgrounds & Borders**
w3.org/TR/css-backgrounds

RELATED
SPECS

10 Parallelograms

Prerequisites

Basic CSS transforms

The problem

FIGURE 3.11

A parallelogram

Parallelograms are a superset of rectangles: their sides are parallel but their corners are not necessarily straight (see **Figure 3.11**). In visual design, they're often useful to make the design appear more dynamic and convey a sense of movement (**Figure 3.12**).

Let's try to create a button-style link with that style in CSS. Our starting point will be a plain flat button, with some simple styling, like the one in **Figure 3.13**. Then, we can create the skewed rectangle shape with a `skew()` transform, like so:

```
transform: skewX(-45deg);
```

FIGURE 3.12

Parallelograms in web design (design by Martina Pitakova)

However, this also results in the content being skewed, which makes it ugly and unreadable (**Figure 3.14**). **Is there a way to only skew the container shape without skewing the contents?**

Nested elements solution

We can **apply an opposite `skew()` transform to the content, which will cancel out the outer transform**, effectively giving us the result we want. Unfortunately, that means we will have to use an extra HTML element to wrap around the content, such as a div:

```html
<a href="#yolo" class="button">
    <div>Click me</div>
</a>
```

FIGURE 3.13

Our button, before any transforms are applied

FIGURE 3.14

Our skewed button, making the text hard to read

FIGURE 3.15

The final result

If you're applying this effect to an element that is inline by default, don't forget to set its **display** property to something else, like **inline-block** or **block**, otherwise **transforms will not apply**. Same goes for the inner element.

```
.button { transform: skewX(-45deg); }
.button > div { transform: skewX(45deg); }
```

As you can see in **Figure 3.15** it works quite well, but it means we have to use an extra HTML element. If markup changes are not an option or you really want markup purity, fear not, as there's also a pure CSS solution.

> ▶ PLAY! play.csssecrets.io/**parallelograms**

Pseudo-element solution

Another idea is to **use a pseudo-element to apply all styling to** (backgrounds, borders, etc.), and then **transform that**. Because our content is not contained in the pseudo-element, it is not affected by the transformation. Let's try to use this technique to style a link in the same way as in the previous section.

We need our pseudo-element box to remain flexible and automatically inherit the dimensions of its parent, even when they are determined by its contents. An easy way to do that is to apply **position: relative** to the parent, **position: absolute** to the generated content, and set all offsets to zero so that it stretches horizontally and vertically to the size of its parent. This is how this code would look:

```
.button {
    position: relative;
    /* text color, paddings, etc. */
}
.button::before {
    content: '';
    position: absolute;
    top: 0; right: 0; bottom: 0; left: 0;
}
```

At this point, the generated box is above the content and once we apply some background to it, it will obscure the contents (**Figure 3.16**). To fix this, we can apply `z-index: -1` to the pseudo-element, so that it moves underneath its parent.

Now it's finally time to apply transforms to our heart's content on it and enjoy the result. The finished code would look like this and produce exactly the same visual result as the previous technique:

FIGURE 3.16

Our pseudo-element is currently above the contents, so applying **background: #58a** to it obscures them

```
.button {
    position: relative;
    /* text color, paddings, etc. */
}
.button::before {
    content: ''; /* To generate the box */
    position: absolute;
    top: 0; right: 0; bottom: 0; left: 0;
    z-index: -1;
    background: #58a;
    transform: skew(45deg);
}
```

These techniques are not only useful for `skew()` transforms. They can also be used with **any other transformation, in order to transform an element's shape without transforming its contents**. For example, using a variation of this technique with a `rotate()` transform on a square element would easily give us a diamond (rhombus) shape.

Also, the idea of using pseudo-elements and positioning to generate a box that is then styled and placed underneath its parent can be used in a number of cases, for very different types of effects, such as:

- It was a common workaround for multiple backgrounds in IE8, discovered by **Nicolas Gallagher** *(nicolasgallagher.com/multiple-backgrounds-and-borders-with-css2)*.

- It could be another solution to effects like the **"Inner rounding" secret on page 36**. Can you guess how?

- It could be used to independently apply properties like **opacity** to a "background," pioneered by **Nicolas Gallagher** *(nicolasgallagher.com/css-background-image-hacks)*.

- It can be used to emulate multiple borders in a more flexible way, in case we can't use the techniques in the **"Multiple borders" secret on page 28**. For example, when we need multiple dashed borders or multiple borders with spacing and transparency between them.

▶ **PLAY!**   `play.csssecrets.io/`**`parallelograms-pseudo`**

- **CSS Transforms**
  w3.org/TR/css-transforms

RELATED
SPECS

11 Diamond images

Prerequisites

CSS transforms, the "Parallelograms" secret on page 84

The problem

Cropping images in a diamond shape is rather common in visual design, but still not quite straightforward to do in CSS. In fact, until recently, it was basically impossible. Therefore, when web designers want to follow this style, they more often than not pre-crop their images via an image editor. Of course, it goes without saying that this is really not a maintainable way to apply any effect and ends up being a mess if one wants to change the image styling in the future.

Surely, these days there must be a better way, right? Actually, there are **two**!

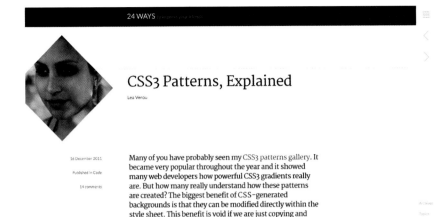

24 WAYS

CSS3 Patterns, Explained

Lea Verou

16 December 2011

Published in Code

14 comments

Many of you have probably seen my CSS3 patterns gallery. It became very popular throughout the year and it showed many web developers how powerful CSS3 gradients really are. But how many really understand how these patterns are created? The biggest benefit of CSS-generated backgrounds is that they can be modified directly within the style sheet. This benefit is void if we are just copying and pasting CSS code we don't understand. We may as well use a data URI instead.

FIGURE 3.17

Following its 2013 redesign, 24ways.org now displays author profile pictures cropped in a diamond shape, using the technique discussed here

transform-based solution

The main idea is the same as the first solution discussed in the previous secret (the **"Parallelograms" secret on page 84**)—we need to wrap our image with a **`<div>`**, then apply opposite **`rotate()`** transforms to them:

```html
<div class="picture">
    <img src="adam-catlace.jpg" alt="…" />
</div>
```

```css
.picture {
    width: 400px;
    transform: rotate(45deg);
    overflow: hidden;
}
.picture > img {
    max-width: 100%;
    transform: rotate(-45deg);
}
```

FIGURE 3.18

Our original image, which we are going to crop in a diamond shape

FIGURE 3.19

Opposite **rotate()** transforms are not enough to achieve this effect (**.picture** div is shown with a dashed outline)

FIGURE 3.20

Our final cropped image

However, as you can see in **Figure 3.19**, this doesn't quite work out of the box and accomplish what we are trying to achieve. Unless, of course, we were trying to crop the image in an **octagon shape**, in which case we can stop now and go do something else with our time. To crop it to a diamond shape, however, there's still some more sweating in order.

The main issue is the `max-width: 100%` declaration. **100%** refers to the side of our `.picture` container. However, we want our image to be **as wide as its diagonal, not its side**. You might have guessed that yes, we need the Pythagorean theorem again (if you need a refresher, there is one in the **"Diagonal stripes" section on page 43**). As the theorem tells us, the diagonal of a square is equal to its side multiplied by $\sqrt{2} \approx 1.414213562$. Therefore, it makes sense to set `max-width` to $\sqrt{2} \times 100\% \approx 141.4213562\%$, or round it up to **142%**, as we don't want it to be smaller under any circumstances (but **slightly larger is OK**, as we're cropping our image anyway).

Actually, it makes even more sense to enlarge the image through a `scale()` transform, for a couple of reasons:

■ We want the size of the image to remain 100% if CSS transforms are not supported.

■ Enlarging an image through a `scale()` transform will scale it from the center (unless a different `transform-origin` is specified). Enlarging it via its `width` property will scale it from the top-left corner, so we will end up having to use negative margins to move it.

Putting it all together, our final code looks like this:

```
.picture {
    width: 400px;
    transform: rotate(45deg);
    overflow: hidden;
}
.picture > img {
    max-width: 100%;
    transform: rotate(-45deg) scale(1.42);
}
```

As you can verify in **Figure 3.20**, this finally gives us the result we wanted.

▶ PLAY!   play.csssecrets.io/**diamond-images**

Clipping path solution

LIMITED SUPPORT

The previous solution works, but it's basically a hack. It requires an extra HTML element, and it's messy, convoluted, and fragile: if we happen to be dealing with non-square images, it will break miserably (**Figure 3.21**).

Actually, there is a much better way to do it. The main idea is to use the **clip-path** property, another feature borrowed from SVG, that these days can be applied to HTML content too (at least in supporting browsers) with a nice, readable syntax, unlike its SVG counterpart, which is known to have driven people to madness. Its main caveat is its (at the time of writing) limited browser support. However, it degrades gracefully (no clipping), so it's an alternative that should at least be considered.

You might be familiar with clipping paths from image editing apps like Adobe Photoshop. Clipping paths allow us to **clip the element** in the shape that we please. In this case, we're going to use a **polygon()** shape to specify a diamond, which allows us to specify any polygon shape as a series of comma-separated points. We can even use percentages, and they refer to the dimensions of the element. The code is as simple as:

FIGURE 3.21

The transform-based solution breaks badly when dealing with non-square images

```
clip-path: polygon(50% 0, 100% 50%, 50% 100%, 0 50%);
```

That's it, believe it or not! The result is identical to **Figure 3.20**, but instead of requiring two HTML elements and eight lines of cryptic CSS code, it's now created with only one simple line.

The wonders of **clip-path** don't stop here. The property is even animatable, as long as we animate between the same shape functions (**polygon()**, in our case), with the same number of points. Therefore, if we want to smoothly uncover the whole image on mouseover, we would do something like this:

FIGURE 3.22

The **clip-path** method adjusts nicely to non-square images

```
img {
    clip-path: polygon(50% 0, 100% 50%,
                       50% 100%, 0 50%);
    transition: 1s clip-path;
}

img:hover {
    clip-path: polygon(0 0, 100% 0,
                       100% 100%, 0 100%);
}
```

Furthermore, this method adjusts nicely to non-square images, as you can verify in **Figure 3.22**. Ah, the joys of modern CSS…

▶ PLAY! play.csssecrets.io/**diamond-clip**

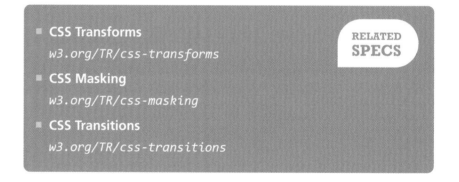

■ **CSS Transforms**
  w3.org/TR/css-transforms

■ **CSS Masking**
  w3.org/TR/css-masking

■ **CSS Transitions**
  w3.org/TR/css-transitions

RELATED
SPECS

12 Cutout corners

Prerequisites

CSS gradients, **background-size**, the "Striped backgrounds" secret on page 40

The problem

FIGURE 3.23

A button with cutout corners, creating an arrow shape that emphasizes its meaning

Cutting corners is not just a way to save money, but also a rather popular style in both print and web design. It usually involves cutting out one or more of an element's corners in a 45° angle (also known as *beveled corners*). Especially lately, with flat design winning over skeuomorphism, there has been an increase in the popularity of this effect. When the cutout corners are only on one side and occupy 50% of the element's height each, it creates an arrow shape that is very popular for buttons and breadcrumb navigation—see **Figure 3.23**.

However, CSS is still not well equipped for creating this effect in an easy, straightforward one-liner. This leads most authors toward using background images to achieve it, either by obscuring the cutout corners with triangles (when the backdrop is a solid color), or by using one or more images for the entire background, with the corner(s) already cut.

FIGURE 3.24

An example of a website where a cutout corner (bottom-left of the semi-transparent "Find & Book" box) really adds to the design

Such methods are clearly inflexible, difficult to maintain, and add latency, both by increasing HTTP requests and the total filesize of the website. Is there a better way?

The solution

One solution comes in the form of the omnipotent CSS gradients. Let's assume we only want **one cutout corner**, say the bottom-right one. The main trick is to take advantage of the fact that **gradients can accept an angle direction** (e.g., `45deg`) and color stop positions in absolute lengths, both of which are **not affected by changes in the dimensions of the element** the background is on.

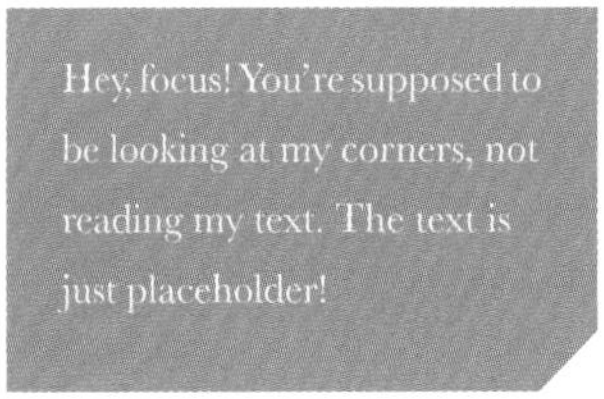

Putting it all together, all we need is **one linear gradient**. It would need a transparent color stop for the cutout corner and another color stop in the same position, with the color we want for our background. The CSS looks like this (for a **15px** size corner):

Hey, focus! You're supposed to be looking at my corners, not reading my text. The text is just placeholder!

FIGURE 3.25

An element with the bottom right corner cut off, through a simple CSS gradient

```
background: #58a;
background:
    linear-gradient(-45deg, transparent 15px, #58a 0);
```

TIP! We are using **separate colors (#58a and #655) for easier debugging**. In practice, both gradients would be the same color.

Simple, wasn't it? You can see the result in **Figure 3.25**. Technically, we don't even need the first declaration. We only included it as a **fall-back**: if CSS gradients are not supported, the second declaration will be dropped, so we still want to get **at least** a solid color background.

Now, let's assume we want **two cutout corners**, say the two bottom ones. We can't achieve this with only one gradient, so we will need two. Our first thought might be something like this:

```
background: #58a;
background:
    linear-gradient(-45deg, transparent 15px, #58a 0),
    linear-gradient(45deg, transparent 15px, #655 0);
```

However, as you can see in **Figure 3.26**, this doesn't work. By default, both gradients occupy the entire element, so **they obscure each other**. We need to make them smaller, by using **`background-size`** to make each gradient occupy only **half the element**:

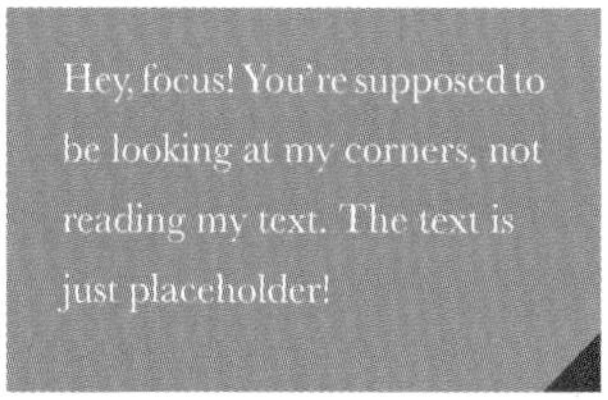

FIGURE 3.26
Failed attempt to apply the cutout effect to both bottom corners

```
background: #58a;
background:
    linear-gradient(-45deg, transparent 15px, #58a 0)
        right,
    linear-gradient(45deg, transparent 15px, #655 0)
        left;
background-size: 50% 100%;
```

FIGURE 3.27
`background-size` is not enough

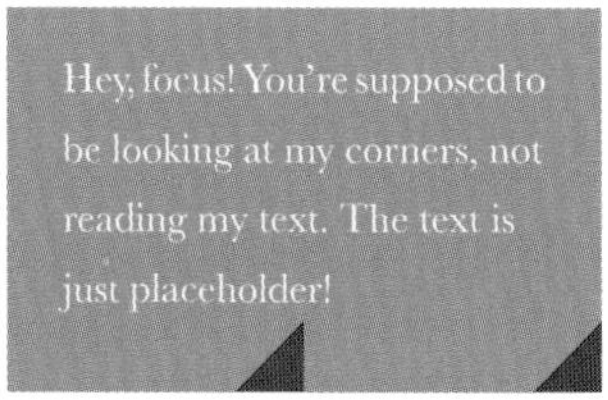

You can see what happens in **Figure 3.27**. As you can see, although **`background-size`** was applied, the gradients are **still covering each other**. The reason for this is that we forgot to turn **`background-repeat`** off, so **each of our backgrounds is repeated twice**. Therefore, our backgrounds are still obscuring each other—by repetition this time. The new code would look like this:

```
background: #58a;
background:
    linear-gradient(-45deg, transparent 15px, #58a 0)
        right,
    linear-gradient(45deg, transparent 15px, #655 0)
        left;
background-size: 50% 100%;
background-repeat: no-repeat;
```

You can see the result in **Figure 3.28** and verify that—finally—it works! At this point, you are probably able to figure out how to **apply this effect to all four corners**. You will need four gradients, and the code looks like this:

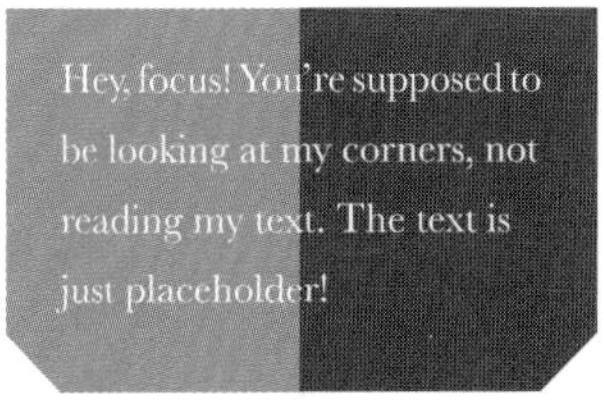

```
background: #58a;
background:
    linear-gradient(135deg,   transparent 15px, #58a 0)
        top left,
    linear-gradient(-135deg, transparent 15px, #655 0)
        top right,
    linear-gradient(-45deg, transparent 15px, #58a 0)
        bottom right,
    linear-gradient(45deg, transparent 15px, #655 0)
        bottom left;
background-size: 50% 50%;
background-repeat: no-repeat;
```

You can see the result in **Figure 3.29**. One issue with the preceding code is that it's not particularly maintainable. It requires **five edits to change the background color** and **four to change the corner size**. A preprocessor mixin could help reduce the repetition. Here's how the code could look with SCSS:

FIGURE 3.28

Our bottom-left and bottom-right cutout corners work now

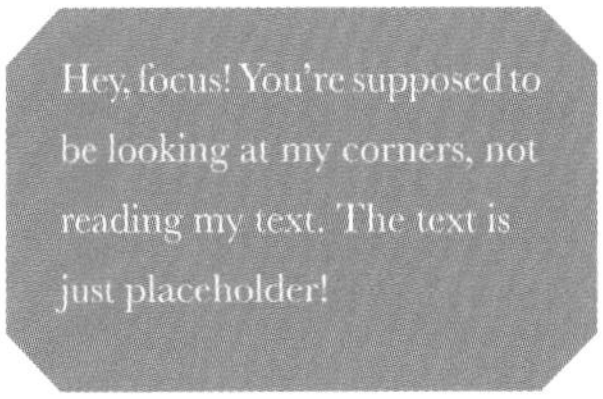

FIGURE 3.29

The effect applied to all four corners, with four gradients

```scss
@mixin beveled-corners($bg,
        $tl:0, $tr:$tl, $br:$tl, $bl:$tr) {
    background: $bg;
    background:
        linear-gradient(135deg, transparent $tl, $bg 0)
            top left,
        linear-gradient(225deg, transparent $tr, $bg 0)
            top right,
        linear-gradient(-45deg, transparent $br, $bg 0)
            bottom right,
        linear-gradient(45deg, transparent $bl, $bg 0)
            bottom left;
    background-size: 50% 50%;
    background-repeat: no-repeat;
}
```

Then, where needed, it would be used like this, with 2–5 arguments:

```scss
@include beveled-corners(#58a, 15px, 5px);
```

In this example, the element we will get a **15px** top-left and bottom-right cutout corner and a **5px** top-right and bottom-left one, similar to how **border-radius** works when we provide fewer than four lengths. This is due to the fact that we provided default values for the arguments in our SCSS mixin, and yes, these default values can refer to other arguments as well.

▶ PLAY! play.csssecrets.io/**bevel-corners-gradients**

Curved cutout corners

A variation of the gradient method works to create curved cutout corners, an effect many people refer to as "inner border radius," as it looks like an

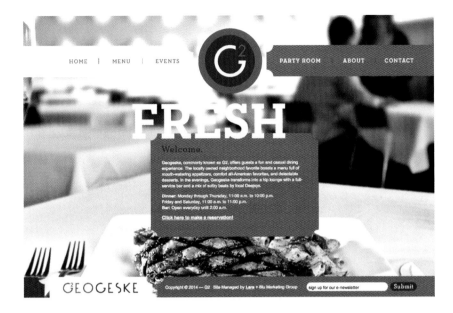

FIGURE 3.30

An excellent use of curved cutout corners in **g2geogeske.com**; the designer has made them the central design element, as they are present in the navigation, the content, and even the footer

inverse version of rounded corners. The only difference is using radial gradients instead of linear ones:

```
background: #58a;
background:
    radial-gradient(circle at top left,
            transparent 15px, #58a 0) top left,
    radial-gradient(circle at top right,
            transparent 15px, #58a 0) top right,
    radial-gradient(circle at bottom right,
            transparent 15px, #58a 0) bottom right,
    radial-gradient(circle at bottom left,
            transparent 15px, #58a 0) bottom left;
background-size: 50% 50%;
background-repeat: no-repeat;
```

Hey, focus! You're supposed to be looking at my corners, not reading my text. The text is just placeholder!

FIGURE 3.31

Curved cutout corners, with radial gradients

You can see the result in **Figure 3.31**. Just like in the previous technique, the corner size can be controlled through the color stop positions and a mixin would make the code more maintainable here as well.

▸ **PLAY!** play.csssecrets.io/**scoop-corners**

Inline SVG & border-image solution

While the gradient-based solution works, it has quite a few issues:

- The code is very **long and repetitive**. In the common case, where we want the same corner size on all four corners, we need to make four edits to modify it. Similarly, we need to make four edits to modify the background color, five counting the fallback.

- It is messy to downright impossible (depending on the browser) to animate between different corner sizes.

Thankfully, there are a couple different methods we could use, depending on our needs. One of them is to use **border-image** with an inline SVG that generates the corners. Given how **border-image** works (if you don't remember, take a look at the quick primer in **Figure 2.58**), can you imagine how our SVG would look?

Because dimensions don't matter (**border-image** takes care of scaling and SVGs scale perfectly regardless of dimensons—ah, the joy of vector graphics!), every measurement could be 1, for easier, shorter, numbers. The corners would be of length 1, and the straight edges would also be 1. The result (zoomed) would look like **Figure 3.32**. The code would look like this:

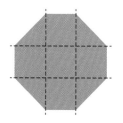

FIGURE 3.32

Our SVG-based border image, with its slicing

```
border: 15px solid transparent;
border-image: 1 url('data:image/svg+xml,\
    <svg xmlns="http://www.w3.org/2000/svg"
        width="3" height="3" fill="%2358a">\
    <polygon points="0,1 1,0 2,0 3,1 3,2 2,3 1,3 0,2"/>\
    </svg>');
```

Note that we used a slice size of **1**. This does not mean 1 pixel; it is referring to the coordinate system of the SVG file (hence the lack of units). If we had specified it in percentages, we would need to approximate $\frac{1}{3}$ of the image with something like **33.34%**. Approximating numbers is always risky, because not all browsers use the same level of precision. However, by using units of the coordinate system of the SVG file, we're saved from precision headaches.

The result is shown in **Figure 3.33**. As you can see, our cutout corners are there, but there is no background. We can solve that in two ways: either by specifying a background, or by adding the keyword `fill` to our `border-image` declaration, **so that it doesn't discard the middle slice**. In this case, we are going to go with specifying a background, because **it will also act as a fallback**.

In addition, you may have noticed that our corners are **smaller than with the previous technique**, which can be baffling. But we specified a **15px** border width! The reason is that with the gradient, the **15px** was along the *gradient line*, which is perpendicular to the direction of the gradient. The border width, however, is not measured diagonally, but horizontally/vertically. Can you see where this is going? Yup, it's the ubiquitous Pythagorean theorem again, that we also saw in the **"Striped backgrounds" secret on page 40**. **Figure 3.34** should help make things clearer. Long story short, to achieve the same size, we need to use a border width that is $\sqrt{2}$ times larger than the size we would use with the gradient method. In this case, that would be $15 \times \sqrt{2} \approx 21.213203436$ pixels, which is sensible to approximate to **20px**, unless we really, absolutely **need** the diagonal size to be as close to **15px** as possible:

FIGURE 3.33

Applying our SVG on the **border-image** property

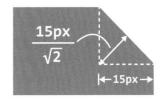

FIGURE 3.34

Specifying a **border-width** of **15px**, results in a (diagonally measured) corner size of $\frac{15}{\sqrt{2}} \approx 10.606601718$, which is why our corners looked smaller

```
border: 20px solid transparent;
border-image: 1 url('data:image/svg+xml,\
    <svg xmlns="http://www.w3.org/2000/svg"
        width="3" height="3" fill="%2358a">\
    <polygon points="0,1 1,0 2,0 3,1 3,2 2,3 1,3 0,2"/>\
    </svg>');
background: #58a;
```

However, as you can see in **Figure 3.35**, this doesn't exactly have the expected result. Where did our laboriously created cutout corners go? Fear not, young padawan, for our corners are still there. You can understand

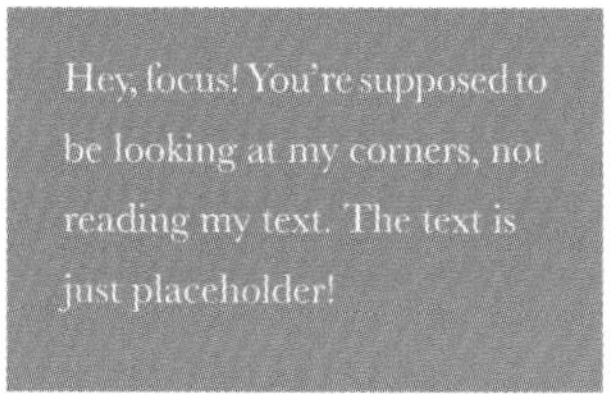

Where did our nice corners go?!

Changing our **background** to
another color solves the …
disappearing corners mystery

Our cutout corners with a radial
gradient background

what's happening if you set the background to a different color, such as
■ #655.

As you can see in **Figure 3.36**, the reason our corners disappeared was
that the background we specified was obscuring them. All we need to do
to fix this is to use **background-clip** to prevent the background from
extending to the border area:

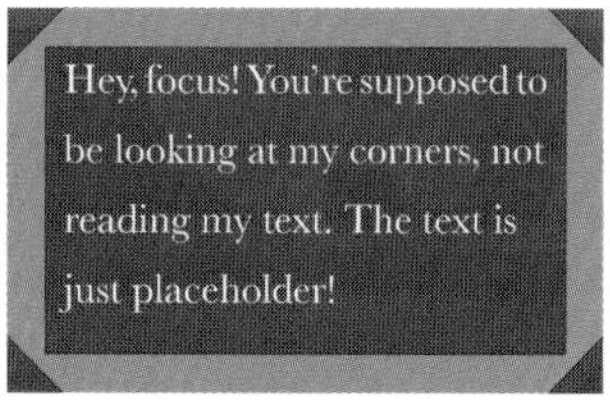

```
border: 20px solid transparent;
border-image: 1 url('data:image/svg+xml,\
    <svg xmlns="http://www.w3.org/2000/svg"\
        width="3" height="3" fill="%2358a">\
    <polygon points="0,1 1,0 2,0 3,1 3,2 2,3 1,3 0,2"/>\
    </svg>');
background: #58a;
background-clip: padding-box;
```

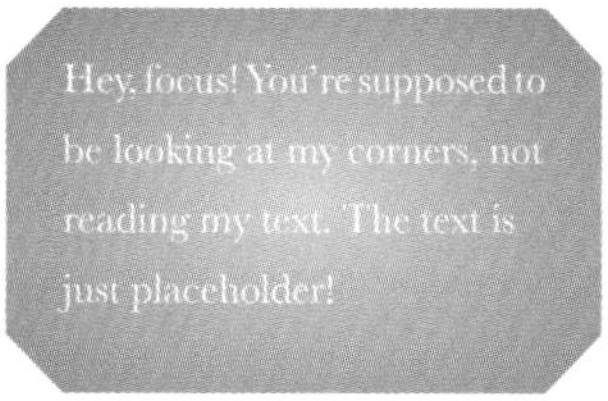

The issue is now fixed and our box now looks exactly like
Figure 3.29. However, we can easily **change the corner size in only one
place**: we just modify the border width. **We can even animate it**, because
border-width is animatable! We can also change the background with
only **two edits instead of five**. In addition, because our background is
now independent of the corner effect, we can even specify a gradient on
it, or any other pattern, as long as it's still ■ **#58a** toward the edges. For
example, check out **Figure 3.37** for an example using a radial gradient from
hsla(0,0%,100%,.2) to **transparent**.

There is only one small issue remaining. If **border-image** is not supported, the fallback is not only the absence of corners. Due to background
clipping, it also looks like there is **less spacing between the box edge
and its content**. To fix that, we could just give our border a color that is
identical to the background:

```
border: 20px solid #58a;
border-image: 1 url('data:image/svg+xml,\
    <svg xmlns="http://www.w3.org/2000/svg"\
```

```
            width="3" height="3" fill="%2358a">\
        <polygon points="0,1 1,0 2,0 3,1 3,2 2,3 1,3 0,2"/>\
        </svg>');
    background: #58a;
    background-clip: padding-box;
```

This color is ignored when **border-image** applies, but will provide a **more
graceful fallback** when it doesn't, which will look like **Figure 3.35**. As a
drawback, this **increases the number of edits** we need to make to change
the background color to three.

▶ PLAY!   play.csssecrets.io/**bevel-corners**

*Hat tip to **Martijn Saly** (twitter.com/martijnsaly) for coming up with
the initial idea of using **border-image** and inline SVG as a solution for
beveled corners, in **a tweet of his from January 5, 2015** (twitter.com/
martijnsaly/status/552152520114855936).*

HAT TIP

Clipping path solution

While the **border-image** solution is very compact and relatively DRY, it
still has its limitations. For example, we still need to have either a solid color
background, or a background that is a solid color toward the edges. What
if we want a different kind of background, such as a texture, a pattern, or
a linear gradient?

**LIMITED
SUPPORT**

There is another way that doesn't have these limitations, though it of
course has other limitations of its own. Remember the **clip-path** property
from the **"Diamond images" secret on page 90**? The amazing thing
about CSS clipping paths is that we can mix percentages (which refer to the
element dimensions) with absolute lengths, offering us tremendous
flexibility.

For example, the code for the clipping path to clip an element in a
rectangle with beveled corners of **20px** size (measured horizontally) would
look like this:

```
background: #58a;
clip-path: polygon(
    20px 0, calc(100% - 20px) 0, 100% 20px,
    100% calc(100% - 20px), calc(100% - 20px) 100%,
    20px 100%, 0 calc(100% - 20px), 0 20px
);
```

FIGURE 3.38

An image styled with beveled corners, via `clip-path`

Despite the code being short, this doesn't mean it's DRY, which is one of its biggest issues if you're not using a preprocessor. In fact, it's the most WET of the pure CSS solutions we presented, with eight (!) edits required to change the corner size. On the other hand, we can change the background in only one place, so there's that.

Among its benefits is that we can have **any background we want**, or even **clip replaced elements such as images**. Check out **Figure 3.38** for an image styled with beveled corners. None of the previous methods can do this. In addition, it is also animatable, not only to different corner sizes, but different shapes altogether. All we need to do is use a different clipping path.

Beyond its WETness and its limited browser support, it also has the drawback that **it will clip text, if there is no sufficient padding**, as it just clips the element without distinguishing between its parts. In contrast, the

FUTURE Cutout corners

In the future, we won't have to resort to CSS gradients, clipping, or SVG for this effect. A new property, **corner-shape**, is coming in **CSS Backgrounds & Borders Level 4** *(dev.w3.org/csswg/css-backgrounds-4/)* to save us from these pains. It will be used in conjunction with **border-radius** to produce cutout corners of different shapes, with their sizes defined in **border-radius**. For example, specifying **15px** cutout corners on all sides would be as simple as:

```
border-radius: 15px;
corner-shape: bevel;
```

gradient method will just let the text overflow beyond the corners (because they're just a background) and the **border-image** method will act just like a border and make the text wrap.

▶ **PLAY!** `play.csssecrets.io/`**`bevel-corners-clipped`**

RELATED
SPECS

- **CSS Backgrounds & Borders**
  w3.org/TR/css-backgrounds
- **CSS Image Values**
  w3.org/TR/css-images
- **CSS Transforms**
  w3.org/TR/css-transforms
- **CSS Masking**
  w3.org/TR/css-masking
- **CSS Transitions**
  w3.org/TR/css-transitions
- **CSS Backgrounds & Borders Level 4**
  dev.w3.org/csswg/css-backgrounds-4

13 Trapezoid tabs

Prerequisites

Basic 3D transforms, the "Parallelograms" secret on page 84

FIGURE 3.39

Trapezoid shapes, faked through borders on pseudo-elements (for clarity, the pseudo-elements are shown here in darker blue)

The problem

Trapezoids are even more generalized than parallelograms: only two of their sides are parallel. The other two can be at any angle. Traditionally, they have been **notoriously difficult shapes to create in CSS**, although they are also very frequently useful, especially for tabs. When authors were not emulating them through carefully crafted background images, they were usually created as a rectangle with two triangles on each side, faked through borders (**Figure 3.39**).

Although this technique saves us the extra HTTP request we would spend on an image, and can easily adjust to different widths, it's still suboptimal. It wastes both available pseudo-elements, and is also very inflexible styling-wise. For example, good luck adding a border, a background texture, or some rounding on that tab.

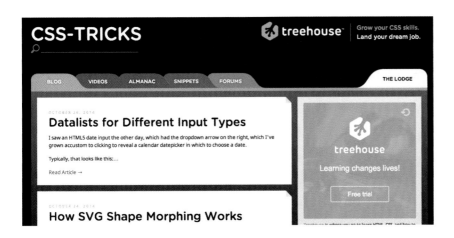

Because all of the well-known techniques for trapezoids are quite messy and/or difficult to maintain, most tabs we see on the Web are not slanted, although real-life tabs usually are. Is there a sane, flexible way to make trapezoid tabs?

The solution

If a combination of 2D transforms existed that could create a trapezoid shape, we could just apply a variation of the solutions discussed in the **"Parallelograms" secret on page 84** and be done with it. Unfortunately, there isn't.

However, think about rotating a rectangle in the physical, three-dimensional world. The two-dimensional image we usually end up seeing is a trapezoid, due to perspective! Thankfully, we can emulate this effect in CSS by using a 3D rotation:

```
transform: perspective(.5em) rotateX(5deg);
```

You can see how this creates a trapezoid shape in **Figure 3.42**. Of course, because we applied the 3D transform to our entire element, the text is also distorted. **3D transforms cannot be "canceled" inside the element in the same way as 2D transforms can** (i.e., via an opposite transform). Canceling them on the inner element is technically possible, but very complicated. Therefore, the only pragmatic way to take advantage of 3D transforms to create a trapezoid shape is to apply the transform to a pseudo-element, akin to the approach taken for parallelograms in the **"Parallelograms" secret on page 84**:

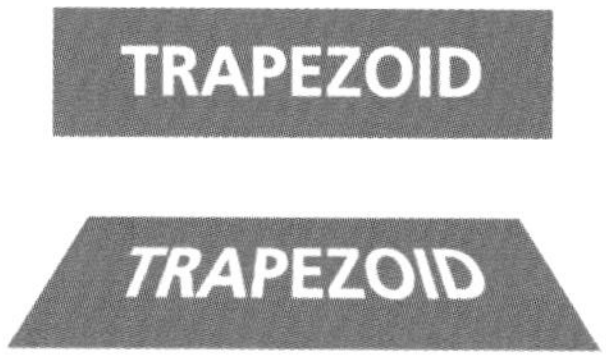

FIGURE 3.42

Creating a trapezoid shape through 3D rotation
Top: Before
Bottom: After

```
.tab {
    position: relative;
    display: inline-block;
    padding: .5em 1em .35em;
    color: white;
}

.tab::before {
    content: ''; /* To generate the box */
    position: absolute;
    top: 0; right: 0; bottom: 0; left: 0;
    z-index: -1;
    background: #58a;
    transform: perspective(.5em) rotateX(5deg);
}
```

FIGURE 3.43

Applying the 3D transform to the box generated by the pseudo-element, so that our text is not affected

As you can see in **Figure 3.43**, this works to create a basic trapezoid shape. There is still one issue, though. When we apply a transform without setting a **transform-origin**, the element is rotated in space around its center. Therefore, its dimensions on the 2D projection in our screen change in many ways, as **Figure 3.44** highlights: its width increases, it shifts a bit to the top, there is a small decrease in its height, and so on, which makes it hard to design around.

To make its metrics a bit more manageable, we can specify `transform-origin: bottom;` so that **its base remains fixed as it rotates in space**. You can see the difference in **Figure 3.45**. Now it's much more predictable: only its height decreased. However, the decrease in height is much sharper, because the entire element rotates away from the viewer, whereas before, half of it rotated "behind" the screen and the other half above it, so the entire element was closer to the viewer in the three-dimensional space. To fix this, we might think of applying some extra top padding. However, the result will then look awful in browsers with no 3D transforms support (**Figure 3.46**). Instead, we will **increase its size via a transform as well**, so that the entire thing is dropped when 3D transforms are not supported. With a little experimentation, we find that some vertical scaling (i.e., the `scaleY()` transform) of about 130% is sufficient to make up for the lost space:

```
transform: scaleY(1.3) perspective(.5em)
           rotateX(5deg);
transform-origin: bottom;
```

You can see both the result and the fallback in **Figure 3.47**. At this point, the result is visually equivalent to the old border-based technique discussed earlier; it's only the syntax that is considerably more concise. However, the superiority of this technique begins to emerge when you start applying some styling to the tabs. For example, take a look at the following code, which is used for styling the tabs in **Figure 3.48**:

```
nav > a {
    position: relative;
    display: inline-block;
    padding: .3em 1em 0;
}
```

FIGURE 3.44

Our trapezoid overlaid on its pre-transform version, to highlight the changes its metrics go through

FIGURE 3.45

Our trapezoid overlaid on its pre-transform version, to highlight the changes its metrics go through when using `transform-origin: bottom;`

FIGURE 3.46

Fixing the issue with extra padding results in a very weird-looking fallback (shown at the top)

FIGURE 3.47

Making up the lost height with `scale()` provides a much better fallback (shown at the top)

```
nav > a::before {
    content: '';
    position: absolute;
    top: 0; right: 0; bottom: 0; left: 0;
    z-index: -1;
    background: #ccc;
    background-image: linear-gradient(
                        hsla(0,0%,100%,.6),
                        hsla(0,0%,100%,0));
    border: 1px solid rgba(0,0,0,.4);
    border-bottom: none;
    border-radius: .5em .5em 0 0;
    box-shadow: 0 .15em white inset;
    transform: perspective(.5em) rotateX(5deg);
    transform-origin: bottom;
}
```

As you can see, we've applied backgrounds, borders, rounded corners, and box shadows—and they just worked, no questions asked! Furthermore, by merely changing the **transform-origin** to **bottom left** or **bottom right**, we can get left- or right-slanted tabs, respectively! (For an example, see **Figure 3.49**.)

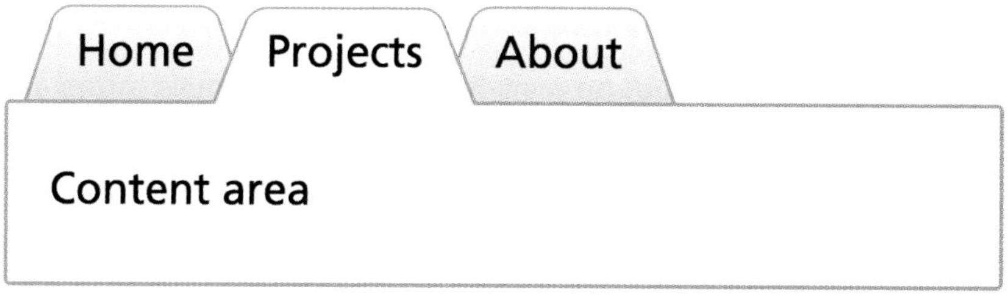

FIGURE 3.48

The advantage of this technique is its flexibility regarding styling

FIGURE 3.49

Slanted tabs by changing the
`transform-origin`

Despite all its virtues, this technique is not perfect by any means. It involves a pretty major drawback: **the angle of the sides depends on the width of the element**. Therefore, it's tricky to get trapezoids with the same angles when dealing with variable content. However, this works great for elements that involve **small width variations**, such as a navigation menu. In those cases, the difference is hardly noticeable.

▶ **PLAY!** play.csssecrets.io/**trapezoid-tabs**

■ **CSS Transforms**
   w3.org/TR/css-transforms

RELATED
SPECS

14 Simple pie charts

Prerequisites

CSS gradients, basic SVG, CSS animations, the "Striped backgrounds" secret on page 40, the "Flexible ellipses" secret on page 76

The problem

Pie charts, even in their simplest two-color form, have traditionally been anything but simple to create with web technologies, despite being incredibly common for things ranging from simple stats to progress indicators and timers.

Implementations usually involved either using an external image editor to create multiple images for multiple values of the pie chart, or large JavaScript frameworks designed for much more complex charts.

Although the feat is not as impossible as it once was, there's still no simple one-liner for it. However, there are many better, more maintainable ways to achieve it today.

transform-based solution

This solution is the best in terms of markup: it only needs one element and the rest is done with pseudo-elements, transforms, and CSS gradients. Let's start with a simple element:

```html
<div class="pie"></div>
```

For now, let's assume we want a pie chart that displays the hardcoded percentage **20%**. We will work on making it flexible later. Let's first style the element as a circle, which will be our background (**Figure 3.50**):

```css
.pie {
    width: 100px; height: 100px;
    border-radius: 50%;
    background: yellowgreen;
}
```

Our pie chart will be green (specifically ▪ `yellowgreen`) with brown (▪ `#655`) showing the percentage. We might be tempted to use skew transforms for the percentage part, but as a little experimentation shows, they prove to be a very messy solution. Instead, we will color the left and right parts of our circle in our **two colors**, and use a **rotating pseudo-element to uncover only the percentage we need**.

To color the right part of our circle brown, we will use a simple linear gradient:

```css
background-image:
    linear-gradient(to right, transparent 50%, #655 0);
```

As you can see in **Figure 3.51**, this is all that's needed. Now, we can proceed to styling the pseudo-element that will act as a mask:

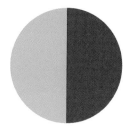

FIGURE 3.51

Coloring the right part of our circle brown, with a simple linear gradient

```
.pie::before {
    content: '';
    display: block;
    margin-left: 50%;
    height: 100%;
}
```

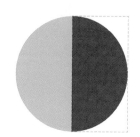

FIGURE 3.52

The pseudo-element that will act as a mask is shown here with dashed lines

> Careful not to use **background: inherit;**, instead of the **background-color: inherit;**, otherwise the gradient will be inherited too!

You can see in **Figure 3.52** where our pseudo-element currently lies relative to the pie element. Currently, it's not styled and it doesn't cover anything. It's merely an invisible rectangle. To start styling it, let's make a few observations:

- Because we want it to **cover the brown part of our circle**, we need to apply a green background to it, using **background-color: inherit** to avoid duplication, as we want it to have the same background color as its parent.

- We want it to **rotate around the circle's center**, which is on the middle of the pseudo-element's left side, so we should apply a **transform-origin** of **0 50%** to it, or just **left**.

- We don't want it to be a rectangle, as it makes it bleed past the edges of the pie chart, so we need to either apply **overflow: hidden** to the **.pie**, or an appropriate **border-radius** to make it a semicircle.

Putting it all together, our pseudo-element's CSS will look like this:

```
.pie::before {
    content: '';
    display: block;
    margin-left: 50%;
    height: 100%;
    border-radius: 0 100% 100% 0 / 50%;
    background-color: inherit;
    transform-origin: left;
}
```

Our pie currently looks like **Figure 3.54**. This is where the fun begins! We can start **rotating the pseudo-element**, by applying a `rotate()` transform. For the **20%** we were trying to achieve, we can use a value of **72deg** (0.2 × 360 = 72), or `.2turn`, which is much more readable. You can see how it looks for a few other values as well, in **Figure 3.53**.

We might be tempted to think we're done, but unfortunately it's not that simple. Our pie chart works great for displaying percentages from 0 to 50%, but if we try to depict a 60% percentage (by applying a `.6turn` rotation), **Figure 3.55** happens. Don't lose hope yet though, as we can— and we will—fix this!

If we think about 50%–100% percentages as a separate problem, we might notice that we can use **an inverted version of the previous solution** for them: a brown pseudo-element, rotating from `0` to `.5turn`, respectively. So, for a 60% pie, the pseudo-element code would look like this:

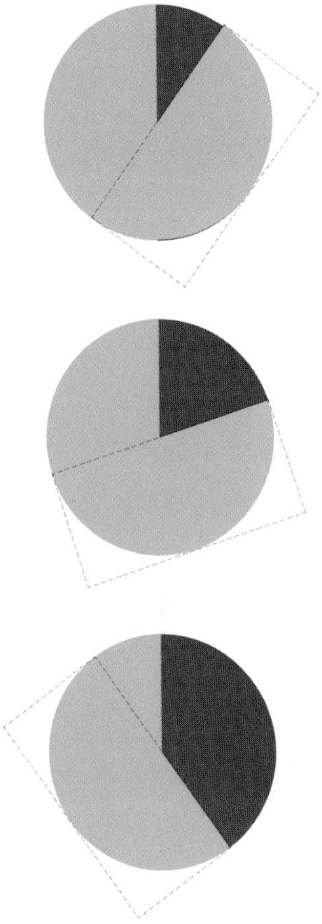

```
.pie::before {
    content: '';
    display: block;
    margin-left: 50%;
    height: 100%;
    border-radius: 0 100% 100% 0 / 50%;
    background: #655;
    transform-origin: left;
    transform: rotate(.1turn);
}
```

FIGURE 3.53

Our simple pie chart showing different percentages; from top to bottom: 10% (**36deg** or **.1turn**), 20% (**72deg** or **.2turn**), 40% (**144deg** or **.4turn**)

You can see this in action in **Figure 3.56**. Because we've now figured out a way to depict any percentage, we could even **animate the pie chart from 0% to 100% with CSS animations**, creating a **fancy progress indicator**:

```
@keyframes spin {
    to { transform: rotate(.5turn); }
}
```

FIGURE 3.54

Our pseudo-element (shown here with a dashed outline) after we finished styling it

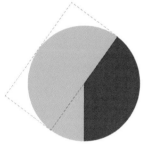

FIGURE 3.55

Our pie chart breaks for percentages greater than **50%** (shown here: **60%**)

FIGURE 3.56

Our now correct 60% pie

```
@keyframes bg {
    50% { background: #655; }
}

.pie::before {
    content: '';
    display: block;
    margin-left: 50%;
    height: 100%;
    border-radius: 0 100% 100% 0 / 50%;
    background-color: inherit;
    transform-origin: left;
    animation: spin 3s linear infinite,
               bg 6s step-end infinite;
}
```

▶ **PLAY!** play.csssecrets.io/**pie-animated**

All this is good, but **how do we style multiple static pie charts with different percentages**, which is the most common use case? Ideally, we want to be able to type something like this:

```
<div class="pie">20%</div>
<div class="pie">60%</div>
```

HTML

...and get two pie charts, one showing **20%**, and the other one showing **60%**. First, we will explore how we can do it with **inline styles**, and then we could always write a short script to parse the text content and add said inline styles, for **code elegance**, **encapsulation**, **maintainability**, and perhaps most importantly, **accessibility**.

The challenge to controlling the pie chart percentage with inline styles is that the CSS code that is responsible for setting the percentage is set on the pseudo-element. As you already know, **we cannot set inline styles on pseudo-elements**, so **we need to be inventive**.

The solution comes from one of the most unlikely places. We are going to use the **animation we already presented**, but it will be **paused**. Instead of running it like a normal animation, we are going to use **negative animation delays** to **step through to any point in the animation** statically and stay there. Confused? Yes, a negative `animation-delay` is not only allowed by the specification, but is very useful for cases like this:

> "A negative delay is **valid**. Similar to a delay of `0s`, it means that the animation executes immediately, but is automatically progressed by the absolute value of the delay, as if the animation had started the specified time in the past, and so it appears to start partway through its active duration."
>
> — **CSS Animations Level 1** (w3.org/TR/css-animations/#animation-delay)

Because our animation is paused, the first frame of it (defined by our negative `animation-delay`), will be **the only one displayed**. The percentage shown on the pie chart will be **the percentage of the total duration our** `animation-delay` **is**. For example, with the current duration of **6s**, we would need an `animation-delay` of **-1.2s** to display a **20%** percentage. To simplify the math, we will set a duration of **100s**. Keep in mind that **because the animation is paused forever, the duration we specify has no other effect**.

There is one last issue: the **animation is on the pseudo-element, but we want to set an inline style on the** `.pie` element. However, because there is no animation on the `<div>`, we can set the `animation-delay` on that as an inline style, and then use `animation-delay: inherit;` on the pseudo-element. To put it together, our markup for the **20%** and **60%** pie charts will look like this:

```html
<div class="pie"
    style="animation-delay: -20s"></div>
<div class="pie"
    style="animation-delay: -60s"></div>
```

TIP! You can use the same technique for other cases where you want to use **values from a spectrum** without repetition and complex calculations, as well as for **debugging animations** by stepping through them. For a simpler, isolated example of the technique, check out **play.csssecrets.io/static-interpolation**.

And the CSS code we just presented for this animation would now become (not including the **.pie** rule, as that stays the same):

```
@keyframes spin {
    to { transform: rotate(.5turn); }
}

@keyframes bg {
    50% { background: #655; }
}

.pie::before {
    /* [Rest of styling stays the same] */
    animation: spin 50s linear infinite,
               bg 100s step-end infinite;
    animation-play-state: paused;
    animation-delay: inherit;
}
```

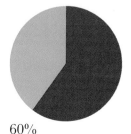

FIGURE 3.57

Our text, before we hide it

At this point, we can convert the markup to use percentages as content, like what we originally aimed for, and add the **animation-delay** inline styles via a simple script:

```
$$('.pie').forEach(function(pie) {
    var p = parseFloat(pie.textContent);
    pie.style.animationDelay = '-' + p + 's';
});
```

Note that we left the text intact, because we need it for **accessibility** and **usability** reasons. Currently, our pie charts look like **Figure 3.57**. We need to hide the text, which we can do accessibly via **color: transparent**, so that it remains **selectable and printable**. As extra polish, we can **center the percentage in the pie chart**, so that it's not in a random place when the user selects it. To do that, we need to:

- Convert the pie's **height** to **line-height** (or add a **line-height** equal to the **height**, but that's pointless code duplication, because **line-height** would set the computed height to that as well).

- Size and position the pseudo-element via **absolute positioning**, so that it doesn't push the text down

- Add **text-align: center;** to horizontally center the text.

The final code looks like this:

```
.pie {
    position: relative;
    width: 100px;
    line-height: 100px;
    border-radius: 50%;
    background: yellowgreen;
    background-image:
        linear-gradient(to right, transparent 50%, #655 0);
    color: transparent;
    text-align: center;
}

@keyframes spin {
    to { transform: rotate(.5turn); }
}
@keyframes bg {
    50% { background: #655; }
}

.pie::before {
    content: '';
    position: absolute;
    top: 0; left: 50%;
    width: 50%; height: 100%;
    border-radius: 0 100% 100% 0 / 50%;
    background-color: inherit;
```

```
    transform-origin: left;
    animation: spin 50s linear infinite,
               bg 100s step-end infinite;
    animation-play-state: paused;
    animation-delay: inherit;
}
```

▶ PLAY! play.csssecrets.io/**pie-static**

SVG solution

SVG makes a lot of graphical tasks easier, and pie charts are no exception. However, instead of creating a pie chart with paths, which would require complex math, we are going to use a little trick instead.

Let's start from a circle:

```
<svg width="100" height="100">
<circle r="30" cx="50" cy="50" />
</svg>
```

Now, let's apply some basic styling to it:

```
circle {
    fill: yellowgreen;
    stroke: #655;
    stroke-width: 30;
}
```

You can see our stroked circle in **Figure 3.58**. SVG strokes don't just consist of the **stroke** and **stroke-width** properties. There are many other less popular stroke-related properties to fine-tune strokes. One of

FIGURE 3.58

Our starting point: a green SVG circle with a fat  **#655** stroke

As you might know, these **CSS properties are also available as attributes** on the SVG element, which might be convenient if portability is a concern.

them is `stroke-dasharray`, intended for creating dashed strokes. For example, we could use it like this:

```
stroke-dasharray: 20 10;
```

This means we want dashes of length **20** with gaps of length **10**, like the ones in **Figure 3.59**. At this point, you might have started wondering what on Earth this SVG stroke primer has to do with pie charts. It starts getting clearer when we apply a stroke with a dash width of **0** and a gap width greater than or equal to the circumference of our circle (C = 2πr, so in our case C = 2π × 30 ≈ 189):

```
stroke-dasharray: 0 189;
```

As you can see in the first circle in **Figure 3.60**, this **completely removes any stroke**, and we're left with just a green circle. However, the fun begins when we start **increasing the first value** (**Figure 3.60**): because the gap is so long, we no longer get a dashed stroke, just a stroke that covers the percentage of the circle's circumference that we specify.

You might have started to figure out where this is going: if we reduce the radius of our circle enough that it's **completely covered by its stroke**, we end up with something that resembles a pie chart quite closely. For example, you can see in **Figure 3.61** how that looks when applied to a circle with a radius of **25** and a `stroke-width` of **50**, like what's produced by the following code:

Remember: SVG strokes are always half inside and half outside the element they're applied to. In the future, we will be able to control this behavior.

```
<svg width="100" height="100">
    <circle r="25" cx="50" cy="50" />
</svg>
```

SVG

```
circle {
    fill: yellowgreen;
    stroke: #655;
    stroke-width: 50;
    stroke-dasharray: 60 158; /* 2π × 25 ≈ 158 */
}
```

Now, turning it into a pie chart like the ones we made with in the previous solution is rather easy: we just need to add **a larger green circle underneath the stroke**, and **rotate it 90° counterclockwise** so that it starts from the top middle. Because the **<svg>** element is also an HTML element, we can just style that:

FIGURE 3.62

The final SVG pie chart

```
svg {
    transform: rotate(-90deg);
    background: yellowgreen;
    border-radius: 50%;
}
```

You can see the final result in **Figure 3.62**. This technique makes it even easier to animate the pie chart from **0%** to **100%**. We just need to create a CSS animation that animates **stroke-dasharray** from **0 158** to **158 158**:

```
@keyframes fillup {
    to { stroke-dasharray: 158 158; }
}
```

```
circle {
    fill: yellowgreen;
    stroke: #655;
    stroke-width: 50;
    stroke-dasharray: 0 158;
    animation: fillup 5s linear infinite;
}
```

As an additional improvement, we can specify a certain radius on the circle so that **the length of its circumference is** (infinitesimally close to) **100**, so that we can **specify the `stroke-dasharray` lengths as percentages**, without having to make calculations. Because the circumference is 2πr, our radius needs to be $\frac{100}{2\pi} \approx 15.915494309$, which for our needs could be rounded up to 16. We will also specify the SVG's dimensions in the **viewBox** attribute instead of the **width** and **height** attributes, to make it adjust to the size of its container.

After these modifications, the markup for the pie chart of **Figure 3.62** would now become:

```
<svg viewBox="0 0 32 32">
    <circle r="16" cx="16" cy="16" />
</svg>
```

And the CSS would become:

```
svg {
    width: 100px; height: 100px;
    transform: rotate(-90deg);
    background: yellowgreen;
    border-radius: 50%;
}

circle {
```

```css
  fill: yellowgreen;
  stroke: #655;
  stroke-width: 32;
  stroke-dasharray: 38 100; /* for 38% */
}
```

Note how **easy it now is to change the percentage**. Of course, even with this simplification, we don't want to have to repeat all this SVG markup for every pie chart. It's time for JavaScript to lend us its helping hand for a little bit of automation. We will write a small script to take simple HTML markup like the following…

HTML

```html
<div class="pie">20%</div>
<div class="pie">60%</div>
```

…and add an inline SVG inside every `.pie` element, with all necessary elements and attributes. It will also add a `<title>` element, for **accessibility**, so that screen reader users can also know what percentage is displayed. The final script will look like this:

JS

```js
$$('.pie').forEach(function(pie) {
    var p = parseFloat(pie.textContent);
    var NS = "http://www.w3.org/2000/svg";
    var svg = document.createElementNS(NS, "svg");
    var circle = document.createElementNS(NS, "circle");
    var title = document.createElementNS(NS, "title");
    circle.setAttribute("r", 16);
    circle.setAttribute("cx", 16);
    circle.setAttribute("cy", 16);
    circle.setAttribute("stroke-dasharray", p + " 100");
    svg.setAttribute("viewBox", "0 0 32 32");
    title.textContent = pie.textContent;
    pie.textContent = '';
```

```
      svg.appendChild(title);
      svg.appendChild(circle);
      pie.appendChild(svg);
   });
```

Pie charts

Remember conical gradients from the **"Checkerboards" section on page 55**? They would be immensely helpful here too. All it would take for a pie chart would be a circular element, with a conical gradient of two color stops. For example, the **40%** pie chart in **Figure 3.53** would be as simple as:

```
.pie {
    width: 100px; height: 100px;
    border-radius: 50%;
    background: conic-gradient(#655 40%, yellowgreen 0);
}
```

Furthermore, once the updated **attr()** function defined in **CSS Values Level 3** *(w3.org/TR/css3-values/#attr-notation)* is widely implemented, you will be able to control the percentage with a simple HTML attribute:

```
background: conic-gradient(#655 attr(data-value %), yellowgreen 0);
```

This also makes it incredibly easy to add a third color. For example, for a pie chart like the one shown on the top right of this box, we would just add two more color stops:

```
background: conic-gradient(deeppink 20%, #fb3 0, #fb3 30%, yellowgreen 0);
```

That's it! You **might be thinking that the CSS method is better**, because its code is simpler and less alien. However, **the SVG method has certain benefits** that the pure CSS solution lacks:

- It's **very easy to add a third color**: just add another stroked circle and shift its stroke with `stroke-dashoffset`. Alternatively, add its stroke length to the stroke length of the circle before (underneath) it. How exactly do you picture adding a third color to pie charts made with the first solution?

- We **don't have to take any extra care for printing**, as SVG elements are considered content and are printed, just like `<img>` elements. The first solution depends on backgrounds, and thus, will not print.

- We can **change the colors with inline styles**, which means we can easily change them via **scripting** (e.g., depending on **user input**). The first solution relies on pseudo-elements, which cannot take inline styles except via inheritance, which is not always convenient.

▸ **PLAY!** play.csssecrets.io/**pie-svg**

- **CSS Transforms**
  w3.org/TR/css-transforms
- **CSS Image Values**
  w3.org/TR/css-images
- **CSS Backgrounds & Borders**
  w3.org/TR/css-backgrounds
- **Scalable Vector Graphics**
  w3.org/TR/SVG
- **CSS Image Values Level 4**
  w3.org/TR/css4-images

RELATED
SPECS

Visual
Effects

4

15 One-sided shadows

The problem

One of the most common questions I see being asked about **box-shadow** on Q&A websites is how a shadow could be applied on one (or, more rarely, two) sides only. A quick search on **stackoverflow.com** reveals close to a thousand results for this. This makes sense, as showing a shadow only on one side creates a subtler, but equally realistic effect. Often, frustrated developers will even write to the CSS Working Group mailing list requesting new properties like **box-shadow-bottom** to be able to do this. However, such effects are already possible with clever use of the good ol' **box-shadow** property we've learned and love.

Shadow on one side

Most people use **box-shadow** with three lengths and a color, like so:

```
box-shadow: 2px 3px 4px rgba(0,0,0,.5);
```

The following series of steps is a good (albeit not completely technically accurate) way to visualize how this shadow is drawn (**Figure 4.1**):

FIGURE 4.1

Example mental model of a **box-shadow** being painted

1. A `rgba(0,0,0,.5)` rectangle is drawn with the same dimensions and position as our element.

2. It's moved **2px** to the right and **3px** to the bottom.

3. It's blurred by **4px** with a Gaussian blur algorithm (or similar). This essentially means that the color transition on the edges of the shadow between the shadow color and complete transparency will be approximately as long as double the blur radius (**8px**, in our example).

4. The blurred rectangle is then **clipped where it intersects with our original element**, so that it appears to be "behind" it. This is a little different from the way most authors visualize shadows (a blurred rectangle underneath the element). However, for some use cases, it's important to realize that **no shadow will be painted underneath the element**. For example, if we set a semi-transparent background on the element, we will not see a shadow underneath. This is different than `text-shadow`, which is not clipped underneath the text.

> Unless otherwise noted, referring to an element's dimensions here means the dimensions of its *border box*, **not** its CSS width and height.

The use of **4px** blur radius means that the dimensions of our shadow are approximately **4px** larger than our element's dimensions, so part of the shadow will show through from every side of the element. We could change the offsets to hide any shadow from the top and left, by increasing them to at least **4px**. However, then this results in a way too conspicuous shadow, which doesn't look nice (**Figure 4.2**). Also, even if this wasn't a problem, we wanted a shadow on only one side, not two, remember?

The solution lies in the lesser known **fourth length parameter**, specified after the blur radius, which is called the *spread radius*. **The spread radius increases or (if negative) decreases the size of the shadow by**

> To be precise, we will see a **1px** shadow on the top (**4px** - **3px**), **2px** on the left (**4px** - **2px**), **6px** on the right (**4px** + **2px**), and **7px** on the bottom (**4px** + **3px**). In practice, it will look smaller because the color transition on the edges is not linear, like a gradient would be.

FIGURE 4.2

Trying to hide the shadow from the top and left sides by using offsets equal to the blur radius

FIGURE 4.3

box-shadow on the bottom side only

FIGURE 4.4

box-shadow on two adjacent sides only

the amount you specify. For example, a spread radius of **-5px** will reduce the width and height of the shadow by **10px** (**5px** on each side).

It logically follows that if we apply a negative spread radius whose absolute value is equal to the blur radius, then the shadow has the exact same dimensions as the element it's applied on. Unless we move it with offsets (the first two lengths), **we will not see any of it**. Therefore, if we apply a positive vertical offset, we will start seeing a shadow on the bottom of our element, but not on any of the other sides, which is the effect we were trying to achieve:

```
box-shadow: 0 5px 4px -4px black;
```

You can see the result in **Figure 4.3**.

▶ **PLAY!** play.csssecrets.io/**shadow-one-side**

Shadow on two adjacent sides

Another frequently asked question concerns applying a shadow on two sides. If the two sides are adjacent (e.g., right and bottom), then this is easier: you can either settle for an effect like the one in **Figure 4.2** or apply a variation of the trick discussed in the previous section, with the following differences:

- We don't want to shrink the shadow to account for blurring in both sides, but only one of them. Therefore, instead of the spread radius having the opposite value of the blur radius, it will be half of that.
- We need both offsets, as we want to move the shadow both horizontally and vertically. Their value needs to be greater or equal to half the blur radius, as we want to hide the remaining shadow from the other two sides.

For example, here is how we can apply a ■ black, **6px** shadow to the right and bottom sides:

```
box-shadow: 3px 3px 6px -3px black;
```

You can see the result in **Figure 4.4**.

▸ **PLAY!**   `play.csssecrets.io/`**`shadow-2-sides`**

Shadow on two opposite sides

It starts getting trickier when we want a shadow on two opposite sides, such as the left and right. Because the spread radius is applied on all sides equally (i.e., there is no way to specify that we want to enlarge the shadow horizontally and shrink it vertically), the only way to do this is to use **two shadows, one on each side**. Then we basically apply the trick discussed in the **"Shadow on one side" section on page 130** twice:

There are discussions in the CSS WG about allowing for **separate horizontal/vertical spread radius** values in the future, which would simplify this.

FIGURE 4.5

`box-shadow` on two opposite sides

```
box-shadow: 5px 0 5px -5px black,
           -5px 0 5px -5px black;
```

You can see the result in **Figure 4.5**.

▸ **PLAY!**   `play.csssecrets.io/`**`shadow-opposite-sides`**

■ **CSS Backgrounds & Borders**
w3.org/TR/css-backgrounds

RELATED SPECS

16 Irregular drop shadows

The problem

box-shadow works great when we want to cast a drop shadow on a rectangle or any shape that can be created with **border-radius** (refer to the **"Flexible ellipses" secret on page 76** for a few examples on that). However, it becomes less useful when we have **pseudo-elements or other semi-transparent decorations**, because box-shadow shamelessly ignores transparency. Some examples include:

- Semi-transparent images, background images, or **border-image**s (e.g., a vintage gold picture frame)
- Dotted, dashed, or semi-transparent borders with no background (or when **background-clip** is not **border-box**)
- Speech bubbles, with their pointer created via a pseudo-element

- Cutout corners like the ones we saw in the **"Cutout corners" secret on page 96**
- Most folded corner effects, including the one later in this chapter
- Shapes created via `clip-path`, like the diamond images in the **"Diamond images" secret on page 90**

FIGURE 4.6

Elements with CSS styling that renders `box-shadow` useless; the value of the `box-shadow` applied is `2px 2px 10px rgba(0,0,0,.5)`

The results of the futile attempt to apply **box-shadow** to some of them is shown in **Figure 4.6**. Is there a solution for such cases, or do we have to give up shadows altogether?

The solution

The **Filter Effects specification** (w3.org/TR/filter-effects) offers a solution to this problem, through a new **filter** property, borrowed from SVG. However, although CSS filters are basically **SVG filters**, they do **not require any SVG knowledge**. Instead, they are specified through a number of convenient functions, such as **blur()**, **grayscale()**, or—wait for it—**drop-shadow()**! You may even daisy-chain multiple filters if you want to, by whitespace separating them, like this:

LIMITED SUPPORT

```
filter: blur() grayscale() drop-shadow();
```

The **drop-shadow()** filter accepts the same parameters as basic **box-shadow**s, meaning no spread radius, no **inset** keyword, and no multiple, comma-separated shadows. For example, instead of:

```
box-shadow: 2px 2px 10px rgba(0,0,0,.5);
```

we would write:

```
filter: drop-shadow(2px 2px 10px rgba(0,0,0,.5));
```

! These might use different blur
algorithms, so you might need
to adjust your blur value!

You can see the result of this **drop-shadow()** filter when applied on the same elements as **Figure 4.6** in **Figure 4.7**.

FIGURE 4.7

A **drop-shadow()** filter, applied to the elements from **Figure 4.6**

The best thing about CSS filters is that they **degrade gracefully**: when they are not supported, nothing breaks, there is just no effect applied. You can get **slightly better browser support** by using an **SVG filter alongside**, if you absolutely need this effect to work in as many browsers as possible. You can find the corresponding SVG filters for every filter function in the **Filter Effects specification** *(w3.org/TR/filter-effects/)*. You can include both the SVG filter and the simplified CSS one alongside and let the cascade take care of which one wins:

```
filter: url(drop-shadow.svg#drop-shadow);
filter: drop-shadow(2px 2px 10px rgba(0,0,0,.5));
```

Unfortunately, if the SVG filter is a separate file, it's not as customizable as a nice, human-friendly function that's right in your CSS code, and if it's inline, it clutters the code. The parameters are fixed inside the file, and it's not practical to have multiple files if we want a slightly different shadow. We could use data URIs (which would also save the extra HTTP request), but they would still contribute to a large filesize. Because this is a fallback, it makes sense to use one or two variations, even for slightly different **drop-shadow()** filters.

Another consideration to keep in mind is that **every non-transparent area will cast a shadow** indiscriminately, including text (when your background is transparent), as you have already seen in **Figure 4.7**. You might think you can cancel this by using **text-shadow: none;**, but **text-shadow** is completely separate and will **not** cancel the effects of a **drop-shadow()** filter on text. In addition, if you're using **text-shadow** to cast an actual shadow on the text, this shadow will also be shadowed by a **drop-shadow()** filter, **essentially creating a shadow of a shadow**! Take a look at the following example CSS code (and excuse the cheesiness of the result—it's trying to demonstrate the issue in all its weirdness):

FIGURE 4.8

text-shadows also cast a shadow through the **drop-shadow()** filter

```
color: deeppink;
border: 2px solid;
text-shadow: .1em .2em yellow;
filter: drop-shadow(.05em .05em .1em gray);
```

You can see a sample rendering in **Figure 4.8**, showing both the **text-shadow** and the **drop-shadow()** it casts.

▶ **PLAY!** play.csssecrets.io/**drop-shadow**

■ **Filter Effects**
w3.org/TR/filter-effects

RELATED SPECS

Color tinting

The problem

Adding a color tint to a grayscale image (or an image that has been converted to grayscale) is a popular and elegant way to give visual unity to a group of photos with very disparate styles. Often, the effect is applied statically and removed on **:hover** and/or some other interaction.

    Traditionally, we use an image editing application to create two versions of the image, and write some simple CSS code to take care of swapping them. This approach works, but it adds bloat and extra HTTP requests, and is a maintenance nightmare. Imagine deciding to change the color of the effect: you would have to go through all the images and create new monochrome versions!

Our awesome speakers

Angelina Fabbro
@angelinamagnum

Antoine Butler
@aebsr

Jenn Schiffer
@jennschiffer

Lea Verou
@leaverou

Nicole Sullivan
@stubbornella

Patrick Hamann
@patrickhamann

FIGURE 4.9

The CSSConf 2014 website used this effect for speaker photos, but showed the full color picture on hover and focus

Other approaches involve overlaying a semi-transparent color on top of the image or applying opacity to the image and overlaying it on a solid color. However, this is not a real tint: in addition to not converting all the colors in the image to tints of the target color, it also reduces contrast significantly.

There are also scripts that turn images into a `<canvas>` element and apply the tint through JavaScript. This does produce proper tinting, but is fairly slow and restrictive.

Wouldn't it be so much easier to be able to apply a color tint to images straight from our CSS?

Filter-based solution

Because there is no single filter function specifically designed for this effect, we need to get a bit crafty and combine **multiple filters**.

The first filter we will apply is `sepia()`, which gives the image a **de-saturated orange-yellow tint**, with most pixels having a hue of around 35–40. If this is the color we wanted, then we're done. However, in most cases it won't be. If our color is more saturated, we can use the `saturate()` filter to increase the saturation of every pixel. Let's assume

LIMITED SUPPORT

FIGURE 4.10

Top: Original image
Bottom: Image after `sepia()` filter

FIGURE 4.11

Our image after adding a
`saturate()` filter

FIGURE 4.12

Our image after adding a **hue-
rotate()** filter as well

we want to give the image a tint of ▓ `hsl(335, 100%, 50%)`. We need to increase saturation quite a bit, so we will use a parameter of 4. The exact value depends on your case, and we generally have to eyeball it. As **Figure 4.11** demonstrates, this combined filter gives our image a **warm golden tint**.

As nice as our image now looks, we didn't want to colorize it with this orangish yellow, but with a deep, bright pink. Therefore, we also need to apply a **hue-rotate()** filter, to **offset the hue of every pixel** by the degrees we specify. To make the hue 335 from around 40, we'd need to add around 295 (335 - 40) to it:

```
filter: sepia() saturate(4) hue-rotate(295deg);
```

At this point, we've colorized our image and you can check out how it looks in **Figure 4.12**. If it's an effect that gets toggled on **:hover** or other states, we could even apply CSS transitions to it:

```
img {
    transition: .5s filter;
    filter: sepia() saturate(4) hue-rotate(295deg);
}

img:hover,
img:focus {
    filter: none;
}
```

▶ **PLAY!** play.csssecrets.io/**color-tint-filter**

Blending mode solution

The filter solution works, but you might have noticed that the result is not exactly the same as what can be obtained with an image editor. Even though we were trying to colorize with a very bright color, the result still looks rather **washed out**. If we try to increase the parameter in the `saturate()` filter, we start getting a **different, overly stylized effect**. Thankfully, there is a better way to approach this: **blending modes!**

If you've ever used an image editor such as Adobe Photoshop, you are probably already familiar with blending modes. When two elements overlap, **blending modes control how the colors of the topmost element blend with the colors of whatever is underneath it**. When it comes to colorizing images, the blending mode you need is `luminosity`. The `luminosity` blending mode **maintains the HSL lightness of the topmost element, while adopting the hue and saturation of its backdrop**. If the backdrop is our color and the element with the blending mode applied to it is our image, isn't this essentially what color tinting is supposed to do?

FIGURE 4.13

Comparison of the filter method (top) and the blending mode method (bottom)

To apply a blending mode to an element, there are two properties available to us: `mix-blend-mode` for applying blending modes to **entire elements** and `background-blend-mode` for applying blending modes to **each background layer** separately. This means that to use this method on an image we have two options, neither of them ideal:

- Wrapping our image in a container with a background color of the color we want

- Using a `<div>` instead of an image, with its `background-image` set to the image we want to colorize and a second background layer underneath with our color

Depending on the specific use case, we can choose either of the two. For example, if we wanted to apply the effect to an `<img>` element, we would need to wrap it in another element. However, if we already have another element, such as an `<a>`, we can use that:

`HTML`

```
<a href="#something">
```

```
    <img src="tiger.jpg" alt="Rawrrr!" />
</a>
```

Then, you only need two declarations to apply the effect:

```
a {
    background: hsl(335, 100%, 50%);
}

img {
    mix-blend-mode: luminosity;
}
```

Just like CSS filters, blending modes degrade gracefully: if they are not supported, no effect is applied but the image is still perfectly visible.

An important consideration is that while **filters are animatable, blending modes are not**. We already saw how you can animate the picture slowly fading into monochrome with a simple CSS transition on the `filter` property, but you cannot do the same with blending modes. However, do not fret, as this does not mean animations are out of the question, it just means we need to think outside the box.

As already explained, `mix-blend-mode` blends the whole element with whatever is underneath it. Therefore, if we apply the `luminosity` blending mode through this property, the image is always going to be blended with **something**. However, using the `background-blend-mode` property blends each background image layer with the ones underneath it, unaware of anything outside the element. What happens then when we only have one background image and a **transparent** background color? You guessed it: **no blending takes place**!

We can take advantage of that observation and use the **background-blend-mode** property for our effect. The HTML will have to be a little different:

```html
<div class="tinted-image"
    style="background-image:url(tiger.jpg)">
</div>
```

Then we only need to apply CSS to that one `<div>`, as this technique does not require any extra elements:

```css
.tinted-image {
    width: 640px; height: 440px;
    background-size: cover;
    background-color: hsl(335, 100%, 50%);
    background-blend-mode: luminosity;
    transition: .5s background-color;
}


.tinted-image:hover {
    background-color: transparent;
}
```

However, as mentioned previously, **neither of the two techniques are ideal**. The main issues at play here are:

- The **dimensions of the image need to be hardcoded** in the CSS code.
- **Semantically**, this is not an image and will not be read as such by screen readers.

Like most things in life, there is no perfect way to do this, but in this section we've seen three different ways to apply this effect, each with its own pros and cons. The one you choose depends on the specific needs of your project.

▶ PLAY! play.csssecrets.io/**color-tint**

HAT TIP

Hat tip to **Dudley Storey** (demosthenes.info) for coming up with **the animating trick for blending modes** (demosthenes.info/blog/888/ Create-Monochromatic-Color-Tinted-Images-With-CSS-blend).

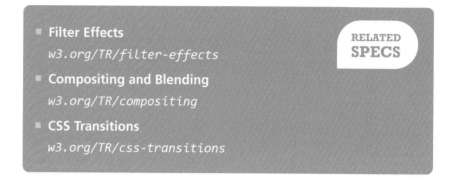

- **Filter Effects**
  w3.org/TR/filter-effects

- **Compositing and Blending**
  w3.org/TR/compositing

- **CSS Transitions**
  w3.org/TR/css-transitions

RELATED
SPECS

18 Frosted glass effect

The problem

We are using the term "backdrop" here to mean **the part of the page that is underneath an element**, which shows through its semi-transparent background.

One of the first use cases of semi-transparent colors was using them as backgrounds, over photographic or otherwise busy backdrops, to decrease contrast and make the text possible to read. The result is quite impressive, but can still be hard to read, especially with very low opacity colors and/or busy backdrops. For example, take a look at **Figure 4.14**, where the main element has a semi-transparent white background. The markup looks like this:

```html
<main>
    <blockquote>
        "The only way to get rid of a temptation[…]"
```

```
        <footer>—
            <cite>
                Oscar Wilde,
                The Picture of Dorian Gray
            </cite>
        </footer>
    </blockquote>
</main>
```

And the CSS looks like this (with all irrelevant bits omitted for brevity):

```
body {
    background: url("tiger.jpg") 0 / cover fixed;
}


main {
    background: hsla(0,0%,100%,.3);
}
```

As you can observe, the text is really hard to read, due to the image behind it being busy and the background color only being 25% opaque. We could

FIGURE 4.14

Our semi-transparent white background makes the text hard to read

FIGURE 4.15

Increasing the alpha value of our
background color does fix the
readability issue, but also makes our
design less interesting

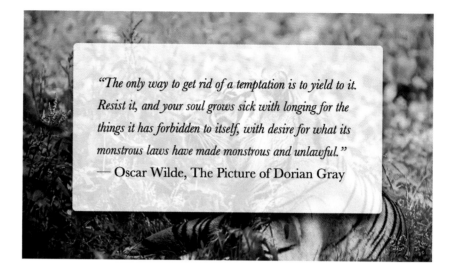

of course improve readability by increasing the alpha parameter of the
background color, but then the effect will not be as interesting (see
Figure 4.15).

In traditional print design, this issue is often addressed by **blurring the
part of the photo that is underneath our text container**. Blurred backgrounds are not as busy, and thus, text on them is easier to read. Because
blurring is computationally expensive, in the past its toll on resources was
prohibitive for using this technique in websites and UI design. However, with
GPUs improving and hardware acceleration becoming more commonplace
for more and more things, these days it's used quite frequently. In the past
few years, we have seen this technique in newer versions of both Microsoft
Windows, as well as Apple iOS and Mac OS X (**Figure 4.16**).

FIGURE 4.16

Translucent UIs with a blurred
backdrop have been becoming
increasingly common in the past few
years, as the toll of blurring on
resources has stopped being
prohibitively expensive (**Apple iOS
8.1** is shown on the left and **Apple
OS X Yosemite** is shown on the
right)

We also got the ability to blur elements in CSS, via the **blur()** filter, which is essentially a hardware-accelerated version of the corresponding SVG blur filter primitive that we always had for SVG elements. However, if we directly apply a **blur()** filter to our example, the entire element is blurred, which makes it even less readable. (**Figure 4.17**). Is there any way to just apply it to the element's backdrop (i.e., the part of the background that is **behind** our element)?

FIGURE 4.17
Applying a **blur()** filter to the element itself makes things worse

The solution

Provided that our element has a **background-attachment** of **fixed**, this is possible, albeit a bit tricky. Because we cannot apply the blurring to our element itself, **we will apply it to a pseudo-element that is positioned behind the element and whose background seamlessly matches the one on <body>**.

It's also possible even with non-fixed backgrounds, just messier.

First, we add the pseudo-element and position it absolutely, with all offsets being **0**, so that it covers the entire **<main>** element:

```
main {
    position: relative;
    /* [Rest of styling] */
```

```
    }

main::before {
    content: '';
    position: absolute;
    top: 0; right: 0; bottom: 0; left: 0;
    background: rgba(255,0,0,.5); /* for debugging */
}
```

Be careful when using a negative **z-index** to move a child underneath its parent: if said parent is nested within other elements with backgrounds, the child will go below those as well.

Why not just use **background: inherit** on **main::before**? Because then it will inherit from **main**, not **body**, so the pseudo-element will get a semi-transparent white background as well.

We also applied a semi-transparent ⬛ **red** background, so we can see what we're doing, otherwise debugging becomes difficult when we're dealing with a transparent (and therefore, invisible) element. As you can see in **Figure 4.18**, our pseudo-element is currently **above** our content, thus obscuring it. We can fix this by adding **z-index: -1;** (**Figure 4.20**).

Now it's time to replace that semi-transparent red background, with one that actually matches our backdrop, either by copying over the **<body>** background, or by splitting it into its own rule. Can we blur now? Let's try it:

```
body, main::before {
    background: url("tiger.jpg") 0 / cover fixed;
}

main {
    position: relative;
    background: hsla(0,0%,100%,.3);
}

main::before {
    content: '';
    position: absolute;
    top: 0; right: 0; bottom: 0; left: 0;
    filter: blur(20px);
}
```

FIGURE 4.18

The pseudo-element is currently obscuring the text

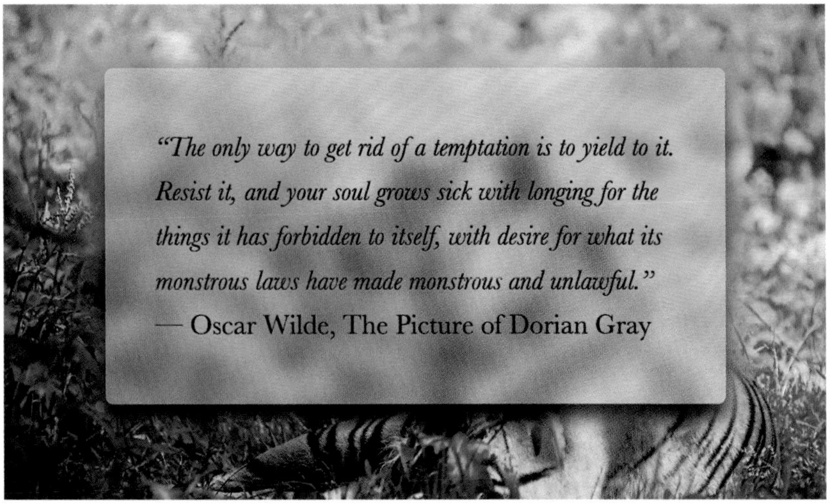

FIGURE 4.19

We fixed the faded blurring at the edges, but now there is some blurring outside our element too

As you can see in **Figure 4.21**, we're pretty much there. The blurring effect looks perfect toward the middle, but is less blurred closer to the edges. This happens because blurring reduces the area that is covered by a solid color by the blur radius. Applying a ■ red background to our pseudo-element helps clarify what's going on (**Figure 4.22**).

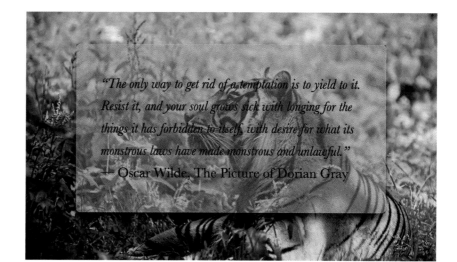

To circumvent this issue, we will make the pseudo-element **at least 20px**
(as much as our blur radius) **larger than the dimensions of its container**, by applying a margin of **-20px** or less to be on the safe side, as different
browsers might use different blurring algorithms. As **Figure 4.19** demon-
strates, this fixes the issue with the faded blurring at the edges, but now
there is also **some blurring outside** our container, which makes it look like
a smudge instead of frosted glass. Thankfully, this is also easy to fix: we will
just apply **overflow: hidden;** to **main**, in order to clip that extraneous
blurring. The final code looks as follows, and its result can be seen in
Figure 4.23:

```css
body, main::before {
    background: url("tiger.jpg") 0 / cover fixed;
}

main {
    position: relative;
    background: hsla(0,0%,100%,.3);
    overflow: hidden;
}

main::before {
```

```
content: '';
position: absolute;
top: 0; right: 0; bottom: 0; left: 0;
filter: blur(20px);
margin: -30px;
}
```

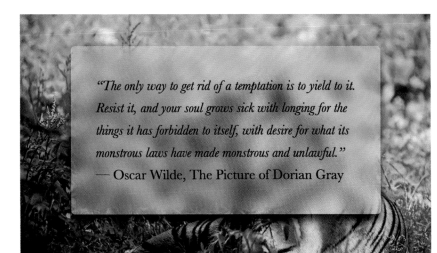

FIGURE 4.21

Blurring our pseudo-element almost works, but its less blurry on the edges, diminishing the frosted glass illusion

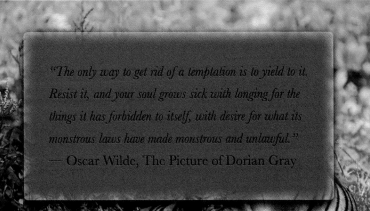

FIGURE 4.22

Adding a ■ red background helps make sense of what's happening

FIGURE 4.23

Our final result

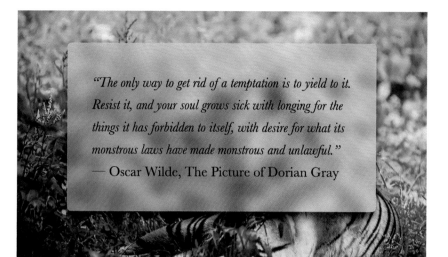

Note how much more readable our page has now become, and how much more elegant it looks. It's debatable whether the fallback for this effect constitutes graceful degradation. If filters are not supported, we will get the result we saw in the beginning (**Figure 4.14**). We can make our fallback a bit more readable by increasing the opacity of the background color.

▸ **PLAY!**   play.csssecrets.io/**frosted-glass**

■ **Filter Effects**
w3.org/TR/filter-effects

RELATED
SPECS

19 Folded corner effect

The problem

Styling one corner (usually the top-right or bottom-right one) of an element in a way that makes it look **folded**, with various degrees of realism, has been a very popular decoration for years now.

These days, there are **several helpful pure CSS solutions**, the first of which was published as easly as 2010 by the pseudo-element master, **Nicolas Gallagher** (*nicolasgallagher.com/pure-css-folded-corner-effect*). Their main premise is usually adding two triangles on the top-left corner: one for the page flip and a white one, to obscure the corner of the main element. These triangles are usually created with the old border trick.

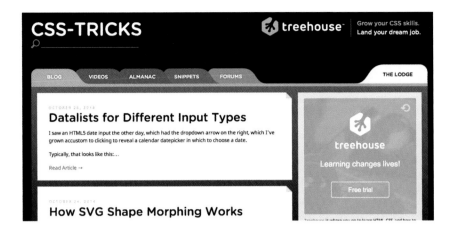

Impressive as these solutions were for their time, today they are very limiting and fall short in several cases:

- When the background behind our element is not a solid color, but a pattern, a texture, a photo, a gradient, or any other kind of background image
- When we want a different angle than 45° and/or a rotated fold

Is there a way to create a more flexible folded corner effect with CSS that doesn't fail on these cases?

The 45° solution

We will start from an element with a beveled top-right corner, which is created with the gradient-based solution in the **"Cutout corners" secret on page 96**. To create a top-right bevel corner of size **1em** with this technique, the code looks like this and the sample rendering can be seen in **Figure 4.25**:

> "The only way to get rid of a temptation is to yield to it."
> ——Oscar Wilde, The Picture of Dorian Gray

```
background: #58a; /* Fallback */
background:
    linear-gradient(-135deg, transparent 2em, #58a 0);
```

At this point, we're already halfway done: all we need to do is to **add a darker triangle for the page flip**. We will do that by **adding another**

gradient to create the triangle, which we will resize to our needs with `background-size` and position on the **top-right corner**.

To create the triangle, all we need is an angled linear gradient with two stops that meet in the middle:

```
background:
    linear-gradient(to left bottom,
        transparent 50%, rgba(0,0,0,.4) 0)
        no-repeat 100% 0 / 2em 2em;
```

You can see the result of having **only** this background in **Figure 4.26**. The last step would be to combine them, and we'll be done, right? Let's try that, making sure that the page flip triangle is **above** our cutout corner gradient:

FIGURE 4.26

Our second gradient for the folded triangle, isolated; the text is shown here as faint gray instead of white, so you can see where it is

```
background: #58a; /* Fallback */
background:
    linear-gradient(to left bottom,
        transparent 50%, rgba(0,0,0,.4) 0)
        no-repeat 100% 0 / 2em 2em,
    linear-gradient(-135deg, transparent 2em, #58a 0);
```

As you can see in **Figure 4.27**, the result is not exactly what we expected. Why don't the sizes match? They're both **2em**!

The reason is that (as we've discussed in the **"Cutout corners" secret on page 96**) the **2em** corner size in our second gradient is in the color stop, and thus is **measured along the gradient line**, which is diagonal. On the other hand, the **2em** length in `background-size` is the **width and height of the background tile**, which is measured horizontally and vertically.

To make the two align, we need to do one of the following, depending on which of the two sizes we want to keep:

FIGURE 4.27

Combining the two gradients doesn't produce exactly the expected result

■ To keep the diagonal **2em** size, we can **multiply** the `background-size` with $\sqrt{2}$.

- To keep the horizontal and vertical **2em** size, we can **divide** the color stop position of our cutout corner gradient by $\sqrt{2}$.

Because the `background-size` is repeated twice, and most other CSS measurements are **not** measured diagonally, going with the latter is usually preferable. The color stop position will become $\frac{2}{\sqrt{2}} = \sqrt{2} \approx 1.414213562$, which we will round up to **1.5em**:

```
background: #58a; /* Fallback */
background:
    linear-gradient(to left bottom,
        transparent 50%, rgba(0,0,0,.4) 0)
        no-repeat 100% 0 / 2em 2em,
    linear-gradient(-135deg,
        transparent 1.5em, #58a 0);
```

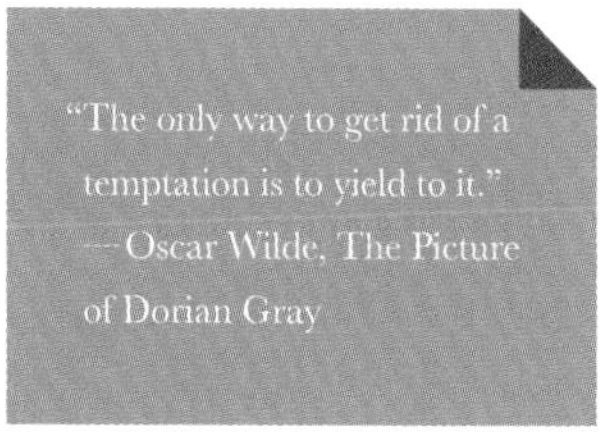

As you can see in **Figure 4.28**, this finally gives us a nice, flexible, minimalistic rounded corner.

▶ **PLAY!** play.csssecrets.io/**folded-corner**

Solution for other angles

Folded corners in real life are rarely exactly 45°. If we want something a tad more realistic, we can use a slightly different angle, for example **-150deg** for a 30° one. If we just change the angle of the beveled corner, however, the triangle representing the flipped part of the page will not adjust, resulting in breakage that looks like **Figure 4.29**. However, adjusting its dimensions is not straightforward. The size of that triangle is not defined by an angle, but by its width and height. How can we find what width and height we need? Well, it's time for some—gasp—trigonometry!

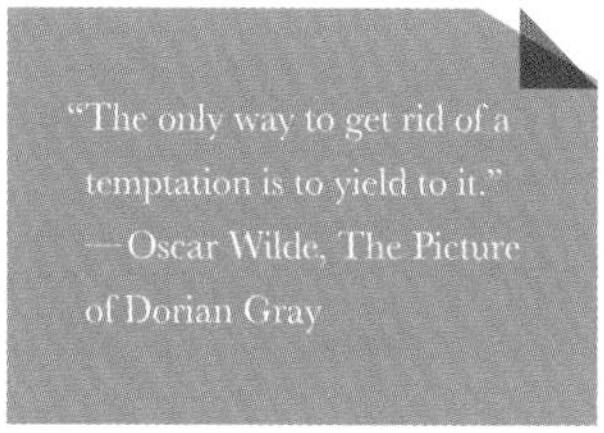

"The only way to get rid of a temptation is to yield to it."
—Oscar Wilde, The Picture of Dorian Gray

FIGURE 4.28

After changing the color stop position of the blue gradient, our folded corner finally works

! Make sure to have **at least as much padding as the corner size**, otherwise the text will overlap the corner (because it's just a background), spoiling the folded corner illusion.

"The only way to get rid of a temptation is to yield to it."
—Oscar Wilde, The Picture of Dorian Gray

FIGURE 4.29

Changing the angle of our cutout corner causes this breakage

The code currently looks like this:

```
background: #58a; /* Fallback */
background:
    linear-gradient(to left bottom,
        transparent 50%, rgba(0,0,0,.4) 0)
        no-repeat 100% 0 / 2em 2em,
    linear-gradient(-150deg,
        transparent 1.5em, #58a 0);
```

A *30-60-90 right triangle* is a right triangle whose other two angles are 30° and 60°.

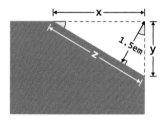

FIGURE 4.30

Our cutout corner, enlarged (the gray marked angles are 30°)

As you can see in **Figure 4.30**, we basically need to calculate the length of the hypotenuse from two *30-60-90 right triangles* when we know the length of one of their legs. As the trigonometric circle shown in **Figure 4.31** reminds us, if we know the **angles** and the **length** of **one of a right triangle's sides**, we can calculate the length of its other two sides by using sines, cosines, and the Pythagorean theorem. We know from math (or a calculator) that $\cos 30° = \frac{\sqrt{3}}{2}$ and $\sin 30° = \frac{1}{2}$. We also know from the trigonometric circle that in our case, $\sin 30° = \frac{1.5}{x}$ and $\cos 30° = \frac{1.5}{y}$. Therefore:

$$\tfrac{1}{2} = \tfrac{1.5}{x} \Rightarrow x = 2 \times 1.5 \Rightarrow x = 3$$

$$\tfrac{\sqrt{3}}{2} = \tfrac{1.5}{y} \Rightarrow y = \tfrac{2 \times 1.5}{\sqrt{3}} \Rightarrow y = \sqrt{3} \approx 1.732050808$$

FIGURE 4.31

Sines and cosines help us calculate the legs of right triangles based on their angle and hypotenuse

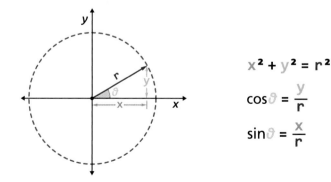

$$x^2 + y^2 = r^2$$

$$\cos \vartheta = \frac{y}{r}$$

$$\sin \vartheta = \frac{x}{r}$$

At this point, we can also calculate *z*, via the Pythagorean theorem:

$$z = \sqrt{x^2 + y^2} = \sqrt{\sqrt{3}^2 + 3^2} = \sqrt{3 + 9} = \sqrt{12} = 2\sqrt{3}$$

We can now resize the triangle to match:

```
background: #58a; /* Fallback */
background:
    linear-gradient(to left bottom,
        transparent 50%, rgba(0,0,0,.4) 0)
        no-repeat 100% 0 / 3em 1.73em,
    linear-gradient(-150deg,
        transparent 1.5em, #58a 0);
```

At this point, our corner looks like **Figure 4.32**. As you can see, the triangle now **does match our cutout corner**, but the result looks even **less realistic**! Although we might not be able to easily figure out why, our eyes have seen many folded corners before and instantly know that this grossly deviates from the pattern they are used to. You can help your conscious mind understand why it looks so fake by **trying to fold an actual sheet of paper** in approximately this angle. There is **literally no way** to fold it and make it look even vaguely like **Figure 4.32**.

As you can see in an actual, real-life folded corner, such as the one in **Figure 4.33**, the triangle we need to create is **slightly rotated** and has the same dimensions as the triangle we "cut" from our element's corner. Because we cannot rotate backgrounds, it's time to move the effect to a pseudo-element:

"The only way to get rid of a temptation is to yield to it."
—Oscar Wilde, The Picture of Dorian Gray

FIGURE 4.32

Although we did achieve the result we wanted, it turns out that it looks even less realistic than before

```
.note {
    position: relative;
    background: #58a; /* Fallback */
    background:
        linear-gradient(-150deg,
            transparent 1.5em, #58a 0);
```

FIGURE 4.33

An analog version of the folded
corner effect (fancy sheet of paper
courtesy of Leonie and Phoebe
Verou)

```
}
.note::before {
    content: '';
    position: absolute;
    top: 0; right: 0;
    background: linear-gradient(to left bottom,
        transparent 50%, rgba(0,0,0,.4) 0)
        100% 0 no-repeat;
    width: 3em;
    height: 1.73em;
}
```

At this point, we've just replicated the same effect as in **Figure 4.32** with
pseudo-elements. Our next step would be to change the orientation of the
existing triangle by **swapping its `width` and `height`** to make it **mirror
the cutout corner** instead of complementing it. Then, we will rotate it by
30° ((90° – 30°) – 30°) counterclockwise, so that its **hypotenuse becomes
parallel to our cutout corner**:

```
.note::before {
    content: '';
    position: absolute;
    top: 0; right: 0;
    background: linear-gradient(to left bottom,
        transparent 50%, rgba(0,0,0,.4) 0)
        100% 0 no-repeat;
    width: 1.73em;
    height: 3em;
    transform: rotate(-30deg);
}
```

You can see how our note looks after these changes in **Figure 4.34**.
As you can see, we're basically there and we just need to move the triangle
so that the hypotenuses of our two triangles (the dark one and the cutout

one) coincide. As things currently stand, we need to move the triangle both horizontally and vertically, so it's more difficult to figure out what to do. We can make things easier for ourselves by setting `transform-origin` to `bottom right`, so that **the bottom-right corner of the triangle becomes the center of rotation**, and thus, stays fixed in the same place:

```
.note::before {
    /* [Rest of styling] */
    transform: rotate(-30deg);
    transform-origin: bottom right;
}
```

As you can see in **Figure 4.35**, we now only need to move our triangle vertically toward the top. To find the exact amount, we can use some geometry again. As you can see in **Figure 4.36**, the vertical offset our triangle needs is $x - y = 3 - \sqrt{3} \approx 1.267949192$, which we can round up to **1.3em**:

```
.note::before {
    /* [Rest of styling] */
    transform: translateY(-1.3em) rotate(-30deg);
    transform-origin: bottom right;
}
```

The sample rendering in **Figure 4.37** confirms that this finally gives us the effect we were going for. Phew, that was *intense*! In addition, now that our triangle is generated via pseudo-elements, we can make it **even more realistic**, by adding rounded corners, (actual) gradients, and **box-shadow**s! The final code looks as follows:

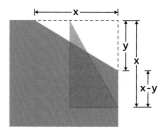

FIGURE 4.34

We're starting to get there, but we need to move the triangle

FIGURE 4.35

Adding `transform-origin: bottom right;` makes things easier: now we only need to move our triangle vertically

FIGURE 4.36

Figuring out how much to move our triangle isn't as difficult as it first looks

Make sure to put the **translateY()** transform **before** the rotation, otherwise our triangle will move along its 30° angle, as **every transformation also transforms the entire coordinate system** of the element, not just the element per se!

"The only way to get rid of a temptation is to yield to it." —Oscar Wilde, The Picture of Dorian Gray

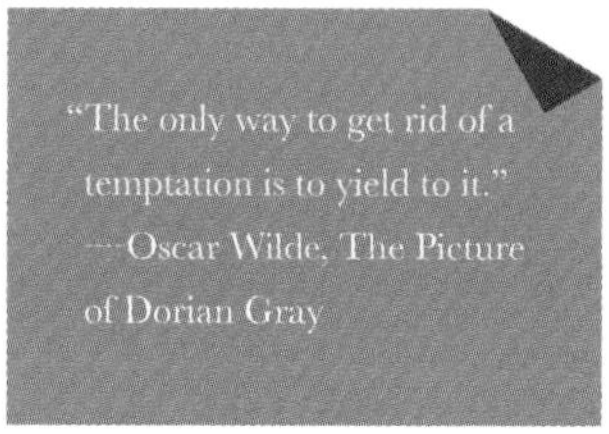

FIGURE 4.37

Our triangles are finally aligned and touching

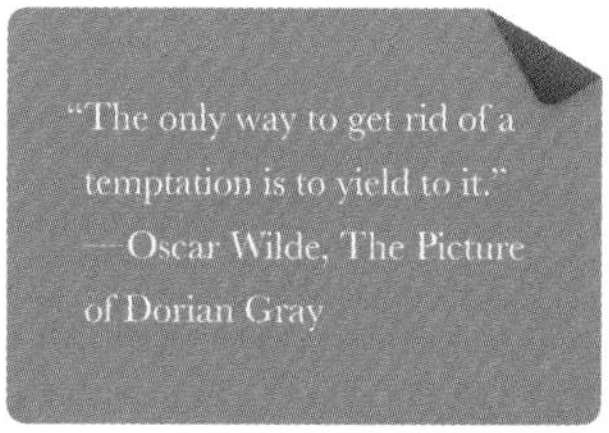

"The only way to get rid of a temptation is to yield to it." —Oscar Wilde, The Picture of Dorian Gray

FIGURE 4.38

With a few more effects, our folded corner comes to life

```
.note {
    position: relative;
    background: #58a; /* Fallback */
    background:
        linear-gradient(-150deg,
            transparent 1.5em, #58a 0);
    border-radius: .5em;
}
.note::before {
    content: '';
    position: absolute;
    top: 0; right: 0;
    background: linear-gradient(to left bottom,
        transparent 50%, rgba(0,0,0,.2) 0, rgba(0,0,0,.4))
        100% 0 no-repeat;
    width: 1.73em;
    height: 3em;
    transform: translateY(-1.3em) rotate(-30deg);
    transform-origin: bottom right;
    border-bottom-left-radius: inherit;
    box-shadow: -.2em .2em .3em -.1em rgba(0,0,0,.15);
}
```

And you can admire the fruits of our labor in **Figure 4.38**.

▶ **PLAY!** play.csssecrets.io/**folded-corner-realistic**

The effect looks nice, but how DRY is it? Let's think about some common edits and variations one might want to make:

- It only takes **one edit** to change the element **dimensions and other metrics** (padding, etc.).
- It only takes **two edits** (one without the fallback) to change the **background color**.

- It takes **four edits and several nontrivial calculations** to change the folded corner **size**.

- It takes **five edits and several even less trivial calculations** to change
  the folded corner **angle**.

The last two are really bad. It might be time for a preprocessor mixin:

```scss
@mixin folded-corner($background, $size,
                     $angle: 30deg) {
    position: relative;
    background: $background; /* Fallback */
    background:
        linear-gradient($angle - 180deg,
            transparent $size, $background 0);
    border-radius: .5em;

    $x: $size / sin($angle);
    $y: $size / cos($angle);

    &::before {
        content: '';
        position: absolute;
        top: 0; right: 0;
        background: linear-gradient(to left bottom,
            transparent 50%, rgba(0,0,0,.2) 0,
            rgba(0,0,0,.4)) 100% 0 no-repeat;
        width: $y; height: $x;
        transform: translateY($y - $x)
                   rotate(2*$angle - 90deg);
        transform-origin: bottom right;
        border-bottom-left-radius: inherit;
        box-shadow: -.2em .2em .3em -.1em rgba(0,0,0,.2);
    }
}
```

```
/* used as... */
.note {
    @include folded-corner(#58a, 2em, 40deg);
}
```

▶ PLAY! play.csssecrets.io/**folded-corner-mixin**

At the time of writing, **SCSS** does not support trigonometric functions natively. To enable support, you could use the **Compass framework** *(compass-style.org)*, among other libraries. You could even write them yourself, using the Taylor expansions of the functions! **LESS**, on the other hand, includes them out of the box.

RELATED SPECS

- **CSS Backgrounds & Borders**
  w3.org/TR/css-backgrounds
- **CSS Image Values**
  w3.org/TR/css-images
- **CSS Transforms**
  w3.org/TR/css-transforms

Typography

5

20 Hyphenation

The problem

"The only way to get rid of a temptation is to yield to it."

FIGURE 5.1

The default effect of CSS justification

Designers love text justification. If you look at any stunningly designed magazine or book, you will see it everywhere. However, on the Web, justification is very sparingly used, and even less so by skilled designers. Why is that, given that we've had `text-align: justify;` since CSS 1?

The reason becomes apparent if you look at **Figure 5.1**. Look at all the *"rivers of white"* created by adjusting spacing to justify the text. Not only does this look bad, it also **hinders readability**. In print, **justification** always goes hand in hand with **hyphenation**. Because hyphenation allows words to be broken down into syllables, much less whitespace adjustment is needed, resulting in the text looking much more natural.

Until recently, there were ways to hyphenate text on the Web, but they were the kind of **solution that is worse than the problem.** The usual way involved using server-side code, JavaScript, online generators, or even just our bare hands and lots of patience to insert soft hyphens (`&shy;`) between syllables, so that the browser knows where each word **could** be broken. Usually, such an overhead was not worth it so the designer decided to go with a different kind of text alignment instead.

The solution

In CSS Text Level 3, a new property came along: **hyphens**. It accepts three values: `none`, `manual`, and `auto`. Its initial value is `manual`, to match the existing behavior: we could always hyphenate manually, with soft hyphens. Obviously, `hyphens: none;` would disable this behavior, but the truly magical results are achieved with this very simple line of CSS:

```
hyphens: auto;
```

That's all it takes. You can see the result in **Figure 5.2**. Of course, **for this to work, you need to have declared a language through the `lang` HTML attribute**, but that's something you should have done regardless.

If you want more fine-grained control over hyphenation (e.g., in short intro text), **you can still use a few soft hyphens (`&shy;`) to help the browser**. The **hyphens** property will **prioritize them**, and then figure out **where else it can break words**.

> "The only way to get rid of a temptation is to yield to it."

FIGURE 5.2
The result of **hyphens: auto**

TRIVIA How does word wrapping work?

Like many things in computer science, word wrapping sounds simple and straightforward, but is actually neither. There are many algorithms to accomplish it, but the most popular are the Greedy algorithm and the Knuth-Pass algorithm. The *Greedy algorithm* works by analyzing one line at a time, filling it with as many words (or syllables, when using hyphenation) as possible and moving on to the next line when it encounters the first word/syllable that doesn't fit.

The *Knuth-Plass algorithm*, derived from the names of the engineers who developed it, is far more sophisticated. It works by taking the entire text into account, and produces much more aesthetically pleasing results, but is also considerably slower to calculate.

Most desktop text processing applications use the Knuth-Plass algorithm. However, browsers currently use the Greedy one for performance reasons, so their justification results are still not as good.

CSS hyphenation degrades very gracefully. If the **hyphens** property is not supported, you just get text justification that looks like **Figure 5.1**. Sure, it's not pretty or particularly pleasant to read, but is still perfectly accessible.

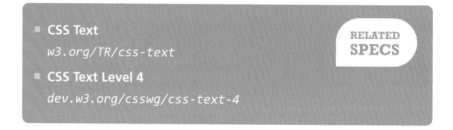

▸ **PLAY!** play.csssecrets.io/**hyphenation**

- **CSS Text**
  w3.org/TR/css-text
- **CSS Text Level 4**
  dev.w3.org/csswg/css-text-4

RELATED
SPECS

FUTURE Control over hyphenation

If you are coming from a more design-oriented background, you might be cringing at the idea of hyphenation as a toggle, with no other settings to control how it breaks words.

You might be happy to hear that in the future, we will have more fine-grained control over hyphenation, with several related properties planned in **CSS Text Level 4** *(dev.w3.org/csswg/css-text-4)*, some of which are:

- **hyphenate-limit-lines**
- **hyphenate-limit-chars**
- **hyphenate-limit-zone**
- **hyphenate-limit-last**
- **hyphenate-character**

21 Inserting line breaks

The problem

The need to insert line breaks via CSS usually arises with definition lists (**Figure 5.3**), but also in several other cases. More often than not, we use a definition list because we want to be good netizens and use proper, semantic markup, even when what we **visually** wanted was just **a few lines of name/value pairs**. For example, consider this markup:

Name: **Lea Verou**
Email: **lea@verou.me**
Location: **Earth**

FIGURE 5.3

A definition list with a name/value pair on each line

Name:
Lea Verou
Email:
lea@verou.me
Location:
Earth

FIGURE 5.4

The default styling of our definition list

```html
<dl>
    <dt>Name:</dt>
    <dd>Lea Verou</dd>

    <dt>Email:</dt>
    <dd>lea@verou.me</dd>

    <dt>Location:</dt>
    <dd>Earth</dd>
</dl>
```

The visual result we wanted was something like the simple styling shown in **Figure 5.3**. The first step is usually to apply some basic CSS like the following:

```css
dd {
    margin: 0;
    font-weight: bold;
}
```

However, because **<dt>**s and **<dd>**s are **block elements**, we end up with something that looks more like **Figure 5.4**, with both names and values on their own line. The next attempt usually involves trying different values of the **display** property on **<dt>**s, **<dd>**s, or both, often even at random as we slowly become more desperate. However, that way, we usually end up with something like **Figure 5.5**.

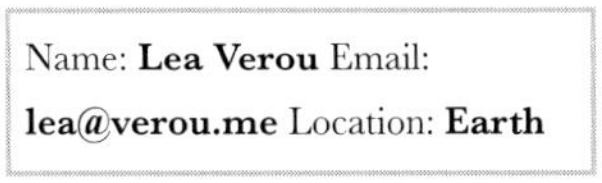

Before we start pulling our hair out, cursing at the CSS gods, or giving up separation of concerns and modifying our markup, is there a way to keep both our sanity and our (coding) morals?

Name: **Lea Verou** Email: **lea@verou.me** Location: **Earth**

FIGURE 5.5
`display: inline` just breaks everything even worse

The solution

Basically, what we need to do is add line breaks at the end of every **<dd>**. If we didn't mind presentational markup, we could have done it with good ol' **
** elements, like so:

```html
<!-- If you do this, kittens die -->
<dt>Name:</dt>
<dd>Lea Verou<br /></dd>
...
```

HTML

Then, we would apply **display:inline;** to both **<dt>**s and **<dd>**s and we'd be done with it. Of course, not only is this a bad practice for maintainability, but it also bloats our markup. If only we could use generated content to add line breaks that work like `<br>` elements, then our problem would be solved! But we can't do that, right? ...*Or can we?*

There is actually a Unicode character that corresponds to line breaks: `0x000A`. In CSS, this would be written as `"\000A"`, or more simply `"\A"`. We could use it as the content of our `::after` pseudo-element in order to add it at the end of every `<dd>`, like so:

```
dd::after {
    content: "\A";
}
```

This looks like it could work, but if we try it out, the results are disappointing: nothing changed from **Figure 5.5**. However, this doesn't mean we're not on the right track; it just means **we forgot something**. What we effectively did with this CSS code is equivalent to adding line breaks in our HTML markup, right before the closing `</dd>` tags. Remember what happens with line breaks in HTML code? By default, they're **collapsed** along with the rest of our whitespace. This is usually a great thing, otherwise we'd have to format our entire HTML page as one line! However, sometimes we want to **retain whitespace and line breaks**, such as in code blocks. Remember what we usually do in such cases? We apply `white-space: pre;`. We can do exactly the same here, and apply it only to the generated line break.

We only have one line break character, so we don't really care whether whitespace will be preserved or not (because there is none), so any **pre** value would work (**pre**, **pre-line**, **pre-wrap**). I would recommend **pre**, for its wider browser support. Let's put it all together:

```
dt, dd { display: inline; }

dd {
    margin: 0;
    font-weight: bold;
}
```

```
dd::after {
    content: "\A";
    white-space: pre;
}
```

If you test this, you will see that it actually works and it renders exactly like **Figure 5.3**! However, is it really flexible? Assume we want to add a second email to the user our definition list was describing:

HTML

```
...
<dt>Email:</dt>
<dd>lea@verou.me</dd>
<dd>leaverou@mit.edu</dd>
...
```

Name: **Lea Verou**

Email: **lea@verou.me**
leaverou@mit.edu

Location: **Earth**

FIGURE 5.6

Our solution breaks with multiple `<dd>`s

Now the result looks like **Figure 5.6**, which is really confusing. Because we have **a line break after every** `<dd>`, every value is on a separate line, even when there's no need to wrap. It would be much better if the multiple values were separated by commas, and on the same line (provided there is sufficient space).

Ideally, we would want to target **the last** `<dd>` before a `<dt>` and only add line breaks in that one, not in all `<dd>`s. However, this is still not possible with the current state of CSS selectors, because they cannot look ahead to elements after the subject in the DOM tree. We need to think of a different way. One idea would be to try adding the line breaks **before** `<dt>`s instead of **after** `<dd>`s:

```
dt::before {
    content: '\A';
    white-space: pre;
}
```

However, this leads to a blank first line, as the selector applies to the first **<dt>** too. To mitigate this, we could try using any of the following selectors instead of **dt**:

- **dt:not(:first-child)**
- **dt ~ dt**
- **dd + dt**

We are going to use the latter, as it also works when there are multiple **<dt>**s for the same value, unlike the first two selectors which would break in that case. We also need to separate the multiple **<dd>**s somehow, unless we're fine with multiple values being space separated (which is perfectly fine for some cases, but not others). Ideally, we want to be able to tell the browser *"add a comma after every <dd> that precedes another <dd>,"* but again, that's not possible with CSS selectors today. So, we will have to resort to adding a comma **before** every **<dd>** that follows another **<dd>**. Here's the CSS we end up with (you can see the result in **Figure 5.7**):

```
dd + dt::before {
    content: '\A';
    white-space: pre;
}

dd + dd::before {
    content: ', ';
    font-weight: normal;
}
```

Name: **Lea Verou**

Email: **lea@verou.me**, **leaverou@mit.edu**

Location: **Earth**

FIGURE 5.7

The final result

Keep in mind that if your markup includes (uncommented) whitespace between the multiple consecutive **<dd>**s, there will be **a space before the comma**. There are many ways to fix this, none perfect. For example, **negative margins**:

```
dd + dd::before {
    content: ', ';
    margin-left: -.25em;
    font-weight: normal;
}
```

This would work, but it's quite flimsy. If your content is displayed on a **different font, with different metrics**, the space might be **wider or narrower** than **0.25em**, in which case the result could look a little off. However, with most fonts, the difference is negligible.

▸ **PLAY!** play.csssecrets.io/**line-breaks**

22 Zebra-striped text lines

Prerequisites

CSS gradients, **background-size**, the "Striped backgrounds" secret on page 40, the "Flexible background positioning" secret on page 32

The problem

When we first got the `:nth-child()`/`:nth-of-type()` pseudo-classes a few years ago, one of the most common use cases was **"zebra-striping" tables** (**Figure 5.8**). While this previously required server-side code, client-side scripts, or tedious handcoding, it had now become as simple as these lines of code:

```
tr:nth-child(even) {
    background: rgba(0,0,0,.2);
}
```

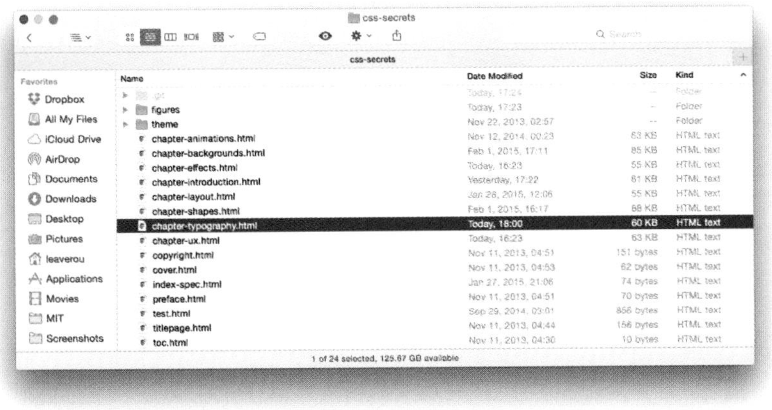

FIGURE 5.8

Tables with zebra-striped rows have always been common both in UI design (such as the Mac OS X Yosemite file listing shown here) as well as print design, as the zebra striping helps our eyes follow a long line more easily

However, we were still left powerless when it came to applying the same effect to **lines of text**, instead of rows in a table. This is especially useful for **making snippets of code more readable**. Many authors ended up using JavaScript to wrap every line in its own `<div>` so they can follow the same `:nth-child()` technique, often abstracting this ugliness away in the syntax highlighters. Not only is this suboptimal for theoretical purity reasons (JS should not be concerned with styling), but also because **too many DOM elements can slow down the page** and it's a **fragile solution anyway** (what happens when you increase the text size and one of the "lines" wraps?). Is there a better way?

Many authors even ended up requesting an `:nth-line()` pseudo-class from the CSS Working Group, which was rejected for performance reasons.

The solution

Instead of applying a darker background to elements that represent rows, let's think about the problem in a different way. Why not apply a background image to the **whole element**, and have the **zebra striping baked in it**? This might sound like an terrible idea at first, but remember that **we can generate backgrounds directly in CSS**, through CSS gradients, and size them in **em**s, so that they **automatically adapt to `font-size` changes**.

Let's give this idea a spin to make the code in **Figure 5.9** zebra striped. First, we need to create horizontal stripes, in the way described in the **"Striped backgrounds" secret on page 40**. The `background-size`

```
while (true) {
  var d = new Date();
  if (d.getDate()==1 &&
      d.getMonth()==3) {
    alert("TROLOLOL");
  }
}
```

FIGURE 5.9

A snippet of code, without any zebra striping, just a plain ol' solid color background needs to be **twice the `line-height`**, as **each stripe accounts for two lines**. The code for our first attempt would look like this:

```css
padding: .5em;
line-height: 1.5;
background: beige;
background-image: linear-gradient(
                      rgba(0,0,0,.2) 50%, transparent 0);
background-size: auto 3em;
```

```
while (true) {
    var d = new Date();
    if (d.getDate()==1 &&
        d.getMonth()==3) {
        alert("TROLOLOL");
    }
}
```

FIGURE 5.10

Our first attempt at zebra-striping our code snippet

As **Figure 5.10** demonstrates, the result is **very close to what we wanted**. We can even try to change the font size, and the stripes shrink or grow as necessary! However, there's a bit of a serious issue: the lines are **misaligned**, which kind of defeats the purpose. Why is that?

If you look more closely at **Figure 5.10**, you will notice that the first stripe begins at the top of our container, as we would expect from a background image. However, **our code doesn't start there**, as then it would look ugly. As you can see, we have applied a `.5em` padding to it, which is exactly the offset our stripes have from where they should be.

One way to solve this would be to use **`background-position`** to move the stripes **`.5em`** to the bottom. However, if we decide to later adjust the padding, we would also need to adjust the background position as well, which is not very DRY. Can we make the **background automatically follow the padding length**?

Let's remember **`background-origin`** from the **"Flexible background positioning" secret on page 32**. This is exactly what we need: a way to tell the browser to **use the content box edge as the reference for resolving `background-position`**, instead of the default, which is the padding box edge. Let's add that to the mix as well:

```
while (true) {
    var d = new Date();
    if (d.getDate()==1 &&
        d.getMonth()==3) {
        alert("TROLOLOL");
    }
}
```

FIGURE 5.11

The final result

```css
padding: .5em;
line-height: 1.5;
background: beige;
background-size: auto 3em;
```

```
background-origin: content-box;
background-image: linear-gradient(rgba(0,0,0,.2) 50%,
                                  transparent 0);
```

As you can see in **Figure 5.11**, this was exactly what we needed to achieve the zebra-striped effect! Because we used semi-transparent colors in the stripes, we can even adjust the background color, and the zebra striping will still work. Basically, it's so flexible that **the only way to break it* would be to change the `line-height`, without changing the `background-size` accordingly**.

Why did we not just use the **background** shorthand for all our background-related values? Because then we would need a separate fall-back declaration for older browsers, so we would need to include **beige** twice, making our code WET.

▶ **PLAY!** play.csssecrets.io/**zebra-lines**

■ **CSS Backgrounds & Borders**
  w3.org/TR/css-backgrounds

■ **CSS Image Values**
  w3.org/TR/css-images

RELATED
SPECS

---

* This assumes we're dealing with code snippets. In the general case, it can also break when there are inline elements that force a larger line height, such as images or inline content with a larger **font-size**.

23 Adjusting tab width

The problem

Code-heavy web pages, such as documentation or tutorials, come with their own styling challenges. The `<pre>` and `<code>` elements that we use to display code do come with some default styling by the user agent, which looks like this:

```
while (true) {
        var d = new Date();
        if (d.getDate()==1
            d.getMonth()==3
                alert("TROL
        }
}
```

FIGURE 5.12

Code displayed with the default tab width of eight characters

```css
pre, code {
    font-family: monospace;
}


pre {
    display: block;
    margin: 1em 0;
    white-space: pre;
}
```

However, this is hardly sufficient to account for all the unique challenges of displaying code. One of the biggest issues is that while **tabs are ideal for indenting code**, they are often avoided on the Web because browsers display them with a width of eight characters (!). Take a look at **Figure 5.12** and see how bad such wide indents look and how wasteful they are: our code didn't even fit in its box!

Did you just wince at the mention of tabs for indentation? The topic is out of scope for this book, but you can find my reasoning **here** *(Lea.verou.me/2012/01/why-tabs-are-clearly-superior).*

The solution

Thankfully, in **CSS Text Level 3**, we got a new CSS property to control that: **tab-size**. It accepts a **number** (of characters) or a **length** (which is rarely useful). We would usually want to set it at **4** (meaning four characters wide), or **2**, which seems to be the latest trend in indent sizes:

```
pre {
    tab-size: 4;
}
```

As you can verify in **Figure 5.13**, it now looks much easier to read. You could even set **tab-size** to **0** to completely disable tabs, but that's rarely (if ever) a good idea, as you can see for yourself in **Figure 5.14**. If the property is not supported, nothing breaks—we just get the default awfully wide tabs that we've learned to live with all these years.

▶ **PLAY!** play.csssecrets.io/**tab-size**

■ **CSS Text**
w3.org/TR/css-text

RELATED SPECS

```
while (true) {
  var d = new Date();
  if (d.getDate()==1 &&
      d.getMonth()==3) {
    alert("TROLOLOL");
  }
}
```

FIGURE 5.13

The same code as **Figure 5.12**, displayed with a tab width of two characters

```
while (true) {
var d = new Date();
if (d.getDate()==1 &&
    d.getMonth()==3) {
alert("TROLOLOL");
}
}
```

FIGURE 5.14

Code displayed with a tab size of 0, making all tab-based indents disappear—don't do this!

24 Ligatures

The problem

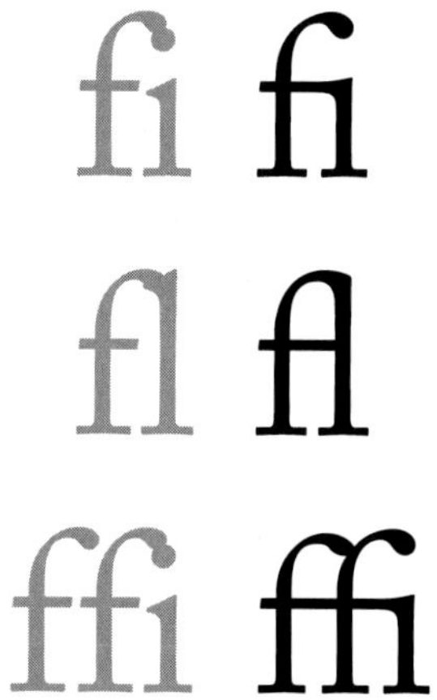

Just like people, not all glyphs go naturally well together. For example, take **f** and **i** in most serif fonts. The dot in the **i** often clashes with the ascender of the **f**, making the pair look clumsy (first example in **Figure 5.15**).

To mitigate this, type designers often include **extra glyphs** in their fonts, called *ligatures*. These are **individually designed pairs and triplets of glyphs**, destined to be used by the typesetting program when their equivalent characters are next to each other. For example, look at **Figure 5.15** for some common ligatures and how much better they look than their equivalent glyphs put together.

There are also the so-called *discretionary ligatures* (**Figure 5.16**), which are designed as a stylistic alternative, and not because there is an issue when their equivalent pairs of characters are next to each other.

However, browsers never use discretionary ligatures by default (which is the correct behavior) and often don't even utilize common ligatures (which is a bug). In fact, until recently, the only way to explicitly use any ligature was to use its equivalent Unicode character—for example, typing `&#xfb01;` for the **fi** ligature. This method brings more problems than it solves:

fi fi

fl fl

ffi ffi

FIGURE 5.15

Common ligatures found in most serif typefaces

- Obviously, it makes the markup difficult to read and even more difficult to write (good luck figuring out what word `de&#xfb01;ne` is!).

- If the current font doesn't include this ligature character, the result will resemble ransom notes (**Figure 5.17**).

- Not every ligature has an equivalent, standardized, Unicode character. For example, the **ct** ligature does not correspond to any Unicode character and any fonts that include it need to place it in the Unicode PUA (Private Use Area) block.

- It can break accessibility of the text, including copy/paste, searches, and voice. Many applications are smart enough to handle this well, but not all. It even breaks search in some browsers.

Surely, at this time and age, there ought to be a better way, right?

The solution

In **CSS Fonts Level 3** *(w3.org/TR/css3-fonts)*, the good ol' **font-variant** was **converted to a shorthand**, comprised of many new longhand properties. One of them is **font-variant-ligatures**, designed specifically for the purpose of turning ligatures on and off. To turn on **all possible ligatures**, you would have to use **three identifiers**:

```
font-variant-ligatures: common-ligatures
                        discretionary-ligatures
                        historical-ligatures;
```

The property is inherited. You might find that discretionary ligatures can hinder readability and you might want to turn them off. In that case, you might want to only turn on common ligatures:

```
font-variant-ligatures: common-ligatures;
```

In fact, the humble ampersand (&) we all know and love started off as a ligature of the letters **E** and **t** ("et" is latin for "and").

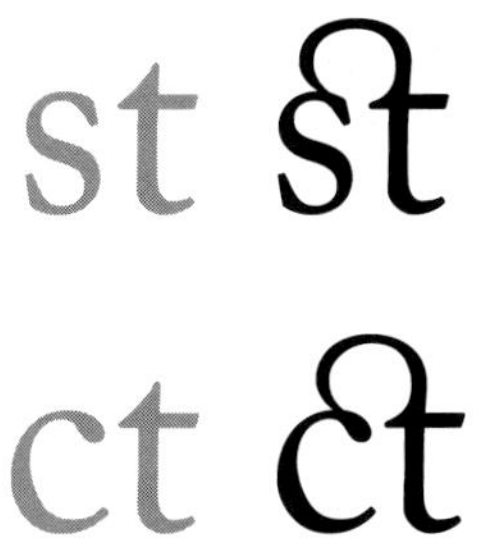

FIGURE 5.16

Discretionary ligatures found in many professionally designed serif typefaces

FIGURE 5.17

Using hardcoded ligatures can often have awful results, when the used font doesn't have a glyph for our ligature

You can even explicitly turn the other two kinds off:

```
font-variant-ligatures: common-ligatures
                        no-discretionary-ligatures
                        no-historical-ligatures;
```

font-variant-ligatures also accepts the value **none**, which turns off ligatures altogether. **Don't use none unless you absolutely know what you're doing.** To reset **font-variant-ligatures** to its initial value, you should use **normal**, not **none**.

▶ **PLAY!** play.csssecrets.io/**ligatures**

CSS Fonts
w3.org/TR/css-fonts

RELATED
SPECS

25 Fancy ampersands

Prerequisites

Basic font embedding through **@font-face** rules

The problem

FIGURE 5.18

A few nice ampersands in fonts that are readily available in most computers; from left to right: Baskerville, Goudy Old Style, Garamond, Palatino (all italic)

You will find many hymns to the humble ampersand in typographic literature. No other character can instantly add the elegance a nicely designed ampersand has the power to add. Entire websites have been devoted to finding the font with the best looking ampersands. However, the font with the nicest ampersand is not necessarily the one you want for the rest of your text. After all, a really beautiful and elegant effect for headlines is **the**

contrast between a nice sans serif font and beautiful, intricate serif ampersands.

Web designers realized this a while ago, but the techniques employed to achieve it are rather crude and tedious. They usually involve wrapping every ampersand with a `<span>`, through a script or manually, like so:

```
HTML <span class="amp">&amp;</span> CSS
```

Then, we apply the font styling we want to just the `.amp` class:

```
.amp {
    font-family: Baskerville, "Goudy Old Style",
                 Garamond, Palatino, serif;
    font-style: italic;
}
```

This works fine and you can see the before and after in **Figure 5.19**. However, the technique to achieve it is rather messy and sometimes even downright impossible, when we cannot easily modify the HTML markup (e.g., when using a CMS). Can't we just tell CSS to style certain characters differently?

The solution

It turns out that we can, indeed, style certain characters (or even ranges of characters) with a different font, but the way to do it is not as straightforward as you might have hoped.

We usually specify multiple fonts (*font stacks*) in **font-family** declarations so that in case our top preference is not available, the browser can fall back to other fonts that would also fit our design. However, many authors forget that **this works on a per-character basis as well**. If a font is available, but only contains a few characters, it will be used for those characters and the browser will fall back to the other fonts for the rest. This

HTML & CSS
HTML *&* CSS

FIGURE 5.19

Our "HTML & CSS" headline, before and after the ampersand treatment applies to **both local and embedded fonts** included through **@font-face** rules.

It follows that if we have a font with only **one character** (guess which one!), it will only be used for that one character, and all others will get the second, third, etc. font from our font stack. So, we have an easy way to only style ampersands: create a web font with just the ampersand we want, include it through **@font-face**, then use it first in your font stack:

```css
@font-face {
    font-family: Ampersand;
    src: url("fonts/ampersand.woff");
}

h1 {
    font-family: Ampersand, Helvetica, sans-serif;
}
```

HTML & CSS

FIGURE 5.20

Including local fonts through **@font-face** results in them being applied to the whole text by default

While this is very **flexible**, it's suboptimal if all we wanted was to style ampersands with one of the **built-in fonts**. Not only is it a hassle to create a font file, it also adds an **extra HTTP request**, not to mention the potential legal issues, if the font you were going for forbids subsetting. **Is there a way to use local fonts for this?**

You might know that the **src** descriptor in **@font-face** rules also accepts a **local()** function, for specifying **local font names**. Therefore, instead of a separate web font, you could instead specify a font stack of local fonts:

```css
@font-face {
    font-family: Ampersand;
    src: local('Baskerville'),
         local('Goudy Old Style'),
         local('Garamond'),
         local('Palatino');
}
```

However, if you try to apply the Ampersand font now, you will notice that our serif font was applied to the **entire text** (**Figure 5.20**), as these fonts include all characters. This doesn't mean we're going the wrong way; it just means **we are missing a descriptor** to declare that we are only interested in the ampersand glyph from these local fonts. Such a descriptor exists, and its name is `unicode-range`.

The `unicode-range` descriptor only works inside `@font-face` rules (hence the term *descriptor*; it is **not** a CSS property) and limits the characters used to a subset. It works with both local and remote fonts. Some browsers are even smart enough to not download remote fonts if those characters are not used in the page!

Unfortunately, `unicode-range` is as **cryptic** in its syntax as it is useful in its application. It works with *Unicode codepoints*, not literal characters. Therefore, before using it, you need to find the hexadecimal codepoint of the character(s) you want to specify. There are numerous online sources for that, or you can just use the following snippet of JS in the console:

```
"&".charCodeAt(0).toString(16); // returns 26
```

Now that you have the hex codepoint(s), you can prepend them with **U+** and you've already specified a single character! Here's how the declaration would look for our ampersand use case:

```
unicode-range: U+26;
```

If you wanted to specify a **range** of characters, you would still need one **U+**, like so: **U+400-4FF**. In fact, for that kind of range, you could have used **wildcards** and specified it as **U+4??** instead. **Multiple characters or ranges are also allowed**, separated by commas, such as **U+26, U+4??, U+2665-2670**. In this case, however, a single character is all we need. Our code now looks like this:

> `String#charCodeAt()` returns **incorrect results** for Unicode characters beyond the BMP (Basic Multilingual Plane). However, 99.9% of the characters you will need to look up will be in it. If the result you get is in the D800-DFFF range, it means you have an "astral" character and you're better off using a proper online tool to figure out what its Unicode codepoint is. The ES6 method `String#codePointAt()` will solve this issue.

```
@font-face {
    font-family: Ampersand;
    src: local('Baskerville'),
         local('Goudy Old Style'),
         local('Palatino'),
         local('Book Antiqua');
    unicode-range: U+26;
}


h1 {
    font-family: Ampersand, Helvetica, sans-serif;
}
```

HTML & CSS

If you try it out (**Figure 5.21**), you will see that we did, in fact, apply a different font to our ampersands! However, the result is still not exactly what we want. The ampersand in **Figure 5.19** was from the italic variant of the Baskerville font, as in general, **italic serif fonts tend to have much nicer ampersands**. We're not styling the ampersands directly, so how can we italicize them?

Our first thought might be to use the **font-style** descriptor in the **@font-face** rule. However, this does not have the effect we want at all. It merely tells the browser to use these fonts in italic text. Therefore, it will make our Ampersand font be completely ignored, unless the whole headline is italic (in which case, we will indeed get the nice italic ampersand).

To find a font's *PostScript Name* in Mac OS X, select it in the **FontBook** application and press ⌘I.

Unfortunately, the only solution here is a bit of a hacky one: instead of using the font family name, we need to use the *PostScript Name* of the **individual font style/weight** we want. So, to get the italic versions of the fonts we used, the final code would look like this:

```
@font-face {
    font-family: Ampersand;
    src: local('Baskerville-Italic'),
         local('GoudyOldStyleT-Italic'),
         local('Palatino-Italic'),
```

```
        local('BookAntiqua-Italic');
    unicode-range: U+26;
}


h1 {
    font-family: Ampersand, Helvetica, sans-serif;
}
```

And this finally works great to give us the ampersands we wanted, just like in **Figure 5.19**. Unfortunately, if we need to customize their styling even more (e.g., to increase their font size, reduce their opacity, or anything else), we would need to go the HTML element route. However, if we only want a different font and font style/weight, this trick works wonders. You can use the same general idea to also style **numbers** with a different **font, symbols, punctuation—the possibilities are endless!**

 ▸ **PLAY!** play.csssecrets.io/**ampersands**

*Hat tip to **Drew McLellan** (allinthehead.com) for coming up with **the first version of this effect** (24ways.org/2011/creating-custom-font-stacks-with-unicode-range).*

HAT TIP

▪ **CSS Fonts**
w3.org/TR/css-fonts

RELATED
SPECS

26 Custom underlines

Prerequisites

CSS gradients, `background-size`, `text-shadow`, the "Striped backgrounds" secret on page 40

The problem

Designers are a picky bunch. We always strive to customize things and carefully craft them to closely match our vision and make our designs more intuitive and easier to use. **The default is rarely good enough.**

Text underlines are one of those things we'd love to customize. Although the default is useful, it's usually **too intrusive**, not to mention it's rendered **differently in every browser**. Although text underlines have been with us since the dawn of the Web, we never really got more ways to customize them. Even after CSS came along, it merely gave us an on/off switch for them:

```
text-decoration: underline;
```

As usual, when we are not given the tools we need, we hack them together. We had no way to customize text underlines, so we started faking them with borders, probably one of the first CSS tricks we ever came up with:

```
a[href] {
    border-bottom: 1px solid gray;
    text-decoration: none;
}
```

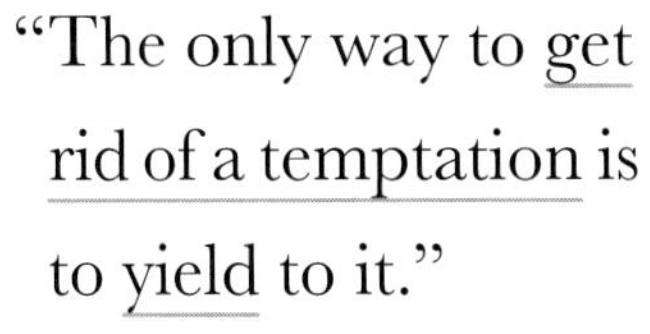

While emulating a text underline with **border-bottom** gave us control over color, thickness, and style, it wasn't perfect. As you can see in **Figure 5.22**, these "underlines" have a **very large distance from the text**, being even underneath the descenders of the glyphs! We could attempt to fix the issue by giving the links a **display** of **inline-block** and a smaller **line-height**, like so:

```
display: inline-block;
border-bottom: 1px solid gray;
line-height: .9;
```

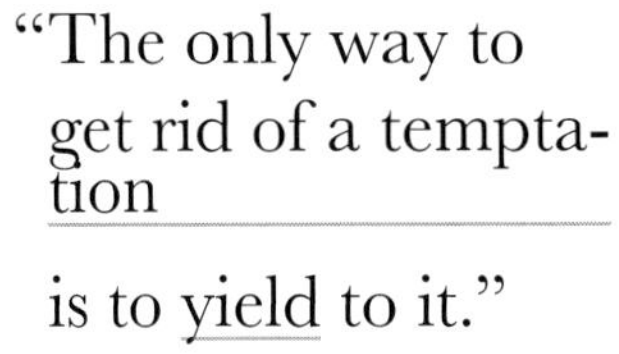

This works to bring the underline closer to the text, but **it prevents proper text wrapping**, as you can see in **Figure 5.23**.

These days, we might try to use an inset **box-shadow** to emulate an underline:

```
box-shadow: 0 -1px gray inset;
```

"The only way to get rid of a temptation is to yield to it."

FIGURE 5.22

Fake underlines created with **border-bottom**

"The only way to get rid of a temptation is to yield to it."

FIGURE 5.23

Trying to fix the issue with border-based "underlines" works, until the text needs to wrap—then hell breaks loose

How much closer? As much as the line thickness, as the only difference of this method is that it's drawn **inside** the box.

However, this has the same issues as **border-bottom**, except that it's drawn slightly closer to the text. Is there any way to get proper, flexible, custom underlines?

The solution

Often the best solutions come from the most unexpected places. In this case, it comes in the form of **background-image** and related properties. You might think this is insane, but bear with me for a bit. Backgrounds follow wrapped text perfectly, and with the new background-related properties we got in **CSS Backgrounds & Borders Level 3** such as **background-size**, we have very fine-grained control over them. We don't even need a separate HTTP request for them, as we can generate the image on the fly, through CSS gradients:

```
background: linear-gradient(gray, gray) no-repeat;
background-size: 100% 1px;
background-position: 0 1.15em;
```

You can see how **elegant** and **unobtrusive** the result looks in **Figure 5.24**. However, we can still make one small improvement. Notice

TRIVIA Text underlines in the future

In the future, we will not have to resort to such hacks for customizing our underlines. There are several properties planned in **CSS Text Decoration Level 3** *(w3.org/TR/css-text-decor-3)*, specifically for this, such as:

- **text-decoration-color** to customize the color of underlines and other decorations
- **text-decoration-style** to customize the style of decorations (e.g., solid, dashed, wavy, etc.)
- **text-decoration-skip** to skip spaces, descenders, and other objects
- **text-underline-position** to fine-tune the exact placement of the underline line

However, these properties currently have very little browser support.

how our underlines **cross the descenders** of letters like p and y. Wouldn't it look so much nicer if there was some breathing space around them? If our background is a solid color, we can fake that with two solid **text-shadow**s in the same color as our background (**Figure 5.25**):

```
background: linear-gradient(gray, gray) no-repeat;
background-size: 100% 1px;
background-position: 0 1.15em;
text-shadow: .05em 0 white, -.05em 0 white;
```

The brilliant thing about using gradients for this is that they are **extremely flexible**. For example, to create a dashed underline, you could do something like (**Figure 5.26**):

```
background: linear-gradient(90deg,
            gray 66%, transparent 0) repeat-x;
background-size: .2em 2px;
background-position: 0 1em;
```

Then you could control the dash and gap proportion via the color stop positions and their size via **background-size**.

▶ **PLAY!** play.csssecrets.io/**underlines**

As an exercise, you could try to create **wavy red underlines**, such as the ones used for **highlighting spelling mistakes**. (**Hint:** *You will need two gradients.*) You will find the solution in the following Play! example, but try to avoid peeking at the solution without giving it a shot—it's more fun that way!

▶ **PLAY!** play.csssecrets.io/**wavy-underlines**

"The only way to get rid of a temptation is to yield to it."

FIGURE 5.24
Our carefully crafted custom underlines, through CSS gradients

"The only way to get rid of a temptation is to yield to it."

FIGURE 5.25
Our custom underlines, treated with **text-shadow** to not cross our descenders

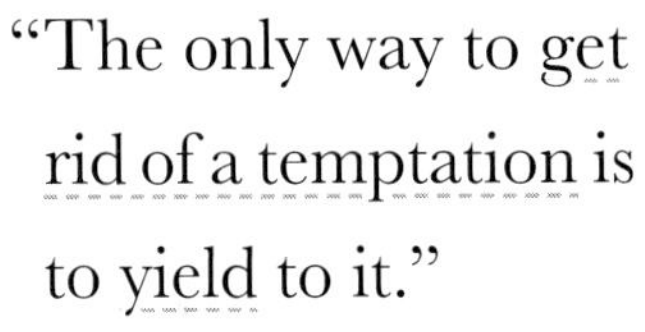

"The only way to get rid of a temptation is to yield to it."

FIGURE 5.26
Fully customized dashed underlines, with CSS gradients

HAT TIP

*Hat tip to **Marcin Wichary** (aresLuna.org) for coming up with **the first version of this effect** (medium.com/designing-medium/crafting-link-underlines-on-medium-7c03a9274f9).*

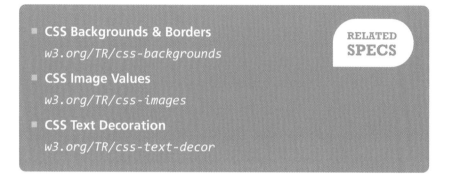

RELATED
SPECS

- **CSS Backgrounds & Borders**
  w3.org/TR/css-backgrounds

- **CSS Image Values**
  w3.org/TR/css-images

- **CSS Text Decoration**
  w3.org/TR/css-text-decor

27 Realistic text effects

The problem

Sometimes, certain text treatments become very widespread on the Web. For example, letterpress text, blurring text on mouseover, extruded (pseudo-3D) text, and so on. These usually depend on a combination of carefully crafted text shadows, and some knowledge of how our eyes work, as many of these are based on **optical illusions** to some degree. They are easy to make, once you know the tricks involved, but not always as easy to reverse engineer through developer tools.

This secret is devoted to creating such effects, so that you never again find yourself wondering, "How on Earth does this effect work?"

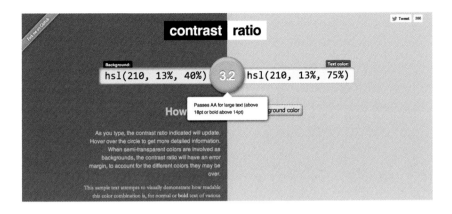

FIGURE 5.27

It's easy to forgo accessibility when using such effects, but never forget to test your contrast ratios (a useful tool for this is **leaverou.github.io/ contrast-ratio**, as it accepts any supported CSS color format)

Letterpress

The letterpress effect is one of the most popular text treatments on skeuomorphic design websites. While skeuomorphic design is not as trendy as it used to be, it will always have its devoted fans.

This effect works best with a medium lightness background with darker text, but it can also be used with lighter text on darker backgrounds, as long as the text is not black and the background is not completely white or black.

It's based on the same premise that has been used since the very first GUIs to create the impression of pressed or extruded buttons: a lighter shadow at the bottom (or a darker one at the top) creates the **illusion that an object is "carved in"** the main surface. Similarly, a darker shadow at the bottom (or a lighter one at the top), creates the illusion that an object is **extruded from the main surface**. The reason this works is that we usually assume that **the light source is above us**, so an extruded object would create a shadow underneath it, and an embossed object would be lit at the bottom.

Let's use the colors in **Figure 5.28** as a starting point. The text color is ■hsl(210, 13%, 30%) and ■hsl(210, 13%, 60%) is the background color:

> "The only way to get rid of a temptation is to yield to it."

> "The only way to get rid of a temptation is to yield to it."

FIGURE 5.28

The letterpress effect on dark text on a lighter background (top: before, bottom: after)

```
background: hsl(210, 13%, 60%);
color: hsl(210, 13%, 30%);
```

When we have darker text on lighter background (like in our example here), **a lighter shadow at the bottom usually works best**. How light depends on the exact colors you have and how subtle you want the effect to be, so you need to experiment a bit with the alpha parameter until it looks good. In this case, we settled on 80% white, but your mileage may vary:

"The only way to get rid of a temptation is to yield to it."

FIGURE 5.29

Letterpress gone wrong: applying the previous effect on text that is lighter than its background

```
background: hsl(210, 13%, 60%);
color: hsl(210, 13%, 30%);
text-shadow: 0 1px 1px hsla(0,0%,100%,.8);
```

You can see the result in **Figure 5.28**. In this case, we used pixels instead of **em**s for the effect, but if you have text that could be any size, from tiny to very large, **em**s might suit your case better:

```
text-shadow: 0 .03em .03em hsla(0,0%,100%,.8);
```

"The only way to get rid of a temptation is to yield to it."

"The only way to get rid of a temptation is to yield to it."

FIGURE 5.30

Letterpress effect when using lighter text on darker background (top: before, bottom: after)

What happens when we have lighter text on a darker background? Our shadow above would yield awful results if the colors were reversed (**Figure 5.29**), making our text blurry. Does this mean we cannot apply a letterpress effect in this case? No, it just means we need to adjust our approach. In these cases, a darker shadow on the top works best, as you can verify in **Figure 5.30**. The CSS code would look like this:

```
background: hsl(210, 13%, 40%);
color: hsl(210, 13%, 75%);
text-shadow: 0 -1px 1px black;
```

▶ **PLAY!** `play.csssecrets.io/letterpress`

Stroked text

In the future, outlined/stroked text will be quite easy, as we will be able to just use the spread parameter of **text-shadow**s to make them larger so that they look like a stroke, akin to how we use **box-shadow** spread to emulate outlines. Unfortunately, browser support for this is currently very limited, so we have to resort to other ways to emulate it, with more or less satisfying results.

The most widespread way is to layer multiple **text-shadow**s with slightly different offsets, like so (**Figure 5.32**):

```
background: deeppink;
color: white;
text-shadow: 1px 1px black, -1px -1px black,
             1px -1px black, -1px 1px black;
```

Alternatively, you could layer multiple slightly blurred shadows, with no offsets:

```
text-shadow: 0 0 1px black, 0 0 1px black,
             0 0 1px black, 0 0 1px black,
             0 0 1px black, 0 0 1px black;
```

However, this doesn't always produce great results and is more expensive performance-wise, due to blurring.

Unfortunately, the thicker the stroke, the worse the result both of these ideas produce. For example, see how bad a 3px outline looks (**Figure 5.33**):

```
background: deeppink;
color: white;
text-shadow: 3px 3px black, -3px -3px black,
             3px -3px black, -3px 3px black;
```

There is always the solution of using SVG, but it adds a lot of cruft to our markup. For example, assume we wanted to use it in a first-level heading. The HTML would look like this:

```
<h1><svg width="2em" height="1.2em">
    <use xlink:href="#css" />
    <text id="css" y="1em">CSS</text>
</svg></h1>
```

FIGURE 5.34

Using SVG for proper thick outlines

Then in our CSS, we'd write something like:

```
h1 {
    font: 500%/1 Rockwell, serif;
    background: deeppink;
    color: white;
}

h1 text {
    fill: currentColor;
}

h1 svg { overflow: visible }

h1 use {
    stroke: black;
    stroke-width: 6;
    stroke-linejoin: round;
}
```

Certainly not ideal, but it produces the best visual results (**Figure 5.34**), and even in ancient browsers where SVG is not supported, the text is still readable, styled, and crawlable.

▶ PLAY! play.csssecrets.io/**stroked-text**

Glowing text

Glowing text is a rather common effect for hovering over links, or headlines in certain types of websites. It's one of the easiest effects to create. In its simplest form you just use a couple layered **text-shadow**s, with no offsets and the same color as the text (**Figure 5.35**):

FIGURE 5.35

Glowing text with only two simple **text-shadow**s

```
background: #203;
color: #ffc;
text-shadow: 0 0 .1em, 0 0 .3em;
```

If used as a hover effect, you should also include a transition, like so:

FIGURE 5.36

Pseudo-blurred text, by hiding the text and showing only its shadows

```
a {
    background: #203;
    color: white;
    transition: 1s;
}
a:hover {
    text-shadow: 0 0 .1em, 0 0 .3em;
}
```

You can create an even more interesting effect by hiding the text itself on **:hover**, effectively making it appear like it's slowly blurring (see **Figure 5.36**):

```
a {
    background: #203;
    color: white;
    transition: 1s;
}
a:hover {
```

```
    color: transparent;
    text-shadow: 0 0 .1em white, 0 0 .3em white;
}
```

However, keep in mind that depending on **text-shadow** for text to appear does not degrade gracefully: if **text-shadow** is not supported, no text will show up. So, you need to be careful to only apply this in environments that support **text-shadow**. Alternatively, you can blur the text through CSS filters:

```
a {
    background: #203;
    color: white;
    transition: 1s;
}
a:hover {
    filter: blur(.1em);
}
```

It may have worse browser support this way, but at least nothing will break when it's not supported.

▶ **PLAY!**   play.csssecrets.io/**glow**

Extruded text

Another popular (and perhaps overused) effect in skeuomorphically de-signed websites is extruded (pseudo-3D) text (**Figure 5.37**). The main idea is having lots of stacked shadows, with no blur and only **1px** difference, getting progressively darker, with a highly blurred dark shadow at the end, emulating the shade the whole thing would create.

Let's use the text on **Figure 5.38** as a starting point, which is styled through this simple CSS code:

```
background: #58a;
color: white;
```

Now let's add a few progressively darker **text-shadow**s:

```
background: #58a;
color: white;
text-shadow: 0 1px hsl(0,0%,85%),
             0 2px hsl(0,0%,80%),
             0 3px hsl(0,0%,75%),
             0 4px hsl(0,0%,70%),
             0 5px hsl(0,0%,65%);
```

As you can see in **Figure 5.39**, we're getting there, but the result still looks quite unrealistic. Believe it or not, all we need to go from this to the finished result in **Figure 5.37** is one more shadow at the bottom:

```
background: #58a;
color: white;
text-shadow: 0 1px hsl(0,0%,85%),
             0 2px hsl(0,0%,80%),
             0 3px hsl(0,0%,75%),
             0 4px hsl(0,0%,70%),
             0 5px hsl(0,0%,65%),
             0 5px 10px black;
```

FIGURE 5.37

Extruded text through multiple CSS **text-shadow**s

FIGURE 5.38

Our starting point

FIGURE 5.39

Almost there, but still looks unrealistic

▶ **PLAY!**   play.csssecrets.io/**extruded**

This kind of repetitive, unwieldy code is a prime candidate for a preprocessor mixin. Here is one way we could do this in SCSS:

SCSS

```
@mixin text-3d($color: white, $depth: 5) {
```

```scss
  $shadows: ();
  $shadow-color: $color;

  @for $i from 1 through $depth {
    $shadow-color: darken($shadow-color, 10%);
    $shadows: append($shadows,
              0 ($i * 1px) $shadow-color, comma);
  }

  color: $color;
  text-shadow: append($shadows,
              0 ($depth * 1px) 10px black, comma);
}

h1 { @include text-3d(#eee, 4); }
```

There are many variations of this effect. For example, by having all shadows be ■ **black** and removing the last blurry shadow, you can emulate a typography effect commonly found in old/retro signage (**Figure 5.40**):

FIGURE 5.40

Retro-style typography

```scss
color: white;
background: hsl(0,50%,45%);
text-shadow: 1px 1px black, 2px 2px black,
             3px 3px black, 4px 4px black,
             5px 5px black, 6px 6px black,
             7px 7px black, 8px 8px black;
```

This one is even easier to convert to a mixin, or—more appropriately for this case—a function:

```scss
@function text-retro($color: black, $depth: 8) {
  $shadows: (1px 1px $color,);
```

SCSS

```
@for $i from 2 through $depth {
    $shadows: append($shadows,
              ($i*1px) ($i*1px) $color, comma);
}

@return $shadows;
}


h1 {
    color: white;
    background: hsl(0,50%,45%);
    text-shadow: text-retro();
}
```

■ **CSS Text Decoration**
w3.org/TR/css-text-decor

RELATED
SPECS

Circular text

The problem

Although it's not a particularly common effect, sometimes the need arises to have a short line of text follow a circular path. When that time comes, CSS leaves us in the cold. There is no CSS property or feature to achieve this and the only CSS ways we can think of are so hacky they make us feel dirty just for thinking about them. Is there any way to achieve such a type treatment without resorting to images and without losing our sanity and self-respect?

The solution

There are a few scripts out there to accomplish this. They rely on wrapping each letter in a separate `<span>` element and rotating them separately to

form a circle. Not only is this extremely hacky, it also adds a lot of bloat and dozens of DOM elements to our page for no good reason.

Although there is currently **no better way to accomplish this with pure CSS**, we can easily do it with **a little inline SVG**. SVG natively supports text on any path, and circles are just a special case of a path. Let's give it a shot!

The basic way text on a path works in SVG is by having a `<textPath>` element containing our text, inside a `<text>` element. The `<textPath>` element also references a `<path>` element defining our path by its id. Text within inline SVG also inherits most of our font styling (except `line-height`, as that's manual in SVG), so we don't have to worry about that, like we do with an external SVG image.

Let's assume we want to style the phrase *"circular reasoning works because"* as circular text, occupying the entire circumference of a circle, like it looks in **Figure 5.42**. We start by adding an inline SVG inside our HTML element, and defining a path for our circle:

Unfortunately, `<textPath>` only works with `<path>` elements, which is why we cannot use the much more readable `<circle>` element for our circle.

```
<div class="circular">
    <svg viewBox="0 0 100 100">
        <path d="M 0,50 a 50,50 0 1,1 0,1 z"
                id="circle" />
    </svg>
</div>
```

FIGURE 5.42

The final result we want to accomplish

Note that we defined its units via **viewBox** and not the **width** and **height** attributes. This enables us to set the coordinate system and aspect ratio of the graphic, without it having an intrinsic size. Not only is this more compact, it also saves us a few lines of CSS, as we no longer need to apply a width and height of 100% to the **<svg>** element—it just naturally adjusts to the size of its container.

If you do not understand the path syntax, do not worry. **Hardly anyone does**, and even those initiated into the secret art of SVG path syntax tend to forget about it in a matter of minutes. If you are curious, the three commands this exceedingly cryptic syntax includes are:

- **M 0,50**: Move to the point (0,50)

- **a** 50,50 **0** 1,1 **0,1**: Draw an arc from the point you are at currently, to a point that is **0** units to the right and **1** unit to the bottom of your current position. The arc should have a radius of 50, both horizontally and vertically. **Out of the two possible angles, pick the largest** and out of those two possible arcs, pick the one on the right of the two points, not the one on the left.

- **z**: Close the path via a straight line segment.

Currently, our path is just a black circle (**Figure 5.43**). We add the text via the **<text>** and **<textPath>** elements and link it to our circle via the **xlink:href** property, like so:

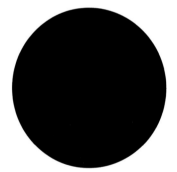

FIGURE 5.43

Our path is currently a circle, with the default ● **black** fill

```
SVG
<div class="circular">
    <svg viewBox="0 0 100 100">
        <path d="M 0,50 a 50,50 0 1,1 0,1 z"
            id="circle" />
        <text><textPath xlink:href="#circle">
            circular reasoning works because
        </textPath></text>
    </svg>
</div>
```

As you can see in **Figure 5.44**, although we still have a lot of work to do to make this presentable and readable, we've already achieved something that we could not in a million years have done with CSS!

The next step would be to **remove the black fill from our circle path**. We don't want the circle to be visible in any way; we only want it to act as a guide for our text. There are many ways to do that, such as nesting it into a **<defs>** element (which is designed for this very purpose). However, here we want to minimize the amount of SVG markup we need for this effect, so we are going to apply a **fill: none** via CSS:

FIGURE 5.44
Although there is a lot left to do, we have already achieved something that CSS simply cannot do

```
.circular path { fill: none; }
```

Now that the black circle is gone (**Figure 5.45**), we can study the other problems more carefully. The next biggest issue is that **most of our text is outside the SVG element**, and **clipped** by it. To correct this, we need to make our containing element smaller, and apply **overflow: visible** to the SVG element, so that it doesn't clip any content outside its viewport:

```
.circular {
    width: 30em;
    height: 30em;
}


.circular svg {
    display: block;
    overflow: visible;
}
```

FIGURE 5.45
After making our path invisible, the other issues become easier to see

You can see the result in **Figure 5.46**. Note that we are almost there, but some text is still clipped. The reason is that the SVG element affects flow only based on its dimensions, not its overflow. Therefore, the fact that there is text overflowing outside the box the **<svg>** element creates does not push the SVG element down. We need to do that manually, via a margin:

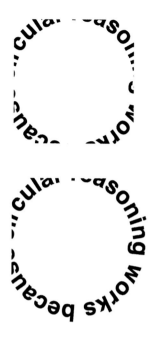

FIGURE 5.46

Top: Applying a width and height to our container element
Bottom: Adding **overflow: visible** to the mix

```css
.circular {
    width: 30em;
    height: 30em;
    margin: 3em auto 0;
}


.circular svg {
    display: block;
    overflow: visible;
}
```

That's it! Our example now looks exactly like **Figure 5.42**, and the text is perfectly accessible. If we only have one instance of circular text (e.g., a website logo), then we are done. However, if we have more than one instance of this type treatment, we **don't want to have to repeat this SVG markup every time**. To avoid that, we can write a short script that generates the necessary SVG elements automatically, from markup like this:

```html
HTML
<div class="circular">
    circular reasoning works because
</div>
```

The code would go through all elements with a class of "**circular**", remove their text and store it in a variable, and add the necessary SVG elements to it:

```js
JS
$$('.circular').forEach(function(el) {
    var NS = "http://www.w3.org/2000/svg";
    var xlinkNS = "http://www.w3.org/1999/xlink";
    var svg = document.createElementNS(NS, "svg");
    var circle = document.createElementNS(NS, "path");
    var text = document.createElementNS(NS, "text");
    var textPath = document.createElementNS(NS, "textPath");
```

```
svg.setAttribute("viewBox", "0 0 100 100");

circle.setAttribute("d", "M0,50 a50,50 0 1,1 0,1z");
circle.setAttribute("id", "circle");

textPath.textContent = el.textContent;
textPath.setAttributeNS(xlinkNS, "xlink:href", "#circle");

text.appendChild(textPath);
svg.appendChild(circle);
svg.appendChild(text);
el.textContent = '';
el.appendChild(svg);
});
```

▶ PLAY! play.csssecrets.io/**circular-text**

■ **Scalable Vector Graphics (SVG)**
w3.org/TR/SVG

RELATED
SPECS

User
Experience

6

29 Picking the right cursor

The problem

The purpose of a mouse pointer is not just to display where the cursor is on the screen, but also to communicate which actions are possible to the user. This common UX practice in desktop applications often gets forgotten in web apps.

Authors are not the only ones to blame for this. Back in the days of CSS 2.1, we didn't really have access to many built-in cursors. We mainly used the `cursor` property to indicate that something is clickable, with a `pointer` cursor, or sometimes to indicate tooltips with a `help` cursor. Some also utilized a the `wait` or `progress` cursors instead of (or alongside) a loader. But that was about it. However, although in **CSS User Interface Level 3** *(w3.org/TR/css3-ui/#cursor)* we got a boatload of new built-in cursors to utilize, most authors comfortably stayed in their old cursor habits. Like many UX improvements, you don't really realize there is a problem, until you reach the solution. Let's advance to that then!

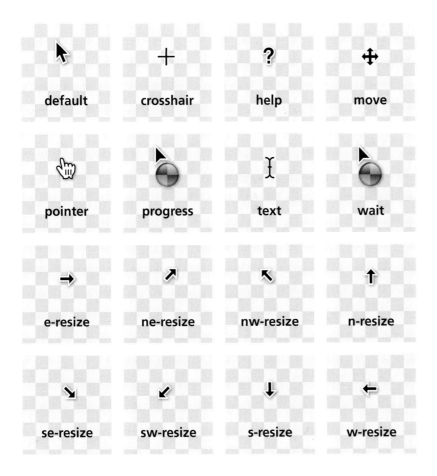

The solution

You can see the full list of new built-in cursors in **Figure 6.2** and read about their purpose in the specification, but as you can imagine, not all of them are useful for most web apps. For example, there's even a `cell` cursor, which *"indicates that a cell or set of cells may be selected."* As you can imagine, there aren't many use cases for that beyond spreadsheets and editable grids.

This secret is not aiming to be an exhaustive reference of the potential use cases of all these new cursors. However, a few of them stand out, as they can instantly improve the usability of a large number of web apps, with very little code.

FIGURE 6.2

The new built-in cursors we got in **CSS User Interface Level 3** *(w3.org/TR/css3-ui/#cursor)* (cursors shown as they're displayed in OS X)

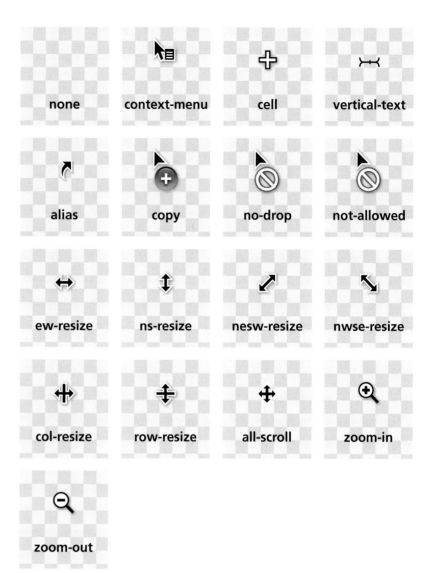

FIGURE 6.2

The new built-in cursors we got in **CSS User Interface Level 3** *(w3.org/TR/css3-ui/#cursor)* (cursors shown as they're displayed in OS X)

Indicating disabled state

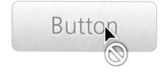

FIGURE 6.3

Using a **not-allowed** cursor to hint that a control is disabled

Arguably, the most widely applicable addition is the **not-allowed** cursor (**Figure 6.3**). It's incredibly useful to hint that interaction with a certain control is not possible for whatever reason—usually because said control is disabled. Especially these days, where most forms are extremely stylized, it can often be difficult to tell whether a form control is enabled or not, and this is a welcome aid. You could use it in a quite generic way, like so:

```
:disabled, [disabled], [aria-disabled="true"] {
    cursor: not-allowed;
}
```

▶ PLAY! play.csssecrets.io/**disabled**

Hiding the cursor

Hiding the cursor sounds like a usability nightmare, doesn't it? Why on Earth would somebody want to do that and why would web standards make it easier for them? Before you get angry at all these people that clearly have some unresolved issues against usability, remember all those times when you used one of those awful public touchscreens (e.g., those used for information booths or in-flight entertainment) and the developers forgot to hide the mouse cursor, so there was one lingering on the screen in weird places. Or those times when you had to move your mouse to the right of the screen while watching a video, because your cursor was in the way.

Clearly, there are multiple use cases where **hiding the cursor can actually improve usability**. This is why one of the new cursor keywords is **none**. Hiding the cursor was possible in CSS 2.1, but it involved using a transparent 1×1 GIF, like so:

```
video {
    cursor: url(transparent.gif);
}
```

> If you hide the cursor over videos, make sure you don't accidentally also hide it over playback controls as well, otherwise you will be causing more harm than good.

These days, we don't need this, as we can just use **cursor: none**. However, you might still want to provide a fallback, for browsers that haven't caught up with Level 3 cursors yet. We can easily do that with the cascade:

```
cursor: url('transparent.gif');
cursor: none;
```

30 Extending the clickable area

The problem

TIP! See Fitts' Law in action, via the interactive visualization at **simonwallner.at/ext/fitts**.

If you are interested in user experience, you have likely heard of *Fitts' Law*. First proposed by American psychologist **Paul Fitts** in as early as **1954**, Fitts' law is the idea that **the time required to rapidly move to a target area is a logarithmic function of the ratio between the distance to the target and the width of the target**. Its most commonly used mathematical formulation is expressed as $T = a + b \log_2 \left(1 + \frac{D}{W}\right)$ where T is the time taken, D is the distance to the center of the target, W is the width of the target, and a and b are constants.

Although graphical user interfaces did not exist at the time, Fitts' Law applies perfectly to pointing devices and has now become the most widely known HCI (Human-Computer Interaction) principle. This may sound surprising at first, but keep in mind that Fitts' Law has more to do with human motor control than with specific hardware.

An obvious corollary is that the bigger the target, the easier it is to reach. Therefore, **it often increases usability to extend the clickable area (hit area)** around smaller controls that might otherwise be difficult to reach, if enlarging them is not an option. With the increasing popularity of touch screens, this has become even more important. **Nobody wants to**

tap a dozen times trying to get that pesky little button and yet, this is still an everyday occurence.

Other times, we want an element to slide in when we hover over a side of the window—for example, an auto-hiding header that slides from the top when the mouse is near, which also involves increasing its hit area (toward one direction only). Can we do this with plain CSS?

The solution

Let's assume we have a simple button like the one shown on **Figure 6.4** and we want to increase its hit area by **10px** in all four directions. We have already applied some simple styling to it, as well as `cursor: pointer`, which both provides an **affordance*** for mouse interaction, but also helps us test where the hit area actually is.

The easiest way to extend our hit area is a transparent solid border, as mouse interaction on borders triggers these mouse events on the element, unlike outlines and shadows. For example, extending an element's hit area by **10px** toward all directions is as simple as this:

FIGURE 6.4

Our starting point in two states: with the cursor on the button (right) or further down (left)

```
border: 10px solid transparent;
```

However, as you can see in **Figure 6.5**, this is no good, as it also makes our button larger! The reason is that backgrounds extend underneath borders by default. Good ol' `background-clip` can help constrain the background where it should be:

FIGURE 6.5

Oops! Extending our hit area with **border** also made our button larger

```
border: 10px solid transparent;
background-clip: padding-box;
```

---

* In usability, an *affordance* is a property of a control that **visibly hints how we can interact with it**. For example, a button's 3D appearance hints that it can be pushed, and a doorknob's appearance that it can be pulled or turned. For more info, check out **en.wikipedia.org/wiki/Affordance**. There is some debate among usability professionals as to whether mouse cursor changes are an affordance or visual feedback.

FIGURE 6.6

Getting our button size back to
normal with **background-clip**

FIGURE 6.7

Using an inset **box-shadow** to
emulate a border

FIGURE 6.8

Adding an actual shadow as well
doesn't work well with this solution

As you can see in **Figure 6.6**, this works fine. Until you end up needing an actual border around the button and realize you've already used up the only one you get to extend the hit area. What happens then? Easy, you could emulate a (solid) border with an inset shadow (**Figure 6.7**):

```
border: 10px solid transparent;
box-shadow: 0 0 0 1px rgba(0,0,0,.3) inset;
background-clip: padding-box;
```

▶ **PLAY!** play.csssecrets.io/**hit-area-border**

Unlike borders, you don't only get one **box-shadow**, so if you need more, you can just use a comma-separated list of shadows instead. However, if we combine inset and outset (non-inset) shadows, we get a very weird effect, because **outset shadows are drawn outside the border box**. For example, we might think of doing something like this to add an actual blurred shadow to make the button "pop out" of the page, which is another affordance for clicking:

```
box-shadow: 0 0 0 1px rgba(0,0,0,.3) inset,
            0 .1em .2em -.05em rgba(0,0,0,.5);
```

However, if we try that, we see that the result is very different from what we might expect (**Figure 6.8**). This solution is not perfect for other reasons too. Borders affect layout, and that might be out of the question in certain cases. What do we do then? We remove the border and take advantage of the fact that **pseudo-elements also capture mouse interaction for their parent element**.

We can then overlay a transparent pseudo-element on our button that is **10px** larger on every direction:

```
button {
    position: relative;
    /* [rest of styling] */
}

button::before {
    content: '';
    position: absolute;
    top: -10px; right: -10px;
    bottom: -10px; left: -10px;
}
```

This just works, and as long as we don't need both pseudo-elements, it doesn't really interfere with anything. The pseudo-element solution is incredibly flexible—we could basically **make the hit area be any size, place, or shape we want**, **even completely disconnected from the element itself**!

▶ **PLAY!** play.csssecrets.io/**hit-area**

■ **CSS Backgrounds & Borders**
w3.org/TR/css-backgrounds

RELATED
SPECS

31 Custom checkboxes

The problem

For readability, we will refer to "checkboxes" throughout this secret, but everything discussed **applies to both checkboxes and radio buttons** unless otherwise noted.

Designers always wanted more control over every element in a web page. When a graphic designer with limited CSS experience is tasked to create a website mockup, they almost always produce one with customized form elements, making the developer tasked to convert it to CSS want to pull their hair out.

When CSS was first introduced, form styling was extremely limited and is still not clearly defined in any of the various CSS specifications. However, browsers got more and more permissive over the years about what CSS properties they allow on form controls, enabling us to style most of them quite extensively.

Unfortunately, **checkboxes and radio buttons** are not among those form controls. To this day, most browsers allow **little to no styling** when it comes to them. As a result, authors end up either coming to terms with their default look or employing awful, inaccessible hacks, such as recreating them with divs and JS.

Is there a way to get around these restrictions and customize the look of our checkboxes, without bloat and without giving up on semantics and accessibility?

The solution

Until a few years ago, this task was impossible without scripting. However, in **Selectors Level 3** *(w3.org/TR/css3-selectors)*, we got a new pseudo-class: `:checked`. This pseudo-class only matches when the checkbox is checked, whether that is done through user interaction, or through script.

It's not very useful when applied directly to checkboxes, as—like we previously mentioned—there aren't many properties we can successfully apply to them. However, we can always **use combinators to style other elements** based on a checkbox state.

You might be wondering what other elements we may want to style based on whether a checkbox is checked or not. Well, there is one kind of element that has special behavior around checkboxes: `<label>`s. **A `<label>` that is associated with a checkbox also acts as a toggle for it.**

Because labels—unlike checkboxes—are not *replaced elements,** we can **add generated content to them and style that based on checkbox state**. Then, we could **hide the real checkbox** in a way that doesn't remove it from the tabbing order, and **have the generated content act as a styled checkbox** instead!

Let's see this in action. We will start from the following simple markup:

```
HTML
<input type="checkbox" id="awesome" />
<label for="awesome">Awesome!</label>
```

The next step is to generate a pseudo-element that will be used as our styled checkbox, and apply some basic styling to it:

Nesting the checkbox in the label would free us from using ids, but then we wouldn't be able to target the label based on the checkbox status, because we do not yet have parent selectors.

FIGURE 6.9

Our rudimentary custom checkbox alongside the original checkbox

---

* From the CSS 2.1 specification: *"[A replaced element is] an element whose content is outside the scope of the CSS formatting model, such as an image, embedded document, or applet."* Replaced elements cannot have generated content applied to them, though some browsers allow it.

```
input[type="checkbox"] + label::before {
    content: '\a0'; /* non-break space */
    display: inline-block;
    vertical-align: .2em;
    width: .8em;
    height: .8em;
    margin-right: .2em;
    border-radius: .2em;
    background: silver;
    text-indent: .15em;
    line-height: .65;
}
```

The style we will apply to our checkboxes in these examples is pretty basic, but the possibilities are endless. You could even skip CSS styling altogether and use images for all different checkbox states!

Awesome!

Styling our pseudo-element as a customized checked checkbox

Be careful when using such permissive selectors. Using **input[type="checkbox"] will also hide checkboxes without a label after them** (e.g., those nested in a label), essentially making them unusable.

You can see how our checkbox and label currently look in **Figure 6.9**. The original checkbox is still visible, but we will hide it later. Now we need to apply a different style to our checkbox when it's checked. This could be as simple as applying a different color and adding a checkmark as content:

```
input[type="checkbox"]:checked + label::before {
    content: '\2713';
    background: yellowgreen;
}
```

As you can see in **Figure 6.10**, this is already functioning as a rudimentary styled checkbox. Now, we need to hide the original checkbox in an accessible way, which means we can't use **display: none**, as that would remove it from the keyboard tabbing order entirely. Instead, we could use something like this:

```
input[type="checkbox"] {
    position: absolute;
    clip: rect(0,0,0,0);
}
```

That's it, we've made a very basic custom checkbox! We could of course improve it further—for example, by changing its style when it's focused or disabled, which you can see in **Figure 6.11**:

Awesome!

Awesome!

Awesome!

```
input[type="checkbox"]:focus + label::before {
    box-shadow: 0 0 .1em .1em #58a;
}


input[type="checkbox"]:disabled + label::before {
    background: gray;
    box-shadow: none;
    color: #555;
}
```

You could even make these effects smoother by applying transitions or animations or go nuts and create things like skeuomorphic switches. The possibilities really are endless!

Although the possibilities are endless, avoid styling checkboxes as circles: most users associate round toggles with radio buttons. Same applies to square radio buttons.

▶ **PLAY!** play.csssecrets.io/**checkboxes**

Hat tip to **Ryan Seddon** *for coming up with the first version of this effect, now known as* **"the checkbox hack"** *(thecssninja.com/css/custom-inputs-using-css). Ryan has since used this idea to* **implement all sorts of widgets that require state persistence** *(Labs.thecssninja.com/bootleg), such as modal dialogs, dropdown menus, tabs, and carousels, though abusing checkboxes this much results in accessibility problems.*

HAT TIP

Toggle buttons

You could use a variation of "the checkbox hack" to emulate toggle buttons, as HTML does not provide a native way to create them. Toggle buttons are push buttons that act like checkboxes: they are used to toggle a setting on or off, and look pressed when checked and unpressed when unchecked.

Awesome!

Awesome!

Semantically, there is no real difference between toggle buttons and checkboxes, so you can both use this trick and maintain semantic purity.

To create toggle buttons with this trick, you would just style the labels as buttons, instead of using pseudo-elements. For example, to create the toggle buttons shown in **Figure 6.12**, the code would look like this:

```css
input[type="checkbox"] {
    position: absolute;
    clip: rect(0,0,0,0);
}


input[type="checkbox"] + label {
    display: inline-block;
    padding: .3em .5em;
    background: #ccc;
    background-image: linear-gradient(#ddd, #bbb);
    border: 1px solid rgba(0,0,0,.2);
    border-radius: .3em;
    box-shadow: 0 1px white inset;
    text-align: center;
    text-shadow: 0 1px 1px white;
}


input[type="checkbox"]:checked + label,
input[type="checkbox"]:active + label {
    box-shadow: .05em .1em .2em rgba(0,0,0,.6) inset;
    border-color: rgba(0,0,0,.3);
    background: #bbb;
}
```

However, be wary about using toggle buttons. In most cases, **toggle buttons hinder usability** as they can easily be confused with regular buttons that perform an action when pressed.

▶ PLAY! play.csssecrets.io/**toggle-buttons**

■ Selectors
w3.org/TR/selectors

RELATED
SPECS

32 De-emphasize by dimming

The problem

Quite often, we need to dim everything behind an element through a semi-transparent dark overlay, to emphasize and draw user attention to a certain UI element. For example, lightboxes (**Figure 6.13**) and interface "quick tours" often benefit from this effect. The most common technique to do this is to add an extra HTML element for the dimming and apply some CSS that looks like this:

```css
.overlay { /* For dimming */
    position: fixed;
    top: 0;
    right: 0;
```

```
    bottom: 0;
    left: 0;
    background: rgba(0,0,0,.8);
}

.lightbox { /* The element to draw attention to */
    position: absolute;
    z-index: 1;
    /* [rest of styling] */
}
```

The overlay is responsible for dimming everything behind the element we want to draw attention to. The `.lightbox` then gets a higher `z-index` to be drawn above the overlay. All this is fine and dandy, but it requires an extra HTML element, which means the effect cannot be applied with CSS alone. This is not a major problem, but it's an inconvenience that we'd rather avoid, if possible. Thankfully, in most cases we can.

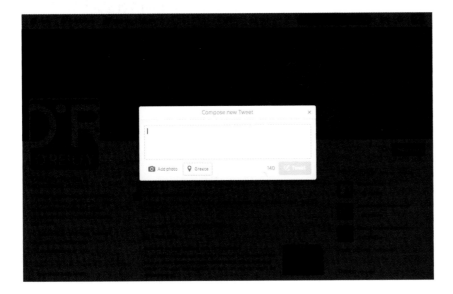

FIGURE 6.13

Twitter is using this effect for its popup dialogs

Pseudo-element solution

We can use pseudo-elements to eliminate the need for an extra HTML element, like so:

```css
body.dimmed::before {
    position: fixed;
    top: 0;
    right: 0;
    bottom: 0;
    left: 0;
    z-index: 1;
    background: rgba(0,0,0,.8);
}
```

This is a slightly better solution, as it means we can now apply this effect directly from CSS. However, the problem is that it's not very portable, as the `<body>` element might already have something else applied on its `::before` pseudo-element. Also, it means that to apply this effect we usually need some sort of JavaScript to apply the `dimmed` class.

We could solve this by **applying the overlay on the element's own `::before` pseudo-element** and giving it a `z-index: -1;` so that it's underneath our element. Although this solves the portability issue, it doesn't give us very fine-grained control over the overlay's Z axis placement. It might end up being underneath our element (which is desirable) or **underneath our element and several of its ancestors**.

Another issue with this is that **pseudo-elements cannot have their own JavaScript event handlers**. When using a separate element for an overlay, we could assign event handlers to it so that—for example—the lightbox closes when the user clicks on the overlay. When using pseudo-elements on the same element we want to highlight, it becomes trickier to detect whether the user clicked on the overlay or the element.

box-shadow solution

The pseudo-element solution is more flexible and usually fits what most people expect from an overlay. However, for simpler use cases or prototyping, we can take advantage of the fact that a **box-shadow**'s spread radius enlarges it by the amount you specify on every side. This means we can create an extremely large shadow with zero offsets and zero blur, to emulate an overlay the quick-and-dirty way:

```
box-shadow: 0 0 0 999px rgba(0,0,0,.8);
```

One obvious problem with this first pass solution is that it won't work with very large resolutions (> 2000px). We can mitigate this either by using a larger number, or solve it completely by using **viewport units**, so that we can be sure that the "overlay" is **always** larger than our viewport. Because we can't use different horizontal and vertical spread radius values, the viewport unit that makes the most sense to use is **vmax**. In case you're not familiar with the **vmax** unit, **1vmax** is equivalent to either **1vw** or **1vh**, whichever is larger. **100vw** is equal to the viewport's width and, similarly, **100vh** is equivalent to its height. Therefore, the minimum value that covers our needs is **50vmax**, as it will be added on each side, so our overlay's final dimensions will be **100vmax** + our element's dimensions:

```
box-shadow: 0 0 0 50vmax rgba(0,0,0,.8);
```

This technique is very quick and easy to apply, but it has two rather serious issues that limit its usefulness. Can you spot them?

First, because the dimensions of our element are viewport related and not page related, **we will see the boundaries of the overlay when we scroll**, unless the element has **position: fixed;** or the page isn't long enough for scrolling. Furthermore, because pages can be *really* long, it wouldn't be wise to attempt to overcome this by just increasing the spread radius even more. Instead, I'd recommend **limiting your use of this**

technique to elements with fixed positioning or pages with minimal to no scrolling.

Second, using a separate element (or a pseudo-element) as the overlay doesn't only visually guide the user's focus to the element we want. It also **prevents them from using the mouse to interact with the rest of the page**, because it captures pointer events. A `box-shadow` does not have this property. Therefore, **it only visually helps draw the user's attention to a particular element, but it will not capture any mouse interaction by itself**. Whether this is acceptable or not depends on your specific use case.

▸ **PLAY!** `play.csssecrets.io/`**`dimming-box-shadow`**

LIMITED SUPPORT

backdrop solution

If the element you want to bring into focus is a modal `<dialog>` (a `<dialog>` element displayed via its `showModal()` method), it already has an overlay, via the User Agent stylesheet. This native overlay can also be styled via the `::backdrop` pseudo-element, for example, to make it darker:

```
dialog::backdrop {
    background: rgba(0, 0, 0, .8);
}
```

The only caveat of this method is that at the time of writing, **browser support for it is very limited**, so make sure to check its current status before using it. Keep in mind, however, that even if it's not supported, nothing will break if a dialog has no overlay because it's just a UX improvement.

▸ **PLAY!** `play.csssecrets.io/`**`native-modal`**

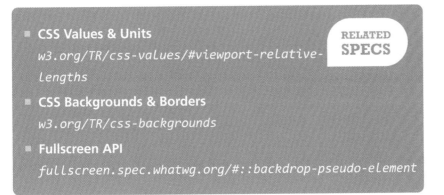

- **CSS Values & Units**
  w3.org/TR/css-values/#viewport-relative-lengths

- **CSS Backgrounds & Borders**
  w3.org/TR/css-backgrounds

- **Fullscreen API**
  fullscreen.spec.whatwg.org/#::backdrop-pseudo-element

33 De-emphasize by blurring

Prerequisites

Transitions, the "Frosted glass effect" secret on page 146, the "De-emphasize by dimming" secret on page 234

The problem

In the **"De-emphasize by dimming" secret on page 234**, we saw a way to de-emphasize parts of a web app by dimming them, through a semi-transparent black overlay. However, when there is a lot going on the page, we need to dim it quite a lot to provide sufficient contrast for text to appear on it, or to draw attention to a lightbox or other element. A more elegant way, shown in **Figure 6.14**, is to blur everything else in addition to (or instead of) dimming it. This is also more realistic, as it creates depth by mimicking **how our vision treats objects that are physically closer to us when we are focusing on them**.

FIGURE 6.14

The gaming website **polygon.com** features an excellent example of drawing user attention to a dialog box by blurring everything else behind it

However, this is a far more difficult effect to achieve. Until **Filter Effects** *(w3.org/TR/filter-effects)*, it was impossible, but even with the `blur()` filter, it is quite difficult. What do we apply the blur filter to, if we want to apply it to everything *except* a certain element? If we apply it to the `<body>` element, everything in the page will be blurred, including the element we want to draw attention to. It's very similar to the problem we addressed in the **"Frosted glass effect" secret on page 146**, but we cannot apply the same solution here, as anything could be behind our dialog box, not just a background image. What do we do?

The solution

Unfortunately, we will need an extra HTML element for this effect: we will need to wrap everything in our page except the elements that shouldn't be blurred in a wrapper element, so that we can apply the blurring to it. The `<main>` element is perfect for this, because it serves a double purpose: it both marks up the main content of the page (dialogs aren't usually main content) and gives us the styling hook we need. The markup could look like this:

LIMITED SUPPORT

`HTML`

```html
<main>Bacon Ipsum dolor sit amet…</main>
<dialog>
```

We assume that all `<dialog>` elements will be initially hidden and at most one of them will be visible at any time.

FIGURE 6.15

A plain dialog with no overlay to de-emphasize the rest of the page

FIGURE 6.16

Blurring the `<main>` element when the dialog is visible

FIGURE 6.17

Applying both blurring and dimming, both via CSS filters

```
              O HAI, I'm a dialog. Click on me to dismiss.
</dialog>
<!-- any other dialogs go here too -->
```

You can see how this looks with no overlay in **Figure 6.15**. Then, we need to apply a class to the `<main>` element every time we make a dialog appear and apply the blur filter then, like so:

```
main.de-emphasized {
    filter: blur(5px);
}
```

As you can see in **Figure 6.16**, this already is a huge improvement. However, right now the blurring is applied immediately, which doesn't look very natural and feels like rather awkward UX. Because **CSS filters are animatable**, we can instead smoothly transition to the blurred page:

```
main {
    transition: .6s filter;
}

main.de-emphasized {
    filter: blur(5px);
}
```

It's often a good idea to combine the two de-emphasizing effects (dimming and blurring). One way to do this is using the **brightness()** and/or **contrast()** filters:

```
main.de-emphasized {
    filter: blur(3px) contrast(.8) brightness(.8);
}
```

You can see the result in **Figure 6.17**. Dimming via CSS filters means that if they are not supported, there is **no fallback**. It might be a better idea to perform the dimming via some other method, which can also serve as a fallback (e.g., the **box-shadow** method we saw in the previous secret). This would also save us from the "halo effect" you can see on the edges of **Figure 6.17**. Notice how in **Figure 6.18** where we used a shadow for the dimming, this issue is gone.

FIGURE 6.18

Applying blurring via CSS filters and dimming via a **box-shadow**, which also serves as a fallback

▶ **PLAY!** play.csssecrets.io/**deemphasizing-blur**

*Hat tip to **Hakim El Hattab** (hakim.se) for coming up with **a smiliar effect** (Lab.hakim.se/avgrund). In addition, in Hakim's version of the effect, the content also becomes smaller via a **scale()** transform, to further enhance the illusion that the dialog is getting physically closer to us.*

HAT TIP

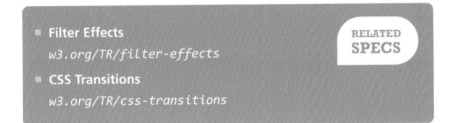

■ **Filter Effects**
  w3.org/TR/filter-effects

■ **CSS Transitions**
  w3.org/TR/css-transitions

**RELATED
SPECS**

34 Scrolling hints

Prerequisites

CSS gradients, **`background-size`**

The problem

Scrollbars are the primary control to indicate that there is more content in an element than meets the eye. However, they are often clunky and visually distracting, so modern operating systems have started to streamline them, often hiding them completely until the user is actually interacting with the scrollable element.

While scrollbars are rarely used to control scrolling these days (users tend to scroll via gestures instead), **indicating that there is more content in an element than what meets the eye** is very useful information that is helpful to convey in a subtle way, even for elements the user is not currently interacting with.

Ada Catlace
Alan Purring
Schrödingcat
Tim Purrners-Lee
WebKitty

FIGURE 6.19
This box has more content and is scrollable, but unless you interact with it, you won't know

The UX designers working on Google Reader, a (now discontinued) feed reader by Google, found a very elegant way to indicate this: when there was more content, a subtle shadow was displayed on the top and/or bottom side of the sidebar (**Figure 6.20**).

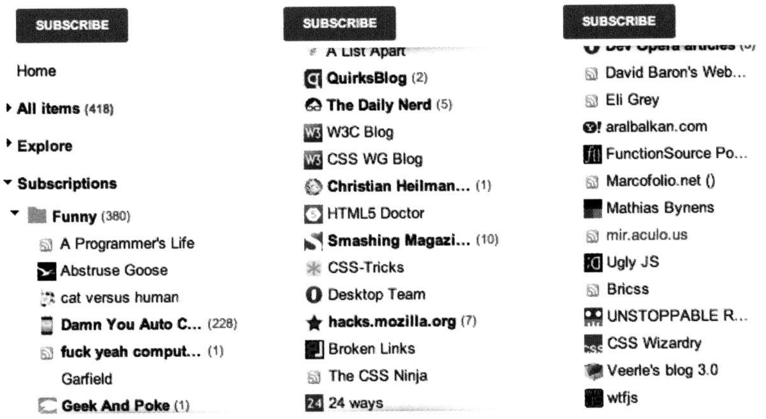

FIGURE 6.20
Google Reader's elegant UX pattern to indicate that scrolling is needed to view the full contents of the sidebar
Left: Scrolled all the way up
Middle: Scrolled to the middle of the feed list
Right: Scrolled all the way to the bottom

However, to achieve this effect in Google Reader, quite a bit of scripting was used. Was that really needed, or can we achieve the same effect with CSS?

The solution

Let's first start with some simple markup, a plain unordered list with some placeholder content (geeky cat names!):

```html
<ul>
    <li>Ada Catlace</li>
    <li>Alan Purring</li>
    <li>Schrödingcat</li>
    <li>Tim Purrners-Lee</li>
    <li>WebKitty</li>
    <li>Json</li>
    <li>Void</li>
    <li>Neko</li>
    <li>NaN</li>
    <li>Cat5</li>
```

```
    <li>Vector</li>
  </ul>
```

We can then apply some basic styling to the `<ul>` to make it smaller than its contents and scrollable:

```
overflow: auto;
width: 10em;
height: 8em;
padding: .3em .5em;
border: 1px solid silver;
```

This is where things start to get interesting. Let's apply a shadow at the top, with a radial gradient:

```
background: radial-gradient(at top, rgba(0,0,0,.2),
                            transparent 70%) no-repeat;
background-size: 100% 15px;
```

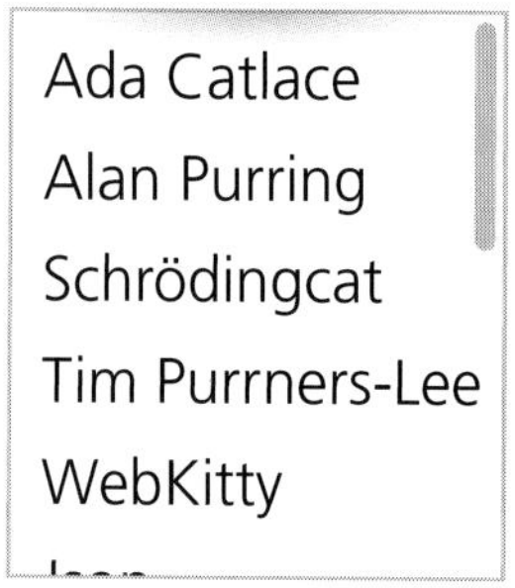

FIGURE 6.21

Our top shadow

You can see the result in **Figure 6.21**. Currently it stays in the same place when we scroll. This is on par with how background images work by default: their position is fixed relative to the element, regardless of how far the element is scrolled. This also applies to images with `background-attachment: fixed`. Their only difference is that they also **stay in place when the page itself scrolls**. Is there any way to get a background image to scroll with an element's contents?

Until a few years ago, this simple thing was impossible. However, the problem was pretty obvious and a new `background-attachment` keyword was added in **Backgrounds & Borders Level 3** *(w3.org/TR/css3-background/#local0)* to address it: `local`.

However, `background-attachment: local` doesn't solve our use case out of the box. If we apply it to our shadow gradient, it gives us the exact opposite result: we get a shadow when we scroll all the way to the top, but when we scroll down, the shadow disappears. It is a start, though —we're starting to get somewhere.

The trick is to use two backgrounds: one for the shadow, and one that is basically **a white rectangle to cover the shadow**, acting as a mask. The background that generates the shadow will have the default `background-attachment` (`scroll`), because we want it to stay in place at all times. However, we will give the masking background a `background-attachment` of `local`, so that it covers the shadow when we are scrolled all the way up, but scrolls with the contents when we scroll down, thus revealing the shadow.

We will use a linear gradient to create the masking rectangle, with the same color as the element's background (in our case, white):

```
background: linear-gradient(white, white),
            radial-gradient(at top, rgba(0,0,0,.2),
                            transparent 70%);
background-repeat: no-repeat;
background-size: 100% 15px;
background-attachment: local, scroll;
```

You can see how this looks in different stages of scrolling in **Figure 6.22**. You may notice that this seems to produce the desired effect, but it has one significant drawback: when we are only slightly scrolled, the way the shadow is revealed is very choppy and awkward. Is there any way to make it smoother?

FIGURE 6.22

Our two backgrounds in different stages of scrolling
Left: Scrolled all the way to the top
Middle: Slightly scrolled down
Right: Scrolled down significantly

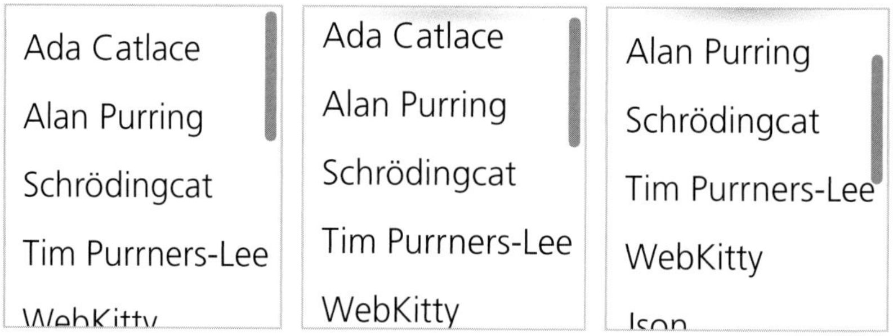

FIGURE 6.23

Using a gradient of **white** to
transparent as a first attempt to
fade the shadow in smoothly

Why transparent white and not just
transparent? The latter is actually
an alias of **rgba(0,0,0,0)**, so the
gradient might include shades of
gray as it transitions from opaque
white to transparent black. If browsers are interpolating colors in what is
called a *premultiplied RGBA space*
per the specification, this shouldn't
happen. Different interpolation algorithms are outside the scope of
this book, but there is a lot of material on this online.

We can take advantage of the fact that our "mask" is a (degenerate)
linear gradient and convert it to a real gradient from **white** to transparent
white (**hsla(0,0%,100%,0)** or **rgba(255,255,255,0)**), so that it
smoothly reveals our shadow:

```
background: linear-gradient(white, hsla(0,0%,100%,0)),
            radial-gradient(at top, rgba(0,0,0,.2),
                            transparent 70%);
```

This is a step in the right direction. As you can see in **Figure 6.23**, it does
progressively reveal the shadow, like we wanted. However, it currently has
a pretty serious flaw: it no longer completely obscures the shadow when
we are scrolled all the way to the top. We can fix this by moving the **white**
color stop a little lower down (**15px** to be precise, equal to our shadow
height), so that we get an area of solid white before the fading starts. Furthermore, we need to increase the size of the "mask" to be larger than the
shadow, otherwise we would get no gradient. The exact height depends on
how smooth we want the effect to be (i.e., how quickly should shadow be
revealed when we scroll?). After some experimentation, it seems that **50px**
is a reasonable value. The final code looks as follows, and you can see the
result in **Figure 6.24**:

FIGURE 6.24

The final result

Ada Catlace	Ada Catlace	Alan Purring
Alan Purring	Alan Purring	Schrödingcat
Schrödingcat	Schrödingcat	Tim Purrners-Lee
Tim Purrners-Lee	Tim Purrners-Lee	WebKitty
WebKitty	WebKitty	Ison

```
background: linear-gradient(white 30%, transparent),
            radial-gradient(at 50% 0, rgba(0,0,0,.2),
                            transparent 70%);
background-repeat: no-repeat;
background-size: 100% 50px, 100% 15px;
background-attachment: local, scroll;
```

Of course, to achieve the original effect, we need **two more gradients for the bottom shadow and its mask**, but the logic is exactly the same, so this can be left as an exercise for the reader (or check out the following Play! example for the solution).

▶ **PLAY!** play.csssecrets.io/**scrolling-hints**

*Hat tip to **Roman Komarov** for coming up with **an early version of this effect** (kizu.ru/en/fun/shadowscroll). His version used pseudo-elements and positioning instead of background images, and might be an interesting alternative for certain use cases.*

HAT TIP

■ **CSS Backgrounds & Borders**
  w3.org/TR/css-backgrounds

■ **CSS Image Values**
  w3.org/TR/css-images

RELATED
SPECS

35 Interactive image comparison

The problem

Sometimes the need arises to showcase the visual differences between two images, usually as a before-and-after comparison. For example, demonstrating the effects of photo manipulation in a portfolio, the results of certain beauty treatments in a beautician's website or the visible results of a catastrophic event in a geographical area.

The most common solution would be to just place the images side by side. However, this way the human eye only notices very conspicuous differences and misses the smaller ones. This is fine if the comparison is unimportant or the differences are large, but in all other cases, we need something more helpful.

There are many solutions to this problem from a UX perspective. A common solution is to show both images in the same place in quick succession, through an animated GIF or a CSS animation. This is much better than showing the images next to each other, but it's time consuming for the user to notice all the differences as they have to wait for several iterations, fixating their eyes at a different area of the images every time.

Fire crews douse Royal Mansions on London Road in Croydon

FIGURE 6.25

An example of an interactive image comparison widget, enabling users to compare the catastrophic results of the 2011 London riots, from major UK news outlet *The Guardian*. The user is supposed to drag the white bar separating the two images, but **there is no affordance to indicate the bar is draggable**, which is why the help text (*"Move the slider…"*) was needed. Ideally, a good, learnable, interface doesn't need help text.

Source: `theguardian.com/uk/`
`interactive/2011/aug/09/`
`london-riots-before-after-`
`photographs`

A solution that is much more usable is what is known as an "image comparison slider." This control superimposes both images and lets the user drag the divisor to reveal one or the other. Of course, such a control does not actually exist in HTML. We have to emulate it via the elements we do have, and there have been many such implementations over the years, usually requiring JavaScript frameworks and a boatload of JS code.

Is there a simpler way to implement such a control? Actually, there are two!

In some variations, the user just moves the mouse instead of dragging. This has the benefit of being easier to notice and use, but the experience can be quite irritating.

CSS resize solution

If we think about it, an image comparison slider basically includes an image and a horizontally resizable element that progressively reveals another image. This is where the JavaScript frameworks usually come in: to make the top image horizontally resizable. However, we don't really need scripting to make an element resizable. In **CSS User Interface Level 3** *(w3.org/TR/ css3-ui/#resize)*, we got a property for that: the humble `resize`!

It's usually a good idea to apply `resize: vertical` to `<textarea>`s to maintain resizability but disable horizontal resizing, which usually breaks layouts.

Once `object-fit` and `object-position` gain more widespread browser support, this won't be an issue, as we'll be able to control how images scale in the same way as we're able to control background image scaling.

Even if you've never heard of this property, you've probably experienced its behavior as it's set to **both** by default on `<textarea>`s, which makes them resizable in both directions. However, it can actually be set on any element, as long as its `overflow` property is **not visible**. In almost every element `resize` is set to **none** by default, which disables resizing. Besides **both**, it also accepts the values **horizontal** and **vertical**, which restrict the direction of the resizing.

This might make one wonder: could we perhaps use this property to implement our image slider? We can't know until we give it a shot!

Our first thought might be to just include two `<img>` elements. However, applying `resize` directly to an `<img>` would look awful, as resizing an image directly distorts it. It makes more sense to apply it to a container `<div>`. Therefore, we end up with markup like the following:

```html
<div class="image-slider">
    <div>
        <img src="adamcatlace-before.jpg" alt="Before" />
    </div>
    <img src="adamcatlace-after.jpg" alt="After" />
</div>
```

Then we need to apply some basic CSS for positioning and dimensions:

FIGURE 6.26

After some basic styling, this is already starting to resemble an image slider, but we can't change the width of the top image yet

```css
.image-slider {
    position:relative;
    display: inline-block;
}

.image-slider > div {
    position: absolute;
    top: 0; bottom: 0; left: 0;
    width: 50%; /* Initial width */
    overflow: hidden; /* Make it clip the image */
}
```

```
.image-slider img { display: block; }
```

Right now the result looks like **Figure 6.26** but is still static. If we manually change the width, we can see it going through all stages that a user would resize it to. To make the width change dynamically with user interaction, through the **resize** property, we need two more declarations:

```
.image-slider > div {
    position: absolute;
    top: 0; bottom: 0; left: 0;
    width: 50%;
    overflow: hidden;
    resize: horizontal;
}
```

The only visual change is that a resize handler now appears at the bottom-right corner of the before image (**Figure 6.27**), but we can now drag it and resize it to our heart's content! However, playing with our widget a little reveals a few weaknesses:

- We can resize the **<div>** past the width of the images.
- The resize handler is difficult to spot.

The first issue is very easy to solve. All we need is to specify a **max-width** of **100%**. However, the second issue is a bit more complicated. Unfortunately, there is still no standard way to style the resize handler. Some rendering engines support proprietary pseudo-elements (such as **::-webkit-resizer**) for this, but their results are limited, both in terms of browser support, as well as styling flexibility. However, hope is not lost: it turns out that overlaying a pseudo-element on the resize handle doesn't interfere with its function, even without **pointer-events: none**. So, a cross-browser solution to style the resize handler would be to just ...overlay another on top of it. Let's do that:

```css
.image-slider > div::before {
    content: '';
    position: absolute;
    bottom: 0; right: 0;
    width: 12px; height: 12px;
    background: white;
    cursor: ew-resize;
}
```

Note the **cursor: ew-resize** declaration: this adds an extra **affordance**, as it hints to the user that they can use this area as a resize handler. However, **we should not depend on cursor changes as our only affordance**, because they are only visible when the user is already interacting with a control.

Right now, our resize handler will appear as a white square (see **Figure 6.28**). At this point, we can go ahead and style it to our liking. For example, to make it a white triangle with **5px** spacing from the sides of the image (**Figure 6.29**), we could write:

```css
padding: 5px;
background:
    linear-gradient(-45deg, white 50%, transparent 0);
background-clip: content-box;
```

As an additional improvement, we could apply **user-select: none** to both images, so that failing to grab the resize handler would not result in them pointlessly being selected. To sum up, the full code would look like this:

```css
.image-slider {
    position:relative;
    display: inline-block;
}
```

```css
.image-slider > div {
    position: absolute;
    top: 0; bottom: 0; left: 0;
    width: 50%;
    max-width: 100%;
    overflow: hidden;
    resize: horizontal;
}

.image-slider > div::before {
    content: '';
    position: absolute;
    bottom: 0; right: 0;
    width: 12px; height: 12px;
    padding: 5px;
    background:
        linear-gradient(-45deg, white 50%, transparent 0);
    background-clip: content-box;
    cursor: ew-resize;
}

.image-slider img {
    display: block;
    user-select: none;
}
```

▶ PLAY! play.csssecrets.io/**image-slider**

Range input solution

The CSS resize method described in the previous section works great and
involves very little code. However, it has a few shortcomings:

- It's **not keyboard accessible**.

- Dragging is the only way to resize the top image, which can be **tedious** for large images or motor-impaired users. Being able to also **click to a point** and have the image resize to that point offers a much better experience.

- The user can only resize the top image from its bottom-right corner, which might be hard to notice, even if we style it in the way previously described.

If we are willing to use a little scripting, we could use a **slider control** (HTML range input) overlaid on top of the images to control the resizing, which solves all three issues. Because we're using JS anyway, we can add all extra elements via scripting, so we can start with the cleanest possible markup:

```HTML
<div class="image-slider">
    <img src="adamcatlace-before.jpg" alt="Before" />
    <img src="adamcatlace-after.jpg" alt="After" />
</div>
```

Then, our JS code will convert it to the following, and add an event on the slider so that it also sets the div's width:

```HTML
<div class="image-slider">
    <div>
        <img src="adamcatlace-before.jpg" alt="Before" />
    </div>
    <img src="adamcatlace-after.jpg" alt="After" />
    <input type="range" />
</div>
```

The JavaScript code is fairly straightforward:

```JS
$$('.image-slider').forEach(function(slider) {
    // Create the extra div and
    // wrap it around the first image
```

```
    var div = document.createElement('div');
    var img = slider.querySelector('img');
    slider.insertBefore(img, div);
    div.appendChild(img);

    // Create the slider
    var range = document.createElement('input');
    range.type = 'range';
    range.oninput = function() {
        div.style.width = this.value + '%';
    };
    slider.appendChild(range);
});
```

The CSS we will use as a starting point is basically the same as in the previous solution. We will only delete the parts we no longer need:

- We don't need the **resize** property.
- We don't need the **.image-slider > div::before** rule, because we no longer have a resizer.
- We don't need **max-width** because the slider will control that.

Here's how our CSS code will look after these modifications:

```
.image-slider {
    position:relative;
    display: inline-block;
}

.image-slider > div {
    position: absolute;
    top: 0; bottom: 0; left: 0;
    width: 50%;
    overflow: hidden;
```

FIGURE 6.30

Our control now works, but we still need to style that range input

```
    }

    .image-slider img {
        display: block;
        user-select: none;
    }
```

TIP! Use `input:in-range`
instead of just **input** to
**only style the range input if
range inputs are supported**. Then
you could use the cascade to hide it
or style it differently in older
browsers.

If we test this code now, you will see that **it already works**, but it
looks awful: there's a range input just randomly placed under our images
(**Figure 6.30**). We need to apply some CSS to **position it on top of
them**, and make it as wide as they are:

FIGURE 6.31

Our range input styled to be overlaid
on the images

```
    .image-slider input {
        position: absolute;
        left: 0;
        bottom: 10px;
        width: 100%;
        margin: 0;
    }
```

As you can see in **Figure 6.31**, this already looks decent. There are several
proprietary pseudo-elements to style range inputs exactly how we want
them. These include `::-moz-range-track`, `::-ms-track`, `::-
webkit-slider-thumb`, `::-moz-range-thumb`, and `::-ms-thumb`.
Like most proprietary features, their results are inconsistent, flimsy, and unpredictable, so I would recommend against using them, unless you **really**
have to. You've been warned.

However, if we just want to **visually unify** the range input with the control a bit more, we could use a blending mode and/or a filter. The blending modes **multiply**, **screen**, or **luminosity** seem to produce good results. Also, **filter: contrast(4)** would make the slider black and white and a contrast value lower than 1 would make it more gray. The possibilities are endless, and there's no universally optimal choice here. You could even **combine blending modes and filters, like so**:

```
filter: contrast(.5);
mix-blend-mode: luminosity;
```

We could also increase the area the user can use for resizing to make it a more pleasant experience (per Fitts' Law), by reducing the width and making up the difference with CSS transforms:

```
width: 50%;
transform: scale(2);
transform-origin: left bottom;
```

You can see the result of both treatments in **Figure 6.32**. Another benefit of this approach—albeit a transient one—is that range inputs currently have better browser support than the **resize** property.

Hat tip to **Dudley Storey** *for coming up with* **the first version of this solution** *(demosthenes.info/blog/819/A-Before-And-After-Image-Comparison-Slide-Control-in-HTML5).*

FIGURE 6.32

Using blending modes and filters to visually unify the range input with our control and CSS transforms to make it larger

HAT TIP

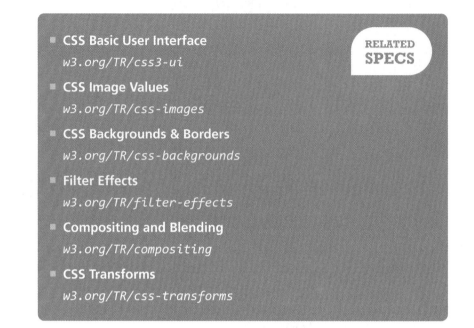

- **CSS Basic User Interface**
  w3.org/TR/css3-ui

- **CSS Image Values**
  w3.org/TR/css-images

- **CSS Backgrounds & Borders**
  w3.org/TR/css-backgrounds

- **Filter Effects**
  w3.org/TR/filter-effects

- **Compositing and Blending**
  w3.org/TR/compositing

- **CSS Transforms**
  w3.org/TR/css-transforms

RELATED
SPECS

Structure & Layout

36 Intrinsic sizing

The problem

As we all know, if we don't set a specific **height** on an element, it automatically adjusts to its contents. What if we want a similar behavior for the **width** as well? For example, let's assume we have HTML5 figures, with markup like the following:

```html
<p>Some text […]</p>
<figure>
    <img src="adamcatlace.jpg" />
    <figcaption>
        The great Sir Adam Catlace was named after
        Countess Ada Lovelace, the first programmer.
    </figcaption>
</figure>
<p>More text […].</p>
```

Let's also assume we're applying some basic styling to them, such as a border around the figures. By default, this looks like **Figure 7.1**. We want to make the figures **as wide as the image they contain** (which could vary in size) and **center them horizontally**. The current rendering is quite far from what we want: the lines of text are much longer than the image. How do we make the width of the figure determined by the width of the image it contains instead of the width of its parent?* Over the course of our career, we have probably built our own list of CSS styles that result in such width behavior, usually as a side effect:

- Floating the `<figure>` gives us the right width, but also drastically alters the layout of the figure, in ways we might not want (**Figure 7.2**).

- Applying `display: inline-block` to the figure does size it based on its contents, but not in the way we want (**Figure 7.3**). In addition, even if the width computation was on par with our expectations, it would be very tricky to horizontally center figures this way. We would need to apply `text-align: center` to its parent and `text-align: left` to any possible child of that parent (`p, ul, ol, dl, ...`).

- As a last resort, developers often apply a fixed `width` or `max-width` to figures, and apply `max-width: 100%` to `figure > img`. However, this underutilizes the available space, might still be off for overly small figures, and is not responsive.

Is there any decent CSS solution to this problem or should we give up and start coding a script to dynamically set the figure widths?

The solution

A relatively new specification, **CSS Intrinsic & Extrinsic Sizing Module Level 3** *(w3.org/TR/css3-sizing)*, defined several new `width` and `height` keywords, one of the most useful of which was `min-content`. This keyword gives us the width of the largest unbreakable element inside the box (i.e., the widest word or image or fixed-width box). This is exactly what we need! Now, giving our figures an appropriate width and horizontally centering them as simple is two lines of code:

FIGURE 7.1

The default way our markup is rendered, after a bit of CSS for borders and padding

FIGURE 7.2

Trying to solve the width issue by floating creates new issues

FIGURE 7.3

Contrary to our expectations, `display: inline-block` does not result in the width we wanted

---

* In CSS spec jargon, we need the width to be *intrinsically* determined instead of *extrinsically*.

Another value, **max-content**, would give us the same width as we saw with **display: inline-block** earlier. And **fit-content** gives us the same behavior as floats (which is often the same as **min-content**, but not always).

```
figure {
    width: min-content;
    margin: auto;
}
```

You can see the result in **Figure 7.4**. To offer a graceful fallback for older browsers, we could combine this technique with a fixed **max-width**, like so:

FIGURE 7.4

The final result

```
figure {
    max-width: 300px;
    max-width: min-content;
    margin: auto;
}

figure > img { max-width: inherit; }
```

On a modern browser, the latter **max-width** declaration would override the former and if the figure is sized intrinsically, **max-width: inherit** has no effect.

▶ **PLAY!** play.csssecrets.io/**intrinsic-sizing**

HAT TIP

Hat tip to **Dudley Storey** *(demosthenes.info) for coming up with* **this use case** *(demosthenes.info/blog/662/Design-From-the-Inside-Out-With-CSS-MinContent).*

▪ **CSS Intrinsic & Extrinsic Sizing**
w3.org/TR/css3-sizing

RELATED SPECS

37 Taming table column widths

The problem

Although we stopped using tables for layout long ago, tables still have their place on modern websites, for tabular data such as statistics, emails, listings of items with lots of metadata, and many other things. Also, we can make other elements behave like table-related elements, by using the table-related keywords for the `display` property. However, convenient as they may seem at times, their layout is very unpredictable for dynamic content. This is due to the fact that column dimensions are adjusted based on their contents and even explicit `width` declarations are treated more like hints, as **Figure 7.5** illustrates.

For this reason, we often end up using different elements even for tabular data or we just accept the unpredictability of it all. Is there any way we could get tables to just behave?

The solution

The solution comes in the form of a little-known **CSS 2.1 property** called `table-layout`. Its default value is `auto`, which results in the so-called *automatic table layout algorithm*, with the familiar behavior shown in

FIGURE 7.5

The default table layout algorithm for tables with 2 columns and varied contents (the container of these tables is shown with a dashed border)

If we don't…	specify a cell width, they will be assigned one that depends on their contents. Notice how the cell with more content here is much wider.

If we don't…	specify a cell width, they will be assigned one that depends on their contents. Notice how the cell with more content here is much wider.
All rows take part in calculating the widths, not just the first one.	Notice how the dimensions here are different than the previous example.

If we specify a width, it will not always be followed. I have a width of **1000px**…	…and I have a width of **2000px**. Because there's not enough space for **3000px**, they are reduced proportionally, to 33.3% and 66.6% of the total width.

If we prevent word wrapping, the table can become so wide it grows beyond its container.	…and `text-overflow: ellipsis` doesn't help either.

Large images and blocks of code can also cause the same issue.	

Figure 7.5. However, there is a second value, `fixed`, which results in **more predictable behavior**. It leaves more up to the author (you, that is!) and less up to the rendering engine. Styling is respected and not treated like some sort of hint, overflow behaves the same way as any other element (including `text-overflow`), and table contents only affect the height of each row and nothing else.

In addition to being more predictable and convenient, the **fixed table layout algorithm is also considerably faster**. Because table contents do not affect cell widths, no redraws/repaints are needed while the page is downloading. We are all familiar with the disruptive image of a table that keeps readjusting the widths of its columns as the page is downloading. This never happens with fixed table layouts.

To use it, we apply the property to `<table>` elements and elements with `display: table`. Note that you need to specify a width to these tables (even if it's **100%**) for the magic to happen. Also, for `text-overflow: ellipsis` to work, we need to set a width to that column as well. That's all! You can see the results in **Figure 7.6**:

```
table {
    table-layout: fixed;
    width: 100%;
}
```

▶ PLAY! play.csssecrets.io/**table-column-widths**

HAT TIP

*Hat tip to **Chris Coyier** (css-tricks.com) for coming up with **this technique** (css-tricks.com/fixing-tables-long-strings).*

FIGURE 7.6

The same tables as in **Figure 7.5**, but with `table-layout: fixed` applied. Note the following, in order:

- When we don't define any widths, all columns get the same width.
- A second row does not affect the column widths.
- Large widths are applied as-is, not shrunk down.
- The `overflow` and `text-overflow` properties are respected.
- Content can overflow table cells (if `overflow` is `visible`)

If we don't…	specify a cell width, they will be assigned one that depends on their contents. Notice how the cell with more content here is much wider.

If we don't…	specify a cell width, they will be assigned one that depends on their contents. Notice how the cell with more content here is much wider.
All rows take part in calculating the widths, not just the first one.	Notice how the dimensions here are different than the previous example.

If we specify a width, it will not always be followed. I have a width of **1000px**…

If we prevent word wrapping, the table can become so wide it grows beyond its container.	…and **text-overflow: ellipsis** doesn't h…

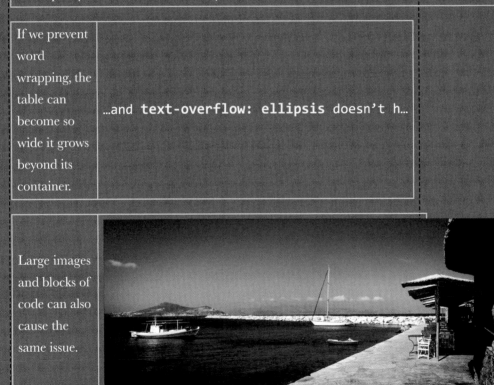

Large images and blocks of code can also cause the same issue.

38 Styling by sibling count

The problem

There are many cases when we need to style elements differently based on how many siblings they have **total**. The main use case is improving UX and conserving screen real estate in an expanding list, by hiding controls or making them more compact as the list grows. Here are a few examples:

- A list of emails or similar text-based items. If we only have a handful of items, we can display a long preview. As the list grows, we reduce the lines of preview we can show. When the length of the list is longer than the viewport height, we might opt to hide previews completely and make any buttons smaller, to minimize scrolling.

- A to-do list app, where we show every item with a large font when there are fewer items, but progressively make the font size smaller (for all items) as the total number of items increases.

- A color palette app, with controls displayed on every color. One might want to make these controls more compact as the number of colors increases and the space they occupy decreases accordingly (**Figure 7.7**).

- An app with multiple `<textarea>`s where every time we add a new one, we make them all smaller (like in **bytesizematters.com**).

FIGURE 7.7

Progressively making controls smaller as the number of colors increases and the available space shrinks. Note the special handling on the case where we only have one color: We then hide the delete button.

Colors are taken from the **Adobe Color** *(color.adobe.com)* palettes:

- **Agave** *(color.adobe.com/ agave-color-theme-387108)*
- **Sushi Maki** *(color.adobe.com/ Sushi-Maki-color- theme-350205)*

However, targeting elements based on their total number of siblings is not trivial with CSS selectors. For example, suppose we want to apply certain styles to a list's items **when their total count is 4**. We could use `li:nth-child(4)` to select the fourth item in the list, but this is not what we needed; we needed to select **every** item, but only **when their total count is 4**.

Our next idea might be to use the generalized sibling combinator (~) together with `:nth-child()`, like `li:nth-child(4), li:nth-child(4) ~ li`. However, this only targets the fourth child and items **after** it (**Figure 7.8**), regardless of the total count. Because there is no combinator that can "look backward" and select previous siblings, is attempting to accomplish this with CSS doomed to fail? Let's not lose hope just yet.

FIGURE 7.8

Which elements get selected with `li:nth-child(4)`, `li:nth-child(4) ~ li`

The solution

For the special case of having exactly **one** item, there is an obvious solution: `:only-child`, which was created exactly for this purpose. This is not only useful as a starting point, but there are several use cases for it, which is why it was added to the specification. For example, note in **Figure 7.7** that we are hiding the delete button when we only have one color; this could be done by a CSS selector using `:only-child`:

We will use `:nth-child()` selectors throughout this section, but everything discussed applies to `:nth-of-type()` selectors equally, **which are often a better fit**, as we usually have siblings of different types and we are only concerned with one type. We will be using list items in the examples, but what we discuss is applicable to elements of any type.

```css
li:only-child {
    /* Styles for when we only have 1 item */
}
```

However, `:only-child` is equivalent to `:first-child:last-child`, for obvious reasons: if the **first** item is also the **last** item, it logically follows that it is the **only** item. However, `:last-child` is also a shortcut, to `:nth-last-child(1)`:

```css
li:first-child:nth-last-child(1) {
    /* Same as li:only-child */
}
```

However, now 1 is a parameter, and we can tweak it to our liking. Can you guess what `li:first-child:nth-last-child(4)` targets? If you answered that it generalizes `:only-child` by targeting list items when their total count is four, you might be overdoing it a bit with the optimism. We're not there yet, but we are on the right track. Think about both pseudo-classes separately: we are looking for elements that match **both `:first-child` and `:nth-last-child(4)`**. Therefore, elements who are—at the same time—the first child of their parent counting from the start, and the fourth child counting from the end. Which elements would fulfill this criteria?

The answer is **the first element in a list with exactly four elements** (**Figure 7.9**). This is not quite what we wanted, but it's very close: because we now have a way to target the first child of such a list, we can use the general sibling combinator (~) to target **every sibling that follows** such a first child, effectively targeting **every list item in a list if and only if it contains four items total**, which is exactly what we were trying to accomplish:

```
li:first-child:nth-last-child(4),
li:first-child:nth-last-child(4) ~ li {
    /* Target list items iff the list
       contains exactly four items */
}
```

FIGURE 7.9

Which elements get selected with **li:first-child:nth-last-child(4)** in lists of three, four, and eight elements

To avoid the verbosity and repetition of the solution just shown, a preprocessor, such as SCSS, could be used, although the syntax of existing preprocessors for this is rather clumsy:

SCSS

```
/* Define mixin */
@mixin n-items($n) {
    &:first-child:nth-last-child(#{$n}),
    &:first-child:nth-last-child(#{$n}) ~ & {
        @content;
    }
}

/* Use it like so: */
li {
    @include n-items(4) {
        /* Properties and values */
    }
}
```

*Hat tip to **André Luís** (andr3.net) for coming up with **an idea that inspired this technique** (andr3.net/blog/post/142).*

TIP! It can be hard to wrap one's head around :nth-* selectors. If you're having trouble, you could use an online tester to experiment with a few expressions. I've written one at **lea.verou.me/demos/nth.html**, but there are plenty of others around.

Selecting by range of sibling count

In most practical applications, we do not want to target specific numbers of items, but ranges thereof. There is a handy trick that we can use to make `:nth-child()` selectors target ranges such as *"select everything **after** the fourth child."* Besides simple numbers as parameters, we can also use **an+b** expressions (e.g., `:nth-child(2n+1)`), where **n** stands for a variable that ranges from 0 to +∞ in theory (in practice, values after a certain point don't select anything anymore because the number of elements we have is finite). If we use an expression of the form **n+b** (where **a** is implied to be 1), then there is no positive integer for **n** that could give us a value smaller than **b**. Therefore, expressions of the form **n+b** can be used to select **every child from the bth onward**; for example, `:nth-child(n+4)` selects every child except the first, second, and third (**Figure 7.10**).

FIGURE 7.10

Which elements get selected with `li:nth-child(n+4)` in lists of three, four, and eight elements

We can take advantage of this to select list items when the total number of items is four or more (**Figure 7.11**). In this case, we could use **n+4** as the expression inside `:nth-last-child()`:

```
li:first-child:nth-last-child(n+4),
li:first-child:nth-last-child(n+4) ~ li {
    /* Target list items iff the list
       contains at least four items */
}
```

Similarly, expressions of the form **-n+b** can be used to select **the first b elements**. Therefore, to select all list items if and only if there are **four or fewer** of them in the same list (**Figure 7.12**), we would write:

```
li:first-child:nth-last-child(-n+4),
li:first-child:nth-last-child(-n+4) ~ li {
    /* Target list items iff the list
       contains at most four items */
}
```

Of course, we could combine the two, but the code now gets even more unwieldy. Assume we want to target list items when the list contains **between 2–6 items**:

```
li:first-child:nth-last-child(n+2):nth-last-child(-n+6),
li:first-child:nth-last-child(n+2):nth-last-child(-n+6) ~ li {
    /* Target list items iff the list
       contains 2-6 items */
}
```

 PLAY! play.csssecrets.io/**styling-sibling-count**

Selectors
w3.org/TR/selectors

RELATED
SPECS

FIGURE 7.11

Which elements get selected with
`li:first-child:nth-last-child(n+4)`,
`li:first-child:nth-last-child(n+4) ~ li` in lists of three, four, and eight elements

FIGURE 7.12

Which elements get selected with
`li:first-child:nth-last-child(-n+4)`,
`li:first-child:nth-last-child(-n+4) ~ li` in lists of three, four, and eight elements

39 Fluid background, fixed content

The problem

In the past few years, there is a certain web design trend that has been growing in popularity: it's what I call *"fluid background width, fixed content width."* The typical characteristics of this pattern are:

- There are multiple sections, each occupying the entire width of the viewport and each with a different background.

- The content is of fixed width, even if that width varies in different resolutions because said fixed width is modified by media queries. In some cases, different sections have different content widths as well.

Sometimes the entire website is comprised of sections styled this way (**Figure 7.15**, or, more subtly, **Figure 7.14**). More frequently, only specific sections follow this pattern, especially footers (**Figure 7.13**).

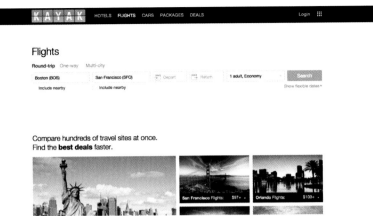

FIGURE 7.14

Popular travel booking website
kayak.com uses this pattern
throughout its homepage, in a very
subtle way

The most common way to accomplish something like this is using **two elements for each section**, one for the fluid background and one for the fixed content width. The latter is centered horizontally via `margin: auto`. For example, the markup for such a footer could look like this:

```html
<footer>
    <div class="wrapper">
        <!-- Footer content here -->
    </div>
</footer>
```

The CSS usually involves rules of this general structure:

```css
footer {
    background: #333;
}
.wrapper {
    max-width: 900px;
    margin: 1em auto;
}
```

Looks familiar? Most web designers/developers have written similar code at some point. Are the extra elements a necessary evil, or can we use modern CSS to avoid them?

The solution

Let's think for a bit about what **margin: auto** does in this case. The margin it produces is equal to half of the viewport width, minus half of our page width. Because percentages here refer to the viewport width (assuming there is no ancestor with an explicit width), we could express this in our case as **50% - 450px**. However, the **calc()** function, defined in **CSS Values and Units Level 3** *(w3.org/TR/css-values-3/#calc)*, allows us to specify this kind of simple math directly in our stylesheet. By substituting **auto** with **calc()**, our wrapper rule will become:

```
.wrapper {
    max-width: 900px;
    margin: 1em calc(50% - 450px);
}
```

The only reason we had to use a second wrapper element was to be able to apply the magic **auto** keyword on its **margin**. However, now we removed the magic and replaced it with **calc()**, so it's just another CSS length value that can be used in any property that accepts lengths. This means that if we want, we can now apply it to the parent instead as **padding**:

```
footer {
    max-width: 900px;
    padding: 1em calc(50% - 450px);
    background: #333;
}
.wrapper {}
```

FIGURE 7.15

The beautiful **Irish website of Cono Sur Vineyards and Winery** *(conosur.ie)* makes extensive use of this pattern

Don't forget to include white-space around any - and + operators in **calc()**, otherwise it's a parsing error! The reason for this weird rule is forward compatibility: in the future, identifiers might be allowed inside **calc()**, and they can contain hyphens.

As you can see, by doing that, we've eliminated any CSS code from the wrapper, which means we don't really need it anymore and we can safely get rid of it from our markup. We have now achieved the style we wanted with no redundant HTML. Can we improve it even further? As usual, the answer to this question is yes.

Notice that if we comment out the **width** declaration, nothing happens. The visual result is exactly the same, and behaves the same regardless of viewport size. Why is that? Because a padding of **50% - 450px** only leaves **900px** (2 × **450px**) of available space anyway. We would see a difference if **width** was anything other than **900px**, smaller or larger. But **900px** is the space we get anyway, so it's redundant and we can remove it, which results in DRY-er code.

Another improvement we can make is to improve backward compatibility, by adding a fallback so that we at least get **some** padding if **calc()** is not supported:

```
footer {
    padding: 1em;
    padding: 1em calc(50% - 450px);
    background: #333;
}
```

This is it: we've achieved a flexible, DRY, backward-compatible result in only three lines of CSS and no extra markup!

 ▶ PLAY!   play.csssecrets.io/**fluid-fixed**

■ **CSS Values & Units**
w3.org/TR/css-values

RELATED
SPECS

FIGURE 7.16
Popular Mac OS productivity application **Alfred** (*alfredapp.com*) also uses this style throughout its website

❗ This solution could end up with no padding if the screen got narrower than the content width! We can fix that with media queries.

40 Vertical centering

The problem

> "44 years ago we put a man on the moon, yet we still can't vertically centre things in CSS."
>
> —**James Anderson** (twitter.com/jsa/status/358603820516917249)

Centering an element **horizontally** in CSS is very straightforward: if it's an inline element, we apply `text-align: center` to its parent, if it's a block element, we apply `margin: auto` to it. However, just the thought of **vertically** centering an element is enough to make our skin crawl.

Over the years, vertical centering has become the holy grail of CSS, as well as a popular inside joke between frontend professionals. The reason being that it has all of the following properties at the same time:

- It's very frequently needed.
- It sounds exceedingly easy and simple in theory.
- It used to be incredibly difficult in practice, especially for elements of variable dimensions.

Frontend developers over the years have exhausted their creativity in coming up with solutions to this conundrum, most of them disturbingly hacky. In this secret, we are going to explore some of the best modern techniques to achieve vertical centering for all needs. Note that there are a few popular techniques that are not discussed here, for various reasons:

- The **table layout method** (using table display modes) is not included, as it requires several redundant HTML elements.
- The **inline-block method** is not included, as it's too hacky for my taste.

However, if you are interested, you can read about both of these techniques on Chris Coyier's excellent article **"Centering in the Unknown"** *(css-tricks.com/centering-in-the-unknown)*.

Unless otherwise noted, we will use the following markup right inside the **<body>** element, although the solutions we will explore should work regardless of container:

```HTML
<main>
    <h1>Am I centered yet?</h1>
    <p>Center me, please!</p>
</main>
```

FIGURE 7.17

Our starting point

We also apply some basic CSS for backgrounds, padding, and so on, in order to get to the starting point shown in **Figure 7.17**.

The absolute positioning solution

One of the earliest vertical centering techniques was the following, which required a fixed width and height:

```
main {
    position: absolute;
    top: 50%;
    left: 50%;
    margin-top: -3em; /* 6/2 = 3 */
    margin-left: -9em; /* 18/2 = 9 */
    width: 18em;
```

```
        height: 6em;
    }
```

Essentially, it places the element's top-left corner at the center of the viewport (or the closest positioned ancestor) and then uses negative margins of
half its width and height to move it up and left so that **the element's center
is at the center of the viewport**. With `calc()` it could be simplified to
use two declarations fewer:

```
main {
    position: absolute;
    top: calc(50% - 3em);
    left: calc(50% - 9em);
    width: 18em;
    height: 6em;
}
```

FIGURE 7.18

Vertical centering with unspecified
dimensions via our CSS transforms
trick

Obviously, the biggest problem with this technique is that it requires
fixed dimensions, while we often need to center elements whose dimensions are determined by their contents. If only we had a way to use percentages that resolve to the element's dimensions, our issue would be solved!
Unfortunately, for most CSS properties (including **margin**), percentages
resolve relative to the dimensions of their parent.

As is common with CSS, often solutions come from the most unlikely
places. In this case, CSS transforms. When we use percentages in
translate() transforms, we are moving the element relative to its own
width and height, which is exactly what we need here. We can thus replace
the negative offsets that hardcode our elements dimensions with
percentage-based CSS transforms and get rid of the hardcoded dimensions:

```
main {
    position: absolute;
    top: 50%;
    left: 50%;
    transform: translate(-50%, -50%);
}
```

You can see the result in **Figure 7.18**, but there aren't really any surprises there: our container is perfectly centered, just like what we'd expect.

Of course, no technique is perfect, and this one has a few caveats:

■ Absolute positioning is often not an option as its effects on the whole layout are quite drastic.

■ If the element to be centered is taller than the viewport, its top is clipped (**Figure 7.19**). There are ways to work around this, but they are incredibly hacky.

■ In some browsers, this can cause elements to appear slightly blurry, due to them being placed on a half pixel. This can be fixed by applying **transform-style: preserve-3d**, although this is a hack and is not guaranteed to be future-proof.

▶ **PLAY!**   play.csssecrets.io/**vertical-centering-abs**

*It proved quite difficult to track down who originally came up with this helpful trick, but the earliest source seems to be the **StackOverflow** (stackoverflow.com) user **"Charlie"** (stackoverflow.com/users/479836/charlie) as a response to the question **"Align vertically using CSS 3?"** (stackoverflow.com/a/16026893/90826) on April 16, 2013.*

FIGURE 7.19

If the element we are trying to center is taller than the viewport, its top is clipped

HAT TIP

The viewport unit solution

Assuming we want to avoid absolute positioning, we could still use the **translate()** trick to move the element by half its width and height. However, how do we give it the initial offsets of 50% from the top and left corner of the container, without **left** and **top**?

Our first thought might be to use percentages in the **margin** property, like so:

```css
main {
    width: 18em;
    padding: 1em 1.5em;
    margin: 50% auto 0;
    transform: translateY(-50%);
}
```

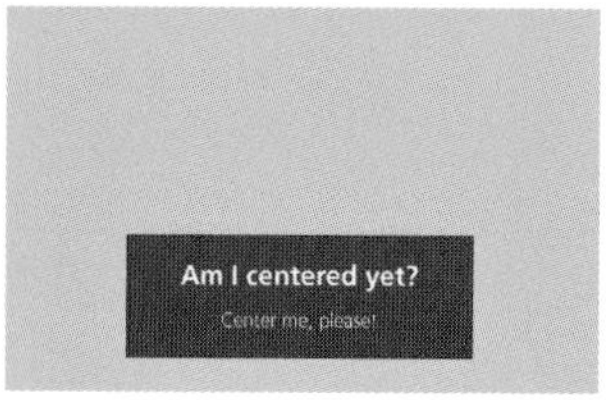

FIGURE 7.20

Using percentages in **margin** to refer to the viewport dimensions does not produce the expected results

However, as you can see in **Figure 7.20**, this produces rather odd results. The reason is that **percentages in margin are computed relative to the width of the parent**. Yes, even percentages for **margin-top** and **margin-bottom**!

Thankfully, if we are trying to center an element on the viewport, there is still hope. **CSS Values and Units Level 3** *(w3.org/TR/css-values-3/ #viewport-relative-lengths)* defined a family of new units, called viewport-relative lengths:

- **vw** is relative to the **viewport width**. Contrary to many expectations, **1vw** stands for 1% of the viewport width, not 100%.
- Similarly to **vw**, **1vh** represents 1% of the **viewport height**.
- **1vmin** is equal to **1vw** if the viewport width is smaller than the height, otherwise it is equal to **1vh**.
- **1vmax** is equal to **1vw** if the viewport width is larger than the height, otherwise it is equal to **1vh**.

In this case, what we need is **vh** for our margins:

```
main {
    width: 18em;
    padding: 1em 1.5em;
    margin: 50vh auto 0;
    transform: translateY(-50%);
}
```

Note that you can also use viewport-relative lengths to create full-screen sections with no scripting. For more details, see **"Make full screen sections with 1 line of CSS"** by Andrew Ckor *(medium.com/@ckor/ make-full-screen-sections- with-1-line-of-css- b82227c75cbd)*.

As you can see in **Figure 7.21**, this works flawlessly. Of course, the usefulness of this technique is severely limited due to the fact that it only works for vertically centering in the viewport.

▶ **PLAY!** play.csssecrets.io/**vertical-centering-vh**

FIGURE 7.21

Using **50vh** as the top margin solved our problem and now our box is vertically centered

The Flexbox solution

This is undoubtedly the best solution available, as **Flexbox** *(w3.org/TR/ css-flexbox)* was designed precisely to help with issues like this. The only reason other solutions are still discussed is because other methods have better browser support, although these days browser support for Flexbox in modern browsers is very good.

All it takes is two declarations: **display: flex** on the parent of the centered element (the **<body>** element in our example) and our familiar **margin: auto** on the child to be centered (**<main>** in our example):

```
body {
    display: flex;
    min-height: 100vh;
    margin: 0;
}

main {
    margin: auto;
}
```

FIGURE 7.22

Using Flexbox to center anonymous text boxes

Note that when using Flexbox, `margin: auto` doesn't only center the element horizontally, but vertically as well. Also note that we didn't even have to set a width (though we could, if we wanted to): the assigned width is equivalent to `max-content` (remember the intrinsic sizing keywords from the **"Intrinsic sizing" secret on page 262**?).

If Flexbox is not supported, the result would look like our starting point in **Figure 7.17** (if we set a width), which is perfectly acceptable, even if not vertically centered.

Another advantage of Flexbox is that it can be used to vertically center anonymous containers (i.e., text without any wrapper). For example, if our markup was the following:

HTML

```html
<main>Center me, please!</main>
```

We could have used the same properties on `<body>` to center the `<main>` element, but the `margin: auto` approach is more elegant and doubles as a fallback.

We could specify fixed dimensions to **main** and **center the text inside it too**, via the **align-items** and **justify-content** properties that Flexbox introduced (**Figure 7.22**):

FUTURE **Align all the things!**

As is already planned in **CSS Box Alignment Level 3** *(w3.org/TR/css-align-3)*, in the future we won't even need to use a different layout mode for easy vertical centering, we will just be able to do it with the following line:

```
align-self: center;
```

This will just work, regardless of what other properties are applied to the element. It may sound too good to be true, but it's coming soon at a browser near you!

```
main {
    display: flex;
    align-items: center;
    justify-content: center;
    width: 18em;
    height: 10em;
}
```

▶ PLAY! play.csssecrets.io/**vertical-centering**

- **CSS Transforms**
  w3.org/TR/css-transforms
- **CSS Values & Units**
  w3.org/TR/css-values
- **CSS Flexible Box Layout**
  w3.org/TR/css-flexbox
- **CSS Box Alignment**
  w3.org/TR/css-align

RELATED
SPECS

41 Sticky footers

The problem

Specifically, the issue appears on pages whose content is shorter than the viewport height minus the footer height.

This is one of the oldest and most common problems in web design, so common that most of us have experienced it at one point or another. It can be summarized as follows: a footer with any block-level styling, such as a background or shadow, works fine when the content is sufficiently long, but breaks on shorter pages (such as error messages). The breakage in this case being that the footer does not "stick" at the bottom of the viewport like we would want it to, but at the bottom of the content.

It is not only its ubiquity that made it popular, but also how **deceptively easy it looks at first**. It's a textbook case of the type of problem that requires significantly more time to solve than expected. In addition, **this is still not a solved problem in CSS 2.1**: almost all classic solutions require a fixed height for the footer, which is flimsy and rarely feasible. Furthermore, all of them are **overly complicated**, **hacky**, and have **specific markup requirements**. Back then, this was the best we could do, given the limitations of CSS 2.1. But can we do better with modern CSS, and if so, how?

Fixed height solution

We will work with an extremely bare-bones page with the following markup inside the **`<body>`** element:

```html
<header>
    <h1>Site name</h1>
</header>
<main>
    <p>Bacon Ipsum dolor sit amet…
    <!-- Filler text from baconipsum.com --></p>
</main>
<footer>
    <p>© 2015 No rights reserved.</p>
    <p>Made with ♥ by an anonymous pastafarian.</p>
</footer>
```

We have also applied some basic styling to it, including a background on the footer. You can see how it looks in **Figure 7.23**. Now, let's reduce the content a bit. You can see what happens then, in **Figure 7.24**. This is the sticky footer problem in all its glory! Great, we have recreated the problem, but how do we solve it?

If we assume that our footer text will never wrap, we can deduce a CSS length for its height:

2 lines × line height + 3 × paragraph margin + vertical padding =

$$2 \times 1.5em + 3 \times 1em + 1em = 7em$$

If you've never had the pleasure of pulling your hair out and diving in the existing literature for this problem, here are a few popular links with existing, widely used solutions that have served many a web developer before CSS Level 3 specs were conceived:

- `cssstickyfooter.com`
- `ryanfait.com/sticky-footer`
- `css-tricks.com/snippets/css/sticky-footer`
- `pixelsvsbytes.com/blog/2011/09/sticky-css-footers-the-flexible-way`
- `mystrd.at/modern-clean-css-sticky-footer`

The last two are the most minimal in the lot, but still have their own limitations.

FIGURE 7.23

How our simple page looks when its content is sufficiently long

> Be careful when using **calc()** with subtraction or addition: the **+** and **-** operators **require** spaces around them. This very odd decision was made for future compatibility. If at some point keywords are allowed in **calc()**, the CSS parser needs to be able to distinguish between a hyphen in a keyword and a minus operator.

FIGURE 7.25

The footer after we've applied CSS to make it stick

Similarly, the header height is **2.5em**. Therefore, by using viewport-relative units and **calc()**, we can "stick" our footer to the bottom with essentially one line of CSS:

```
main {
    min-height: calc(100vh - 2.5em - 7em);
    /* Avoid padding/borders screwing up our height: */
    box-sizing: border-box;
}
```

Alternatively, we could apply a wrapper around our **<header>** and **<main>** elements so that we only need to calculate the footer height:

```
#wrapper {
    min-height: calc(100vh - 7em);
}
```

This works (**Figure 7.25**) and it seems to be slightly better than the existing fixed height solutions, mainly due to its minimalism. However, except for very simple layouts, this is **not practical at all**. It requires us to assume that the footer text will **never wrap**, we need to edit the **min-height every time we change the footer metrics** (i.e., it is not DRY), and unless we're willing to add a wrapper HTML element around our header and content, we need to do the same calculations and modifications for the header as well. Surely, in this day and age we can do better, right?

▶ PLAY!   play.csssecrets.io/**sticky-footer-fixed**

Flexible solution

Flexbox is perfect for these kinds of problems. We can achieve perfect flexibility with only a few lines of CSS and there is no need for weird calculations or extra HTML elements. First, we need to apply **display: flex** to the **<body>** element, as it's the parent of all three of our main blocks, to toggle Flexible Box Layout (Flexbox) for all three of them. We also need to set **flex-flow** to **column**, otherwise they will be all laid out horizontally on a single row (**Figure 7.26**):

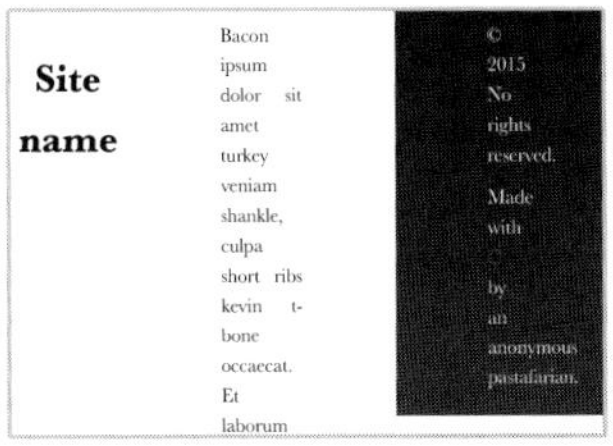

```
body {
    display: flex;
    flex-flow: column;
}
```

FIGURE 7.26
Applying **flex** without applying anything else arranges the children of our element horizontally

At this point, our page looks about the same as it did before all the Flexbox stuff, as every element occupies the entire width of the viewport and its size is determined by its contents. Ergo, we haven't really taken advantage of Flexbox yet.

To make the magic happen, we need to specify a **min-height** of **100vh** on **<body>**, so that it occupies **at least the entire height of the viewport**. At this point, the layout still looks exactly like **Figure 7.24**, because even though we have specified a minimum height for the entire body element, the heights of each box are still determined by their contents (i.e., they are *intrinsically determined*, in CSS spec parlance).

What we need here is for the height of the header and footer to be **intrinsically** determined, but the height of the content should flexibly stretch to all the leftover space. We can do that by applying a **flex** value that is larger than **0** (**1** will work) to the **<main>** container:

```
body {
    display: flex;
    flex-flow: column;
    min-height: 100vh;
}

main { flex: 1; }
```

TIP! The **flex** property is actually a shorthand of **flex-grow**, **flex-shrink**, and **flex-basis**. Any element with a **flex** value greater than **0** becomes flexible and **flex** controls the ratio between the dimensions of different flexible elements. For example, in our case, if **<main>** had **flex: 2** and **<footer>** had **flex: 1**, the height of the footer would be **twice** the height of the content. Same if the values were **4** and **2** instead of **2** and **1**, because **it's their relationship that matters.**

That's it, no more code required! The perfect sticky footer (same visual result as in **Figure 7.25**), with only four simple lines of code. Isn't Flexbox beautiful?

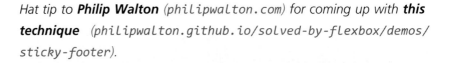

▶ **PLAY!** `play.csssecrets.io/`**sticky-footer**

HAT TIP

*Hat tip to **Philip Walton** (philipwalton.com) for coming up with **this technique** (philipwalton.github.io/solved-by-flexbox/demos/ sticky-footer).*

■ **CSS Flexible Box Layout**
   `w3.org/TR/css-flexbox`

■ **CSS Values & Units**
   `w3.org/TR/css-values`

RELATED
SPECS

Transitions & Animations

42 Elastic transitions

The problem

Elastic transitions and animations (i.e., transitions that "bounce") are a popular way to make an interface feel more playful and realistic—when objects are moving in real life, they rarely go from A to B with no elasticity.

From a technical point of view, a bouncing effect is when a transition reaches the final value, then rewinds for a little bit, then reaches the final value again, one or more times diminishingly, until it reaches the end for good. For example, let's assume we are animating an element styled like a falling ball (see **Figure 8.1**), by transitioning `transform` from `none` to `translateY(350px)`.

Of course, bounces are not just about positional movement. They can greatly enhance almost any kind of transition, including:

Why use transforms and not some other CSS property, like **top** or **margin-top**? At the time of writing, transforms tend to be smoother, whereas other CSS properties often snap to pixel boundaries.

- Size transitions (e.g., making an element larger on `:hover`, displaying a popup that grows from `transform: scale(0)`, animating the bars in a bar chart)

- Angular movement (e.g., rotations, a pie chart whose slices grow from 0 via an animation)

Quite a few JavaScript libraries offer animation capabilities with bounce built in. However, these days we don't need scripting for animations and transitions any longer. However, what's the best way to code a bounce in CSS?

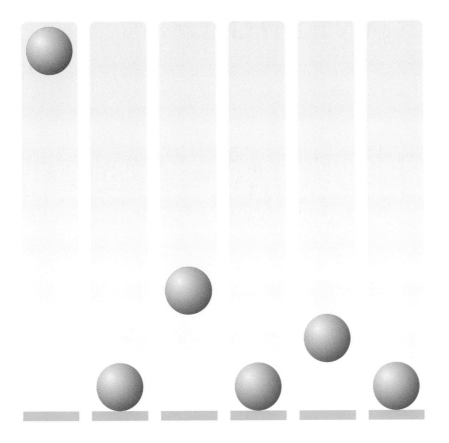

FIGURE 8.1

A real-life bouncing movement

Bouncing animations

Our first hunch might be to use a CSS animation, with keyframes such as the following:

```
@keyframes bounce {
    60%, 80%, to { transform: translateY(350px); }
    70% { transform: translateY(250px); }
    90% { transform: translateY(300px); }
}

.ball {
    /* Dimensions, colors, etc. */
    animation: bounce 3s;
}
```

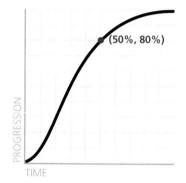

(50%, 80%)

PROGRESSION

TIME

FIGURE 8.2

The default timing function (**ease**) for all transitions and animations

The keyframes in the preceding code specify exactly the same steps as in **Figure 8.1**. However, if you run this animation, you will notice that it looks very artificial. One of the reasons for this is that every time the ball changes direction, it continues accelerating, which looks unnatural. The reason is that its *timing function* is the same across all these keyframes.

"Its timing…what?" you might ask. Every transition and animation is associated with **a curve that specifies how it progresses over time** (also known as "easing" in some contexts). If you don't specify a timing function, it will get the default one, which unlike what you might expect is **not linear** and is shown in **Figure 8.2**. Note (as shown by the pink point in **Figure 8.2**) how when **half of the time has elapsed, the transition is about 80% along the way!**

The default timing function can also be **explicitly** specified with the keyword **ease**, either in the **animation/transition** shorthand or the **animation-timing-function/transition-timing-function** longhands. However, because **ease** is the default timing function, it's not very useful. There are four more pre-baked curves you can use to change the way the animation progresses, shown in **Figure 8.3**.

As you can see, **ease-out is the reverse of ease-in**. This is exactly what we wanted for our bounce effect: we want **to reverse the timing function every time the direction reverses**. We can therefore specify a main timing function in the **animation** property and override it in the keyframes. We want the timing function of the main direction to be the

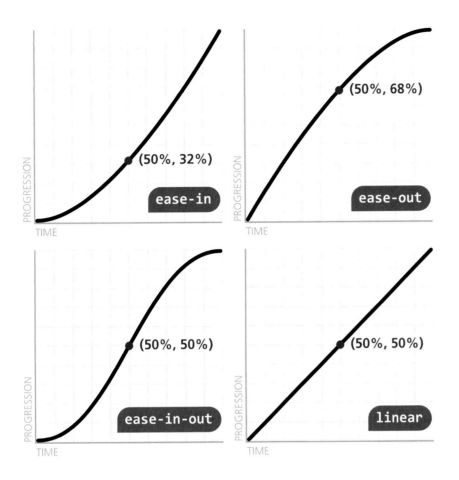

FIGURE 8.3

The available keywords that
correspond to predetermined timing
functions

(50%, 32%) — ease-in

(50%, 68%) — ease-out

(50%, 50%) — ease-in-out

(50%, 50%) — linear

accelerating one (**ease-out**) and the one of the reverse direction to be
decelerating (**ease-in**):

```
@keyframes bounce {
    60%, 80%, to {
        transform: translateY(400px);
        animation-timing-function: ease-out;
    }
    70% { transform: translateY(300px); }
    90% { transform: translateY(360px); }
}


.ball {
```

```
    /* Rest of styling here */
    animation: bounce 3s ease-in;
}
```

If you test the code out, you will see that even this simple change instantly results in a considerably more realistic bounce. However, restricting ourselves to these five predetermined curves is extremely limiting. If we could pick arbitrary timing functions, we would be able to achieve much more realistic results. For example, if the bounce animation is for a falling object, then a **higher acceleration** (such as the one provided by **ease**) would create a more realistic result. But how could we create the inverse of **ease**, when there is no keyword for it?

All five of these curves are specified through *(cubic) Bézier curves*. Bézier curves are the kinds of curves you work with in any vector application (e.g., Adobe Illustrator). They are defined by a number of path segments, with a handle on each end to control their curvature (these handles are often called *control points*). Complex curves contain a large number of such segments, which are joined at their endpoints (**Figure 8.4**). CSS timing functions are **Bézier curves with only one segment**, so they only have **two control points**. As an example, you can see the default timing function (**ease**) with its control points exposed in **Figure 8.5**.

In addition to the five predefined curves we discussed in the previous section, there is also a **cubic-bezier()** function that **allows us to specify a custom timing function**. It takes four arguments, which are the coordinates of the two control points, to create the Bézier curve we are specifying, with the form **cubic-bezier(x_1, y_1, x_2, y_2)** where **(x_1, y_1)** are the coordinates of the first control point and **(x_2, y_2)** of the second. The endpoints of the line segment are fixed at **(0,0)**, which is the beginning of the transition (zero elapsed time, zero progression) and **(1,1)**, which is its end (100% elapsed time, 100% progression).

Note that the restriction on having a single segment whose endpoints are fixed is not the only one. The x values of both control points are restricted to the [0, 1] range (i.e., we cannot move the handles outside of the graph horizontally). This restriction is not arbitrary. As we cannot *(yet?)* travel through time, we cannot specify a transition that begins before it is triggered

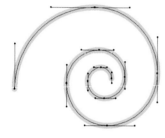

FIGURE 8.4

A cubic Bézier curve for a spiral, with its nodes and control points showing

PROGRESSION

TIME

FIGURE 8.5

The **ease** timing function with its nodes and control points displayed or ends after its duration. The only real limitation here is the number of nodes: restricting the curve to only two nodes limits the result quite considerably, but it also makes the **cubic-bezier()** function simpler to use. Despite these limitations, **cubic-bezier()** allows us to create a very diverse set of timing functions.

It logically follows that we can **reverse any timing function** by **swapping the horizontal with the vertical coordinates for both its control points**. This applies to keywords too; all five keywords we discussed correspond to **cubic-bezier()** values. For example, **ease** is equivalent to **cubic-bezier(.25,.1,.25,1)**, so its reverse is **cubic-bezier(.1,.25,1,.25)** and is shown in **Figure 8.6**. This way, our bounce animation can now use **ease** and look even more realistic:

```
@keyframes bounce {
    60%, 80%, to {
        transform: translateY(400px);
        animation-timing-function: ease;
    }
    70% { transform: translateY(300px); }
    90% { transform: translateY(360px); }
}
.ball {
    /* Styling */
    animation: bounce 3s cubic-bezier(.1,.25,1,.25);
}
```

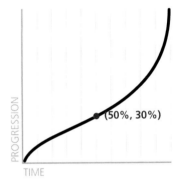

FIGURE 8.6

The reverse timing function for **ease**

Using a graphical tool like **cubic-bezier.com** (**Figure 8.7**) we can experiment further and improve our bounce animation even more.

▶ PLAY!   play.csssecrets.io/**bounce**

Cubic Bézier curves are notoriously hard to specify and understand without a visualization, especially when they are acting as timing functions for a transition; thankfully, there are quite a few online tools for this, such as **cubic-bezier.com** (shown here), made by yours truly

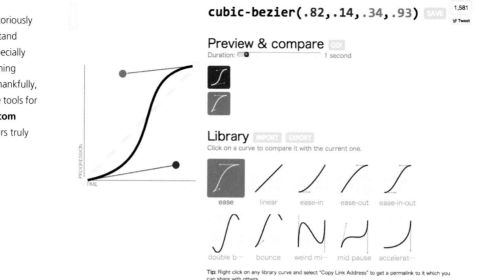

HAT TIP

In the *animate.css* animation library by **Dan Eden** *(daneden.me)*, the timing function used is *cubic-bezier(.215,.61,.355,1)* and *cubic-bezier(.755,.05,.855,.06)* instead of its reverse, which is steeper, for increased realism.

Elastic transitions

Suppose we want to show a callout every time a text field is focused, to supply additional information, such as allowed values. The markup could look like this:

TIP! If you were using a **height** and not a transform to show the callout, you would notice that transitions from **height: 0** (or any other) to **height: auto** do not work, because **auto** is a keyword and cannot be expressed as an animatable value. In those cases, **use max-height instead** with a sufficiently large height.

HTML

```html
<label>
    Your username: <input id="username" />
    <span class="callout">Only letters, numbers,
    underscores (_) and hyphens (-) allowed!</span>
</label>
```

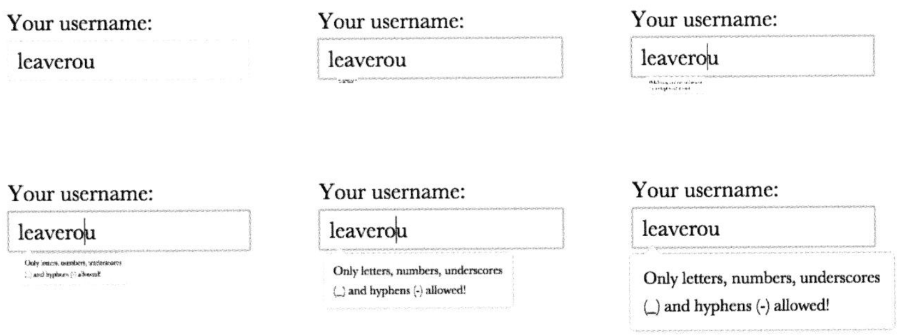

Your username:

leaverou

Your username:

leaverou

Your username:

leaverou

FIGURE 8.8

How our transition looks initially

Your username:

leaverou

Only letters, numbers, underscores
(_) and hyphens (-) allowed!

Your username:

leaverou

Only letters, numbers, underscores
(_) and hyphens (-) allowed!

Your username:

leaverou

Only letters, numbers, underscores
(_) and hyphens (-) allowed!

And the CSS for toggling the display could look like the following (we have omitted everything related to styling or layout):

```css
input:not(:focus) + .callout {
    transform: scale(0);
}


.callout {
    transition: .5s transform;
    transform-origin: 1.4em -.4em;
}
```

As it currently stands, when the user focuses on our text field, there is a half-second transition that looks like **Figure 8.8**. Nothing wrong with that, but it would look more natural and playful if it overshot a bit at the end (e.g., if it grew to 110% its size, and then snapped back to 100%). We can do this by converting the transition to an animation, and applying what we learned in the previous section:

```css
@keyframes elastic-grow {
    from { transform: scale(0); }
    70% {
        transform: scale(1.1);
        animation-timing-function:
            cubic-bezier(.1,.25,1,.25); /* Reverse ease */
```

```
    }
  }

  input:not(:focus) + .callout { transform: scale(0); }

  input:focus + .callout { animation: elastic-grow .5s; }

  .callout { transform-origin: 1.4em -.4em; }
```

If we try it out, we will see that it does indeed work. You can see how it looks in **Figure 8.9** and compare it with the previous transition. However, we've essentially used an animation when we really needed a transition. Animations might be very powerful, but in a case like this where all we needed was to add some elasticity to our transition, it feels a bit overkill, like using a chainsaw to cut ourselves a slice of bread. Is there a way to accomplish something like this with a transition?

The solution lies again in custom **cubic-bezier()** timing functions. So far, we have only discussed curves whose control points were in the 0–1 range. As we mentioned in the previous section, we cannot exceed this range horizontally, although this might change in the future if time machines are ever invented. However, **we are allowed to exceed the 0–1 range vertically** and get our transition to go **below 0% progression** or **above 100%**. Can you guess what that means? It means that if we are moving from a **scale(0)** transform to a **scale(1)** transform, we can make it go further than the final value, and reach values like **scale(1.1)**, or even more, depending on how steep we make the timing function.

FIGURE 8.9

Our UI feels more realistic and playful if we add some elasticity to our transition

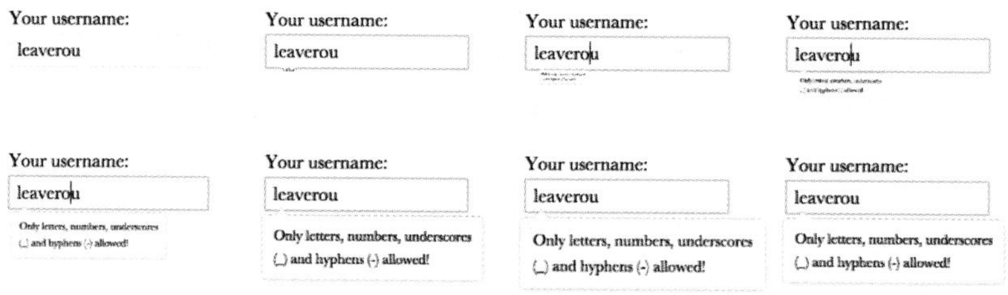

In this case, we only want very little elasticity, so we want our timing function to reach 110% progression (which corresponds to **scale(1.1)**) and then start transitioning back to **100%**. Let's start from the initial **ease** timing function (**cubic-bezier(.25,.1,.25,1)**) and move the second control point toward the top until we reach something like **cubic-bezier(.25,.1,.3,1.5)**. As you can see in **Figure 8.10**, the transition now reaches 100% progression at roughly **50%** of its total duration. However, it does not stop there; it continues moving **past the end value** until it reaches 110% progression at the **70%** time mark and then spends the remaining 30% of its available time transitioning back to the final value, resulting in a transition that is very similar to our animation, but is achieved with only one line of code. For the sake of comparison, our code is now:

```
input:not(:focus) + .callout { transform: scale(0); }

.callout {
    transform-origin: 1.4em -.4em;
    transition: .5s cubic-bezier(.25,.1,.3,1.5);
}
```

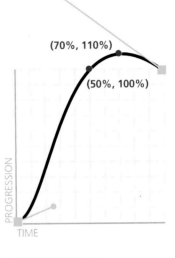

FIGURE 8.10

A custom timing function with vertical coordinates outside the 0–1 range

However, although our transition looks as expected when we focus on the text field and the callout shows up, the results might not be exactly what one would expect when the text field loses focus and the callout shrinks and disappears (**Figure 8.11**). What happened here?! Odd as the result might look, it's actually expected: when we tab out of the input field, the transition that fires has **scale(1)** as its starting value and **scale(0)** as it's final value. Therefore, because the same timing function is applied, the transition will still reach 110% progression after 350ms. Only this time, 110% progression does not translate to **scale(1.1)**, but to **scale(-0.1)**!

Don't give up just yet though, because fixing this issue only adds one more line of code. Assuming we just want a regular **ease** timing function when the callout shrinks, we can do it by overriding the current timing function in the CSS rule that defines its closed state:

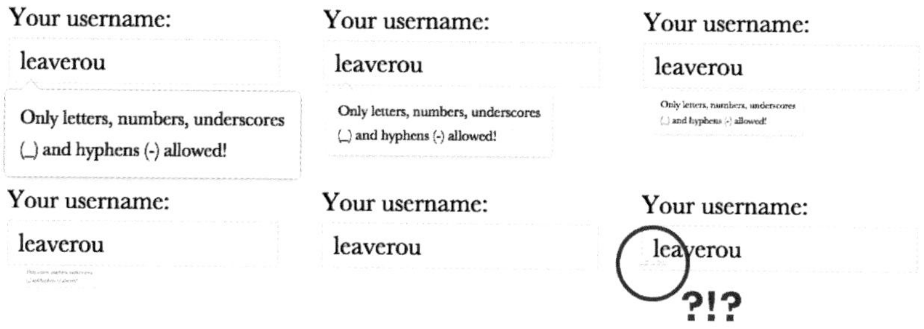

FIGURE 8.11

What happened here?!

Your username:

leaverou

Only letters, numbers, underscores
(_) and hyphens (-) allowed!

Your username:

leaverou

Only letters, numbers, underscores
(_) and hyphens (-) allowed!

Your username:

leaverou

Only letters, numbers, underscores
(_) and hyphens (-) allowed!

Your username:

leaverou

Your username:

leaverou

Your username:

leaverou

?!?

```
input:not(:focus) + .callout {
    transform: scale(0);
    transition-timing-function: ease;
}


.callout {
    transform-origin: 1.4em -.4em;
    transition: .5s cubic-bezier(.25,.1,.3,1.5);
}
```

If you try it again, you will see that it now closes in exactly the same way as it did before our custom **cubic-bezier()** function, but when it opens, it has the nice elastic effect we were going for.

The most vigilant of readers will also notice another issue: **closing the callout feels very slow.** Why is that? Think about it. When it's growing, it reaches **100%** of its final size at **50%** progression (i.e., after **250ms**). However, when it is shrinking, going from 0% to 100% takes up **all of the time** we specified for the transition (500ms), so **it feels half as fast**.

To fix that last issue, we can just override the duration as well, either by using **transition-duration** or by using the **transition** shorthand and overriding everything. If we do the latter, we don't have to explicitly specify **ease**, because it is the initial value:

```
input:not(:focus) + .callout {
    transform: scale(0);
    transition: .25s;
}


.callout {
    transform-origin: 1.4em -.4em;
    transition: .5s cubic-bezier(.25,.1,.3,1.5);
}
```

FIGURE 8.12

An elastic color transition from
■ rgb(100%, 0%, 40%) to
■ gray (rgb(50%, 50%, 50%))
with a timing function of **cubic-
bezier(.25,.1,.2,3)**. Each
RGB coordinate interpolates
individually, so we reach weird colors
like ■ rgb(0%, 100%, 60%).
Check out **play.csssecrets.io/
elastic-color**.

While elastic transitions can be a nice touch in many kinds of transitions (some of which we mentioned in the "The problem" section of this secret), **they are a terrible idea for others**. The typical case where you **don't** want elastic transitions is **colors**. Although elastic transitions on colors can be **quite amusing** (see **Figure 8.12**), they are usually not desirable for a UI.

To guard against accidentally applying elastic transitions to colors, try to **restrict transitions to specific properties**, instead of not specifying any like we did before. When we don't specify any properties in the **transition** shorthand, **transition-property** gets its default value: **all**. This means that **anything that can be transitioned, will be transitioned**. Therefore, if we later add a **background** change on the rule that is applied to open callouts, the elastic transition will now be applied to that too. The final code looks like this:

```
input:not(:focus) + .callout {
```

TIP! Speaking of restricting transitions to specific properties, you can even **queue the transitions** for the different properties, via **transition-delay**, which is the second time value in the **transition** shorthand. For example, if both **width** and **height** are transitioning and you want the height to go first and the width second (an effect popularized by many lightbox scripts), you could do it with something like **transition: .5s height, .8s .5s width;** (i.e., the **delay** of the **width** transition is equal to the duration of the **height** transition).

```
    transform: scale(0);
    transition: .25s transform;
}


.callout {
    transform-origin: 1.4em -.4em;
    transition: .5s cubic-bezier(.25,.1,.3,1.5) transform;
}
```

▶ **PLAY!** play.csssecrets.io/**elastic**

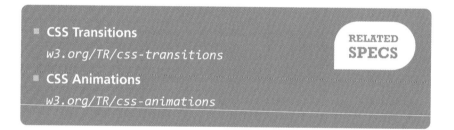

■ **CSS Transitions**
w3.org/TR/css-transitions

■ **CSS Animations**
w3.org/TR/css-animations

RELATED
SPECS

43 Frame-by-frame animations

Prerequisites

Basic CSS animations, the "Elastic transitions" secret on page 294

The problem

Quite often, we need an animation that is difficult or impossible to achieve by transitioning CSS properties on elements. For example, a cartoon moving or a complex progress indicator. In this case, image-based frame-by-frame animations are perfect, but surprisingly challenging to accomplish on the Web in a flexible manner.

At this point, you might be wondering, "Can't we just use animated GIFs?" The answer is yes, for many cases, animated GIFs are perfect. However, they have a few shortcomings that might be a dealbreaker for certain use cases:

- They are limited to a **256 color palette**, **shared across all frames**.

commented line is your dabblet's tit

#f06;
linear-gradient(45deg, #f06, yellow)

FIGURE 8.13

A semi-transparent progress indicator (on **dabblet.com**); this is impossible to achieve with animated GIFs

- They **cannot have alpha transparency**, which can be a big problem when we don't know what will be underneath our animated GIF. For example, this is very common with progress indicators (see **Figure 8.13**).

- There is no way to modify certain aspects from within CSS, such as duration, repetitions, pausing, and so on. Once the GIF is generated, everything is baked into the file and can only be changed by using an image editor and generating another file. This is **great for portability, but not for experimentation**.

Back in 2004, there was an effort by Mozilla to address the first two issues by allowing **frame-by-frame animation in PNG files**, akin to the way we can have both static and animated GIF files. It was called *APNG* and was designed to be backward compatible with non-supporting PNG viewers, by encoding the first frame in the same way as traditional PNG files, so old viewers would at least display that. Promising as it was, APNG never got enough traction and to this day, has very limited browser and image editor support.

For more information about APNG, see **wikipedia.org/wiki/APNG**.

Developers have even used JavaScript to achieve flexible frame-by-frame animations in the browser, by using an image sprite and animating its `background-position` with JS. You can even find small libraries to facilitate this! Is there a straightforward way to achieve this with only nice, readable CSS code?

The solution

Let's assume we have all frames of our animation in a PNG sprite like the one shown in **Figure 8.14**.

FIGURE 8.14
Our spinner's eight frames (dimensions: 800×100)

We also have an element that will hold the loader (don't forget to include some text, for accessibility!), to which we have already applied the dimensions of a single frame:

```html
<div class="loader">Loading…</div>
```

```css
.loader {
    width: 100px; height: 100px;

    background: url(img/loader.png) 0 0;

    /* Hide text */
    text-indent: 200%;
    white-space: nowrap;
    overflow: hidden;
}
```

Currently, the result looks like **Figure 8.15**: the first frame is displayed, but there is no animation. However, if we play with different **background-position** values, we will notice that **-100px 0** gives us the second frame, **-200px 0** gives us the third frame, and so on. Our first thought could be to apply an animation like this:

FIGURE 8.15

The first frame of our loader shows, but there is no animation yet

```css
@keyframes loader {
    to { background-position: -800px 0; }
}

.loader {
    width: 100px; height: 100px;
    background: url(img/loader.png) 0 0;
    animation: loader 1s infinite linear;

    /* Hide text */
    text-indent: 200%;
    white-space: nowrap;
    overflow: hidden;
}
```

However, as you can see in the following stills (taken every 167ms), this doesn't really work:

FIGURE 8.16

Our initial attempt for a frame-by-frame animation failed, as we did not need interpolation between keyframes

It might seem like we're going nowhere, but we are actually very close to the solution. The secret here is to use the **steps()** timing function, instead of a Bézier-based one.

"The what timing function?!" you might ask. As we saw in the previous chapter, all Bézier-based timing functions interpolate between keyframes to give us smooth transitions. This is great; usually, smooth transitions are exactly the reason we are using CSS transitions or animations. However, in this case, **this smoothness is destroying our sprite animation**.

Very unlike Bézier timing functions, **steps()** **divides the whole animation in frames** by the number of steps you specify and **abruptly switches between them** with no interpolation. Usually this kind of abruptness is undesirable, so **steps()** is not talked about much. As far as CSS timing functions go, Bézier-based ones are the popular kids that get invited to all the parties and **steps()** is the ugly duckling that nobody wants to have lunch with, sadly. However, in this case, it's exactly what we need. Once we convert our animation to the following, our loader suddenly starts working the way we wanted it to:

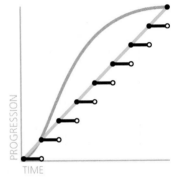

PROGRESSION

TIME

FIGURE 8.17

A comparison of **steps(8)**, linear and the default timing function, ease

```
animation: loader 1s infinite steps(8);
```

Keep in mind that **steps()** also accepts an optional second parameter, **start** or **end** (default) that specifies when the switch happens on every interval (see **Figure 8.17** for the default behavior of **end**), but that is rarely needed. If we only need a single step, there are also shortcuts: **step-start** and **step-end**, which are equivalent to **steps(1, start)** and **steps(1, end)**, respectively.

 ▸ PLAY! `play.csssecrets.io/`**frame-by-frame**

HAT TIP

*Hat tip to **Simurai** (simurai.com/) for coming up with this useful technique in **Sprite sheet animation with steps()** (simurai.com/blog/ 2012/12/03/step-animation).*

■ **CSS Animations**
w3.org/TR/css-animations

RELATED
SPECS

44 Blinking

Prerequisites

Basic CSS animations, the "Frame-by-frame animations" secret on page 308

The problem

Remember the old `<blink>` tag? Of course you do. It has become a cultural symbol in our industry, reminding us of the humble, clumsy beginnings of our discipline, and always willing to serve as an inside joke between old-timers. It is universally despised, both because it violated separation of structure and style, but mainly because its overuse made it a pain for anyone browsing the Web in the late 90s. Even its own inventor, Lou Montulli, has said *"[I consider] the blink tag to be the worst thing I've ever done for the Internet."*

However, now that the nightmare of the `<blink>` tag is long behind us, we sometimes still find ourselves needing a blinking animation. It feels weird at first, a bit like discovering some sort of strange perversion inside us that we never knew we had. The identity crisis stops when we realize that there are a few use cases in which blinking can **enhance usability, rather than reduce it**.

A common UX pattern is blinking a few times (no more than three!) to indicate that a change has been applied somewhere in the UI or to highlight the current link target (the element whose id matches the URL **#hash**). Used in such a limited way, blinking can be very effective to draw the user's attention to an area, but due to the limited number of iterations, it doesn't have the adverse effects the `<blink>` tag did. Another way to keep the good of blinking (directing user attention) without the bad (distracting, annoying, seizure inducing) is to "smoothe" it out (i.e., instead of alternating between an abrupt "on" and "off" state, to have a smooth progression between the two).

However, how do we implement all this? The CSS-only replacement for the `<blink>` tag, `text-decoration: blink`, is too limited to allow us to do what we want, and even if it was powerful enough, its browser support is very poor. Can we use CSS animations for this, or is JS our only hope?

The solution

There are actually multiple ways to use CSS animations to achieve any kind of blinking: on the whole element (via **opacity**), on the text color (via **color**), on its border (via **border-color**), and so on. In the rest of this section, we will assume that we want to blink the text only, as that is the most common use case. However, the solution for other parts of an element is analogous.

Achieving a smooth blink is rather easy. Our first attempt would probably look like this:

```
@keyframes blink-smooth { to { color: transparent } }

.highlight { animation: 1s blink-smooth 3; }
```

This *almost* works. Our text smoothly fades from its text color to transparent, however it then **abruptly jumps back** to the original text color. Plotting the change of text color over time helps us figure out why this happens (**Figure 8.18**).

FIGURE 8.18

The progression of our text color over three seconds (three iterations)

This might actually be desirable. In that case, we are done! However, when we want the blinking to be smooth both when the text fades out and when it fades in, we have a bit more work to do. One way to achieve this would be by changing the keyframes to make the switch happen in the middle of each iteration:

```
@keyframes blink-smooth { 50% { color: transparent } }

.highlight {
    animation: 1s blink-smooth 3;
}
```

This looks like the result we wanted. However, although it doesn't show in this particular animation (because it's difficult to differentiate between timing functions with color/opacity transitions), it's important to keep in mind that the animation is accelerating both when it fades in and when it fades out, which could look unnatural for certain animations (e.g., pulsating animations). In that case, we can pull a different tool out of our toolbox: **animation-direction**.

The only purpose of **animation-direction** is to reverse either all iterations (**reverse**), every even one (**alternate**) or every odd one (**alternate-reverse**). What is great about it is that **it also reverses the timing function**, creating far more realistic animations. We could try it on our blinking element like so:

```
@keyframes blink-smooth { to { color: transparent } }
```

```
.highlight {
    animation: .5s blink-smooth 6 alternate;
}
```

Note that we had to double the number of iterations (instead of the duration, like the previous method), as now one fade-in/fade-out pair consists
of two iterations. For the same reason, we also cut **animation-duration**
in half.

FIGURE 8.19

All four values of **animation-
direction** and their effect on a
color animation from **black** to
transparent over three iterations

If we want a smooth blink animation, we're done at this point. However,
what if we want a classic one? How do we go about it? Our first attempt
might look like this:

```
@keyframes blink { to { color: transparent } }

.highlight {
    animation: 1s blink 3 steps(1);
}
```

However, this will fail spectacularly: absolutely nothing will happen.
The reason is that **steps(1)** is essentially equivalent to **steps(1,
end)**, which means that the transition between the current color and
transparent will happen in one step, and **the value switch will occur
at the end (Figure 8.20)**. Therefore, **we will see the start value for the
entire length of the animation, except one infinitesimally short point**

PROGRESSION

TIME

FIGURE 8.20

What **steps(1)** actually does to our animation

in time at the end. If we change it to **steps(1, start)** the opposite will happen: the switch will occur at the start, so we will only see transparent text, with no animation or blinking.

A logical next step would be to try **steps(2)** in both its flavors (start and end). Now we do see some blinking, but it's between semi-transparent text and transparent or semi-transparent and normal respectively, for the same reason. Unfortunately, because we cannot configure **steps()** to make the switch in the middle, but only at the start and end, the only solution here would be to adjust the animation keyframes to make the switch at **50%**, like we did earlier:

```
@keyframes blink { 50% { color: transparent } }

.highlight {
    animation: 1s blink 3 steps(1); /* or step-end */
}
```

This finally works! Who would have guessed that a classic abrupt blink would have been harder to accomplish than a modern, smooth one? CSS never ceases to surprise….

▶ PLAY!   play.csssecrets.io/**blink**

■ **CSS Animations**
  w3.org/TR/css-animations

RELATED
SPECS

45 Typing animation

The problem

Sometimes we want to make text appear one by one character, to simulate typing. This effect is especially popular on tech websites, using monospace fonts to resemble a terminal command prompt. Used right, it can really contribute to the rest of the design.

Usually, this is done with long, hacky, complicated JS code. Even though this is pure presentation, using CSS for this kind of effect seems like a pipe dream. Or could it be possible?

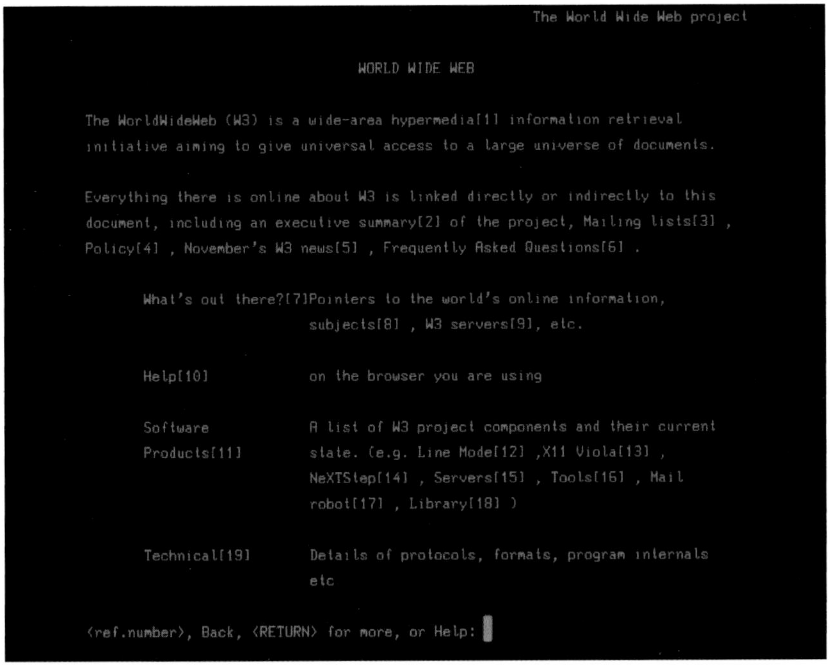

FIGURE 8.21

We used a variation of this kind of animation at CERN, when creating a **web-based simulation of the first line mode browser** *(Line-mode.cern.ch)*

The solution

The main idea is to **animate the width** of the element that contains our text from **0** to its content width one by one character. You might have already realized what the limitation of this approach is: **it will not work for multiline text**. Thankfully, most of the time, you only want to use such styling on single-line text anyway, such as headings.

Another thing to keep in mind is that **every animation effect has diminishing returns as its duration increases**: short duration animations make an interface appear more polished and in some cases can even improve usability. However, the longer the duration of the animation, the more it starts becoming annoying for the user. Therefore, **even if the technique could be used on longer, multiline text, in most cases that would not be a good idea**.

Let's get started with the code! Assume we want to apply this to a top-level heading (**<h1>**) that we've already styled with monospace text, and that looks like the following:

Theoretically, we could make this work for multiline text, but it would involve wrapping each line in its own element and maintaining the appropriate animation delays (i.e., it's the kind of solution that is worse than the problem).

CSS is awesome!

FIGURE 8.22

Our starting point

```html
<h1>CSS is awesome!</h1>
```
HTML

We can easily add an animation that goes from **0** to the final width of the heading, like so:

```css
@keyframes typing {
    from { width: 0 }
}

h1 {
    width: 7.7em; /* Width of text */
    animation: typing 8s;
}
```

**CSS
is
awesome!**

**CSS is
awesome!**

CSS is awesome!

FIGURE 8.23

Our first attempt at a typing animation does not resemble typing at all

CSS

CSS is aw

CSS is aweson

FIGURE 8.24

Our second attempt is closer, but still not quite there

It makes perfect sense, right? However, as you can see in **Figure 8.23**, it's a trainwreck that has nothing to do with what we wanted.

You might have guessed what the problems are. First, we forgot to apply **white-space: nowrap;** to prevent text wrapping, so as the width grows, its number of lines changes. Second, we forgot to apply **overflow: hidden;**, so there is no clipping. If we fix these issues, the real issues with our animation get uncovered (**Figure 8.24**). Namely:

- The obvious problem is that the animation is smooth instead of revealing the text character by character.

- The less obvious problem is that so far we have been specifying the width in **em**s, which is better than doing it in pixels, but still suboptimal. Where did this **7.7** come from? How do we calculate it?

We can fix the first issue by using **steps()**, just like in the **"Frame-by-frame animations" secret on page 308** and the **"Blinking" secret on page 314**. Unfortunately, the number of steps we need is the number of characters in our string, which is difficult to maintain or downright impossible for dynamic text. However, we will see later on that we can automate this with a tiny snippet of JavaScript code.

The second issue could be alleviated by using the **ch** unit. The **ch** unit is one of the new units introduced in **CSS Values and Units Level 3** *(w3.org/TR/css3-values)*, and represents the width of the "0" glyph. It's one of the most unknown new units, because in most cases, we don't care about sizing things relative to the width of the 0 glyph. However, monospace fonts are special. **In monospace fonts, the width of the "0" glyph is the same as the width of every glyph.** Therefore, the width in **ch** is the number of characters: **15** in our example.

Let's put all this together:

```css
@keyframes typing {
    from { width: 0; }
}

h1 {
    width: 15ch; /* Width of text */
    overflow: hidden;
    white-space: nowrap;
    animation: typing 6s steps(15);
}
```

As you can see in the frames in **Figure 8.25**, now we finally got the expected result: our text is revealed character by character. However, it still doesn't look realistic. Can you spot what's missing?

The last touch that will make this way more realistic is adding a **blinking caret**. We have already seen how to create blinking animations in the **"Blinking" secret on page 314**. In this case, we could either implement the caret via a pseudo-element, and use **opacity** for the blinking, or we could save our limited pseudo-elements in case we need them for something else, and use a right border instead:

CS

CSS is a

CSS is aweso

FIGURE 8.25

Now the text is revealed character by character, but something is still missing

```css
@keyframes typing {
    from { width: 0 }
}
```

```
@keyframes caret {
    50% { border-color: transparent; }
}


h1 {
    width: 15ch; /* Width of text */
    overflow: hidden;
    white-space: nowrap;
    border-right: .05em solid;
    animation: typing 6s steps(15),
               caret 1s steps(1) infinite;
}
```

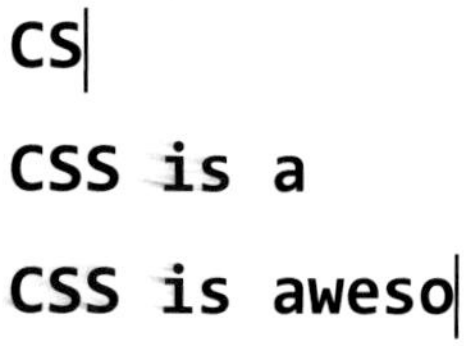

CS|

CSS is a

CSS is aweso|

FIGURE 8.26

Our animation is now complete with
a realistic blinking caret

Note that unlike the text revealing animation, the caret needs to blink indefinitely (even after all of the text has been revealed), hence the **infinite** keyword. Also, we did not have to specify a border color, as we want it to automatically get the text color. You can see a few stills from the result on **Figure 8.26**.

Now our animation works perfectly, although it's still not very maintainable: it requires setting different styles on every heading, depending on the number of characters in the content, and having to update them every time we edit said content. This is exactly the kind of task that JS is perfect for:

```
$$('h1').forEach(function(h1) {
    var len = h1.textContent.length, s = h1.style;

    s.width = len + 'ch';
    s.animationTimingFunction = "steps("+len+"),steps(1)";
});
```

Just with these few lines of JS we can now have our cake and eat it too: our animation is not only realistic, but maintainable as well!

All this is nice and dandy, but what happens with browsers that don't support CSS animations? They will essentially drop all animation-related stuff, so they will only read this:

```css
h1 {
    width: 15ch; /* Width of text */
    overflow: hidden;
    white-space: nowrap;
    border-right: .05em solid;
}
```

CSS is awesome!|

CSS is awesome!

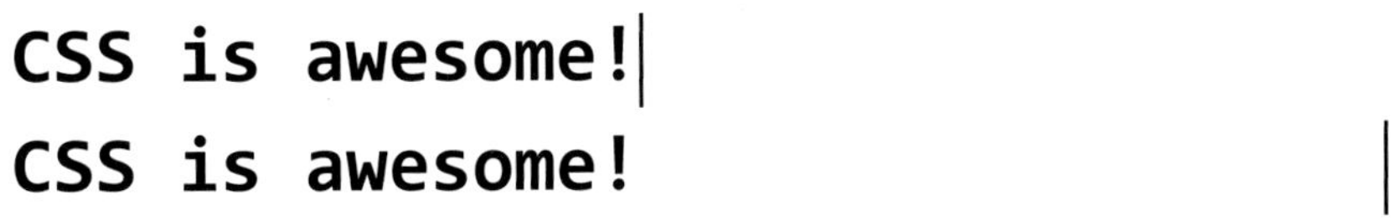

FIGURE 8.27

The potential fallbacks for browsers with no CSS animation support (**top:** with **ch** unit support, **bottom:** without **ch** unit support)

Depending on whether or not they support the **ch** unit, they will see one of the fallbacks in **Figure 8.27**. If you want to avoid the bottom one, you can provide a fallback in **em** units as well. If you do not want a non-blinking caret in your fallback, you could change the caret animation to include the border in the keyframes, so that when it's dropped you only get an invisible transparent border, like so:

```css
@keyframes caret {
    50% { border-color: currentColor; }
}

h1 {
    /* ... */
    border-right: .05em solid transparent;
    animation: typing 6s steps(15),
               caret 1s steps(1) infinite;
}
```

This is pretty much as good as fallbacks get: in older browsers, there is no animation, but nothing breaks at all and the text is perfectly accessible and even styled the same way.

▶ **PLAY!** play.csssecrets.io/**typing**

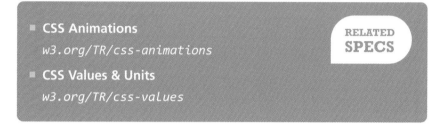

- **CSS Animations**
  w3.org/TR/css-animations
- **CSS Values & Units**
  w3.org/TR/css-values

RELATED
SPECS

46 Smooth state animations

Prerequisites

Basic CSS animations, **animation-direction** (briefly mentioned in the "Blinking" secret on page 314)

The problem

Animations do not always start on page load. More often than not, we want to use **animations in response to a user action**, such as hovering over an element or holding the mouse down on it (`:active`). In that case, we might not have control over the actual number of iterations, as user activity might force the animation to stop before it gets a chance to finish the number of iterations we have specified. For example, the user might trigger a fancy `:hover` animation and mouse out of the element before the animation finishes. What do you expect should happen in these cases?

If you answered something along the lines of *"the animation should stay at its current state"* or *"it should smoothly transition to the pre-animation state"* you are in for a nasty surprise. By default, the animation

FIGURE 8.28

I finally decided to find a solution to this problem when working on a simple one-page website as a birthday gift for my friend **Julian** (`juliancheal.co.uk`). Notice the circular picture on the right. The image file I had was actually landscape. The circle crops its right part, but when the user hovers over it, it slowly starts scrolling to the left, revealing the cropped part. By default, when the user moved their cursor away, it abruptly snapped back to its original position, which made the UI feel broken. Because this was a tiny website, and this picture the centerpiece, I decided I couldn't turn a blind eye to the issue.

will just **stop and abruptly jump back to the pre-animation state**. This might sometimes be acceptable in the case of very subtle animations. However, in most cases it just results in very choppy user experience. Can we change this behavior?

This is yet another reason to use transitions when possible. Instead of abruptly jumping to the pre-animation state, **transitions play in reverse** to smoothly transition back to the original value.

The solution

Assume we have a very long landscape photo, such as the one in **Figure 8.29**, but the space we have available to display it is a 150 × 150 pixel square. One way to solve the problem is animation: show the left edge of the image by default, and make it scroll to reveal the rest when the user

FIGURE 8.29

The entire **naxos-greece.jpg** image file, used in the examples throughout this secret (photo taken by **Chris Hutchison**)

is interacting with it (e.g., hovering over it). We will use a single element for the image and animate its background position:

```
.panoramic {
    width: 150px; height: 150px;
    background: url("img/naxos-greece.jpg");
    background-size: auto 100%;
}
```

Currently, it looks like **Figure 8.30** and there is no animation or interactivity. If we experiment however, we can see that manually changing **background-position** from the original **0 0** to **100% 0** scrolls through the entire image. We just found our keyframes!

FIGURE 8.30

Our image is cropped

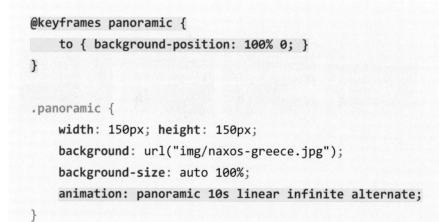

```
@keyframes panoramic {
    to { background-position: 100% 0; }
}

.panoramic {
    width: 150px; height: 150px;
    background: url("img/naxos-greece.jpg");
    background-size: auto 100%;
    animation: panoramic 10s linear infinite alternate;
}
```

This works great. It sort of resembles a panoramic view and it almost feels like being in the place and looking left or right. However, the animation is triggered on page load, which could be **distracting** in the context of, for example, a travel web page, where the user might be trying to focus on reading the text about Naxos, instead of looking at the beautiful panoramic picture. It would be better to **enable the animation when the user hovers over the image**. So, our first thought would be this:

```
.panoramic {
    width: 150px; height: 150px;
    background: url("img/naxos-greece.jpg");
    background-size: auto 100%;
}


.panoramic:hover, .panoramic:focus {
    animation: panoramic 10s linear infinite alternate;
}
```

This does work as expected when we hover over the image: it starts from the initial state of showing the leftmost part of the image and slowly scrolls to reveal the right part of it. However, when we mouse out, it abruptly jumps to the left position again (**Figure 8.31**). We've just stumbled on the problem this secret is about!

FIGURE 8.31

Mousing over is very smooth, but mousing out is abrupt and feels broken

To fix this, we need to think differently about what we are trying to achieve here. What we need is not to apply an animation on :hover, as this implies no memory of its previous position. What we need is to **pause it when there is no :hover happening**. Thankfully, we have a property just for the purpose of pausing an existing animation: animation-play-state!

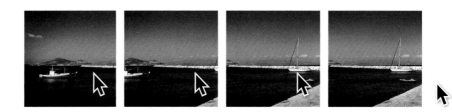

Therefore, we are going to apply our original animation to .panoramic, but have it paused initially, until :hover applies. Because it's no longer a matter of applying and canceling an animation, but just **pausing and resuming an existing animation**, there is **no abrupt rewinding**. The final code looks like this and you can see the result in **Figure 8.32**:

```css
@keyframes panoramic {
    to { background-position: 100% 0; }
}


.panoramic {
    width: 150px; height: 150px;
    background: url("img/naxos-greece.jpg");
    background-size: auto 100%;
    animation: panoramic 10s linear infinite alternate;
    animation-play-state: paused;
}


.panoramic:hover, .panoramic:focus {
    animation-play-state: running;
}
```

47 Animation along a circular path

FIGURE 8.33

Google+ uses animation on a circular path to show that a new member was added to a "circle"

The problem

A few years ago, back when basic CSS animations were still new and exciting, **Chris Coyier** *(css-tricks.com)* asked me if I could think of any way to animate an element on a circular path with CSS animations. At the time, it was just a fun CSS exercise, but in the future I stumbled on many real use cases. For example, Google+ uses such an animation when a new member is added to a circle with more than 11 members: the existing avatars animate on a circular path to make space for the new one.

A different, fun example can be seen on the popular Russian tech website **habrahabr.ru** (**Figure 8.34**). As is often a good practice with 404 pages, it offers a navigation menu to a few main areas of the website.

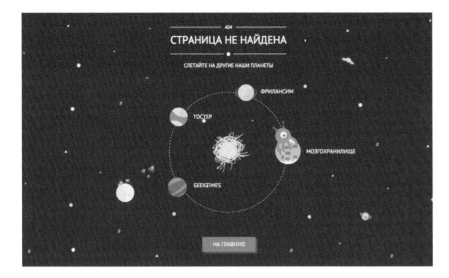

FIGURE 8.34

The 404 page of popular Russian
tech website *habrahabr.ru*

However, each menu item is presented as a planet orbiting on a circle and the text above reads "Fly to other planets of our universe." Of course, it makes sense to just move the planets on a circular path and not also rotate them, which would make their text almost impossible to read.

These are only a few out of many possible examples. But how can we achieve such an effect with CSS animations?

We are going to work on a very simple example of an avatar animating on a circular path, a bit like a simplified version of the aforementioned Google+ effect. The markup would look like this:

HTML

```html
<div class="path">
    <img src="lea.jpg" class="avatar" />
</div>
```

Before we start thinking about our animation, we will apply some basic styling to it (sizes, backgrounds, margins, etc.), so that it looks like **Figure 8.35**. Because this styling is pretty basic, it is not included here, but if you are having difficulty with it, you can find it in the live example. The main thing to keep in mind is that the diameter of the path is **300px**, ergo the radius is **150px**.

After we're done with basic styling, we can start thinking about our animation. We want to move the avatar in a circle, along the orange path.

If you're unsure about how to make circular *shapes* with CSS, take a look at the **"Flexible ellipses" secret on page 76**.

FIGURE 8.35

Our starting point, after applying some basic styling—now we can get our hands dirty with some CSS animation!

How could we possibly use CSS animations to do this? When presented with this problem, some are quick to reply with something like this:

```css
@keyframes spin {
    to { transform: rotate(1turn); }
}


.avatar {
    animation: spin 3s infinite linear;
    transform-origin: 50% 150px; /* 150px = path radius */
}
```

While this is a step in the right direction, it does not only move the avatar on a circular path, it also rotates it around itself (**Figure 8.36**). For example, notice how when the avatar is halfway through, it is also upside down. If it had text, the text would also be upside down, which can be quite a readability issue. We only wanted it to **move *along* the circle**, while still maintaining **the same orientation relative to itself**.

FIGURE 8.36

A few stills from our failed attempt at animating on a circular path

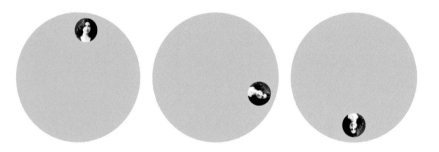

Back then, neither me nor Chris could think of a reasonable way. The best way we could come up with was specifying multiple keyframes to approximate a circle, which is obviously not a good idea by any possible definition of one. There must be a better way, right?

Two element solution

I finally came up with a solution to Chris' challenge a few months later, after thinking about the problem as a background process for quite some time. The main idea behind this solution is the same as in the **"Parallelograms" secret on page 84** or the **"Diamond images" secret on page 90**: **nested transforms canceling each other**. However, instead of doing this statically, in this case it happens on **every single frame of the animation**. The caveat is that, just like the aforementioned secrets, this requires two elements. Therefore, we need to amend our original clean HTML with an extra wrapper div:

```html
<div class="path">
    <div class="avatar">
        <img src="lea.jpg" />
    </div>
</div>
```

Let's apply the initial animation we tried earlier to the `.avatar` wrapper. Now, as we've seen in **Figure 8.36**, this doesn't work because it also rotates the element itself. But what if we applied **another rotation** to the avatar, and **rotate it around itself by the same amount of degrees in the opposite direction**? Then the two rotations would cancel each other, and we would only see the circular movement created by the difference in transform origins!

There is one problem though: we don't have a static rotation that we can cancel, but an animation that goes through a range of angles. For example, if it was **60deg**, we would cancel it with **-60deg** (or **300deg**), if it was **70deg** we would cancel it with **-70deg** (or **290deg**). But now that it's anything between **0-360deg** (or **0-1turn**, which is the same thing), what do we cancel it with? The answer is much easier than it might seem. We just animate over the reverse range (**360-0deg**), like so:

```css
@keyframes spin {
    to { transform: rotate(1turn); }
}
@keyframes spin-reverse {
    from { transform: rotate(1turn); }
}


.avatar {
    animation: spin 3s infinite linear;
    transform-origin: 50% 150px; /* 150px = path radius */
}


.avatar > img {
    animation: spin-reverse 3s infinite linear;
}
```

Now, at any point, when the first animation is rotated by **x** degrees, the second one is rotated by **360 – x** degrees, because one of them is increasing and the other is decreasing. This is exactly what we wanted and as you can see in **Figure 8.37**, it produces the desired effect.

The code, however, could use some improvement. For one, we are repeating all parameters of the animation twice. If we need to adjust its duration, we would need to do it twice, which is not very DRY. We can easily solve this by inheriting all animation properties from the parent, and overriding the animation name:

FIGURE 8.37

We have now achieved the animation we wanted, but the code is unwieldy

```css
@keyframes spin {
    to { transform: rotate(1turn); }
}
@keyframes spin-reverse {
    from { transform: rotate(1turn); }
}


.avatar {
    animation: spin 3s infinite linear;
    transform-origin: 50% 150px; /* 150px = path radius */
}


.avatar > img {
    animation: inherit;
    animation-name: spin-reverse;
}
```

However, we shouldn't need a whole new animation just to reverse our initial one. Remember the **animation-direction** property from the **"Blinking" secret on page 314**? In that secret, we saw why the **alternate** value is useful. Here we are going to use the **reverse** value, to get a **reversed copy of our original animation**, thus eliminating the need for a second one:

```css
@keyframes spin {
    to { transform: rotate(1turn); }
}

.avatar {
    animation: spin 3s infinite linear;
    transform-origin: 50% 150px; /* 150px = path radius */
}

.avatar > img {
```

```
      animation: inherit;
      animation-direction: reverse;
  }
```

And there we go! It might not be ideal, due to the extra element requirement, but we've achieved a rather complex animation, with fewer than 10 lines of CSS!

> ▶ **PLAY!**   play.csssecrets.io/**circular-2elements**

Single element solution

You can read the whole discussion at **lists.w3.org/Archives/Public/ www-style/2012Feb/0201.html**.

The technique described in the previous section works, but is suboptimal, as it requires HTML modifications. When I first came up with that technique, I wrote to the mailing list of the CSS Working Group (of which I was not a part of, at the time) and suggested that it should be possible to specify multiple transform origins for the same element. That should make it possible to implement something like this with a single element, and it seemed like a reasonable thing to ask for in general.

The discussion was in high gear, when at some point **Aryeh Gregor**, one of the editors of the CSS Transforms specification at the time, made a statement that seemed confusing at first:

> *"**transform-origin** is just syntactic sugar. You should always be able to use **translate()** instead."*
>
> — Aryeh Gregor

However, it turns out that every **transform-origin** can be simulated with two **translate()** transforms. For example, the following two code snippets are equivalent:

```
transform: rotate(30deg);
transform-origin: 200px 300px;
```

```
transform: translate(200px, 300px)
           rotate(30deg)
           translate(-200px, -300px);
transform-origin: 0 0;
```

This seems strange at first, but becomes more clear if we keep in mind that **transform functions are not independent**. Each of them doesn't just transform the element it is applied on, **it transforms the entire coordinate system of that element**, thus affecting all transforms that come after it. **This is exactly why transform order matters**, and different orderings of the same transforms can produce entirely different results. If this is still unclear, **Figure 8.38** should help eliminate any confusion.

Therefore, we can use the same **transform-origin** for both our previous animations by using this idea (we are going to use separate animations again as their keyframes are now completely different):

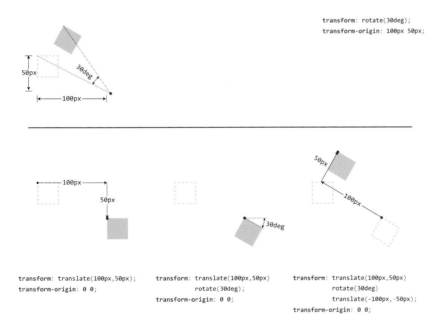

FIGURE 8.38

How we can substitute a transform origin with two translations. The red dot represents the transform origin each time. Top: Using **transform-origin**. Bottom: Using two translations, step by step.

```css
@keyframes spin {
    from {
        transform: translate(50%, 150px)
                   rotate(0turn)
                   translate(-50%, -150px);
    }
    to {
        transform: translate(50%, 150px)
                   rotate(1turn)
                   translate(-50%, -150px);
    }
}
@keyframes spin-reverse {
    from {
        transform: translate(50%,50%)
                   rotate(1turn)
                   translate(-50%,-50%);
    }
    to {
        transform: translate(50%,50%)
                   rotate(0turn)
                   translate(-50%, -50%);
    }
}

.avatar {
    animation: spin 3s infinite linear;
}

.avatar > img {
    animation: inherit;
    animation-name: spin-reverse;
}
```

This looks awfully unwieldy, but do not worry, as we will improve it a lot by the end of this section. Notice that we now no longer have different transform origins, which was the only reason we needed two elements and two animations earlier. Now that everything uses the same origin, we can combine the two animations into one and only work with `.avatar`:

```css
@keyframes spin {
    from {
        transform: translate(50%, 150px)
                    rotate(0turn)
                    translate(-50%, -150px)
                    translate(50%,50%)
                    rotate(1turn)
                    translate(-50%,-50%)
    }
    to {
        transform: translate(50%, 150px)
                    rotate(1turn)
                    translate(-50%, -150px)
                    translate(50%,50%)
                    rotate(0turn)
                    translate(-50%, -50%);
    }
}

.avatar { animation: spin 3s infinite linear; }
```

The code is definitely improving, but is still long and confusing. Can we make it a bit more concise? There are a few potential improvements.

The low-hanging fruit is to combine consecutive **translate()** transforms, specifically **translate(-50%, -150px)** and **translate(50%, 50%)**. Unfortunately, percentages and absolute lengths cannot be combined (unless we use **calc()** which is also quite unwieldy). However, the horizontal translations cancel each other, so we basically have two translations on the Y axis (**translateY(-150px) translateY(50%)**). Also,

Note that we don't need two HTML elements anymore: we can just apply the **avatar** class to the image itself, as we're not styling them separately any longer.

because the rotations cancel each other, we can remove the horizontal translations before and after as well and combine the vertical ones. We currently have these keyframes:

```
@keyframes spin {
    from {
        transform: translateY(150px) translateY(-50%)
                   rotate(0turn)
                   translateY(-150px) translateY(50%)
                   rotate(1turn);


    }
    to {
        transform: translateY(150px) translateY(-50%)
                   rotate(1turn)
                   translateY(-150px) translateY(50%)
                   rotate(0turn);
    }
}

.avatar { animation: spin 3s infinite linear; }
```

This is a bit shorter and less repetitive, but still not great. Can we do any better? If we **start from the avatar in the center** of the circle (like in **Figure 8.39**), we can eliminate the first two translations, which essentially just place it at the center. Then the animation becomes:

```
@keyframes spin {
    from {
        transform: rotate(0turn)
                   translateY(-150px) translateY(50%)
                   rotate(1turn);
    }
    to {
```

```
        transform: rotate(1turn)
                   translateY(-150px) translateY(50%)
                   rotate(0turn);
    }
}

.avatar { animation: spin 3s infinite linear; }
```

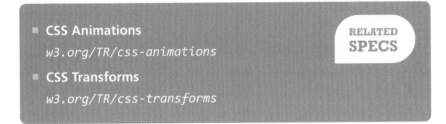

FIGURE 8.39

If we center the avatar as the starting point, our keyframes become a bit shorter; however, note that this state will also be our fallback in case animations are not supported, which may or may not be desirable

This seems to be the best we can do today. It's not the DRY-est possible code, but it's quite short. There is now **minimal repetition and no redundant HTML elements**. To make it completely DRY and avoid repeating the path radius, we could use a preprocessor, which is left as an exercise for the reader.

▸ PLAY!   play.csssecrets.io/**circular**

- **CSS Animations**
  w3.org/TR/css-animations
- **CSS Transforms**
  w3.org/TR/css-transforms

RELATED
SPECS

Index

automatic table layout algorithm, **266**

hyphens: auto, **169**

I

image comparison, interactive, **250-259**
    CSS resize method for, **251-254**
    range input method for, **255-259**
image, as border, **68**
infinite (keyword), **324**
inherit (keyword), **13**
inheritance, **13**
inline SVG, **102-105**, **211**
inner border radius, **100**
inner rounding (borders), **36-38**
interactive image comparison, **250-259**
intrinsic sizing, **262-264**
irregular drop shadows, **134-137**

J

Jacobs, Ian, **5**
JavaScript
    for frame-by-frame animation, **309**
    for typing animation, **324**
justification, text, **168**
justify-content, **286**

K

Knuth-Pass algorithm, **169**
Komarov, Roman, **249**

L

latency, **20**
Law of Leaky Abstractions, **20**
layout, **262-292**
    fluid backgrounds with fixed content, **276-279**
    intrinsic sizing, **262-264**
    sticky footers, **288-292**
    styling by sibling count, **270-275**
    table column widths, **266-268**
    vertical centering, **280-286**

least common multiple (LCM), for (pseudo)random backgrounds, **64**
letterpress effect, **201**
Lie, Håkon Wium, **5**
ligatures, **184-186**
Lilley, Chris, **5**
line breaks, inserting, **172-177**
linear gradient
    and grids, **52**
    and striped backgrounds, **41**
    for cutout corners, **97**
lines, text, zebra-striped, **178-181**
local() function, **190**
longhands, **18**

M

maintainability, brevity vs., **12**
marching ants border, **72**
margin: auto, **277**, **285**
max-width, **264**
McClellan, Drew, **193**
media queries, **15-17**
Meyer, Eric, **66**
min-content (keyword), **263**
mix-blend mode, **141**
modal dialog, **238**
Montulli, Lou, **314**
mouse pointer, **218**
Mozilla, **309**
multiple borders, **28-30**
    box-shadow for, **29**
    outlines for, **30**

N

negative animation delays, **119-121**
nested elements, for parallelograms, **85**
nested transforms, **337**

not-allowed cursor, **220**

O

one-sided shadows, **130-133**
optical illusions, **15**, **200**
outline-offset, **30**
outlines, for multiple borders, **30**
overflow: hidden, **116**, **152**
overflow: visible, **213**

P

parallelograms, **84-87**
pattern, as border, **68**
pie charts
    SVG solution for, **122-128**
    transform-based solution for, **115**
pie charts, simple, **114-128**
PNG sprite animation, **309-312**
polka dot backgrounds, **53**
polygon(), for diamond images, **93**
position: relative/absolute, **86**
preprocessors, **19-22**
    for complex background patterns, **50**
    for folded-corner effect, **165**
prerequisites, **xxv**
prime numbers, for (pseudo)random backgrounds, **65**
pseudo-elements
    for dimming, **236**
    for parallelograms, **86**
    for pie charts, **116**, **117**
    for trapezoids, **110**
    mouse interaction capture by, **226**
Pythagorean theorem, **160**
    and inner-rounded borders, **38**
    and striped backgrounds, **44**

for curved cutout corners, **103**

Q

quarter ellipses, **81**

R

radial gradients
    for curved cutout corners, **100**
    for polka dots, **53**
random backgrounds, **62-65**
readability, justification and, **168**
repeating-linear-gradient(), **45-47**
repeating-radial-gradient(), **45**
resize, for interactive image comparison, **251-254**
Responsive Web Design (RWD), **15-17**
rotate() transform
    for animation along circular path, **337-340**
    for diamond images, **91**
    for parallelograms, **87**
    for pie charts, **117**
rounding, inner (borders), **36-38**

S

Saly, Martijn, **105**
saturate () filter, **139**
scale() transform
    for diamond images, **92**
    for elastic transitions, **302**
scrolling, **244-249**
Seddon, Ryan, **231**
shadows
    irregular drop, **134-137**
    on one side, **130-132**
    on two adjacent sides, **132**
    on two opposite sides, **133**
    one-sided, **130-133**
shapes, **76-128**
    cutout corners, **96-107**
    diamond images, **90-94**
    flexible ellipses, **76-81**